D1498658

JEWISH-CHRISTIAN
RELATIONS

JEWISH-CHRISTIAN RELATIONS
An Annotated Bibliography and Resource Guide

MICHAEL SHERMIS

INDIANA UNIVERSITY PRESS
Bloomington and Indianapolis

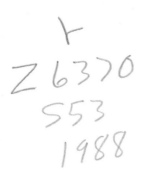

Manufactured in the United States of America

92 91 90 89 88   5 4 3 2 1

Library of Congress Cataloging-in-Publication Data

Shermis, Michael, 1959-
Jewish-Christian relations.

Includes indexes.
l. Judaism--Relations--Christianity--Bibliography.
2. Christianity and other religions--Judaism--
Bibliography. 3. Christianity and antisemitism--
Bibliography. I. Title.
Z6370.S53 1988 [BM535]   016.2612'6   87-46365
ISBN 0-253-33153-6

To my father,

who has inspired in me a love of
learning for learning's sake.

CONTENTS

FOREWORD

If one were to read only the newspapers or watch only the nightly news on television, she or he might conclude that Jewish–Christian relations exist in a constant state of crisis, with each crisis worse than its predecessor. Why, then, our hypothetical observer could question, bother with dialogue at all? Would it not be better to let our two communities go their own ways, interacting as little as possible?

Such thinking, while perhaps tempting to some on both sides of the historic encounter that has been the great privilege of our generation to witness, is wrong. The Christian–Jewish dialogue, as the evidence amassed in this volume by Michael Shermis amply testifies, continually provides each community with ever-deepening insights into areas of vital concern to both.

We Jews and Christians live together in a world made increasingly small by modern communications and transportation. We are, whether we like it or not, intimately interwoven with one another by our histories and essential religious visions.

The question that confronts us is not whether we will interrelate, but how well—or how poorly—we will carry out the moral and spiritual responsibilities of a religious relationship which exists, if we each take our own self-claims seriously, by the will of God.

I do not make the above assertion lightly. Nor, as a Christian, do I wish to impose in any way on the Jewish community's basic right, as a people brought into being by God (such is the clear biblical testimony), to determine its own destiny in response to God's call. But such, I believe, is an objective response one can make to the obvious facts of our complex and intertwined histories over the past two millennia and certainly in the present.

Today, on the eve of the third millennium of our often troubled history, it falls upon this generation to forge an entirely new mode of relating than that which formerly prevailed. Recent, one may say epochal, events make this inevitable. The Shoah, the attempted destruction of European Jewry in the heart of what was once known as "Christendom"; the ingathering of the Jewish people into Eretz Israel, the Land of Israel; the creation there once again of a Jewish state; and Christian responses to these theologically pregnant historical events, such as the Second Vatican Council and the first visit of the Bishop of Rome to the Great Synagogue of Rome since the time of St. Peter—such realities both make possible and mandate a fundamental reassessment, a <u>heshbon</u> <u>ha-nefesh</u>, of essential aspects of our understandings of one another.

Michael Shermis has made a significant contribution to this task by meticulously annotating the contemporary dialogue in its written, media, and colloquium manifestations. He provides here a basic volume for the beginner and the scholar alike which deserves a central place on the bookshelf of every parish, synagogue, and diocesan ecumenical officer.

As one who has labored for a number of years in the vineyard of Christian–Jewish relations, I would like to take the opportunity presented by this Foreword to thank Mr. Shermis for his contribution, and for the patience and painstaking care that went into it. All who use this work, whether professionally or occasionally, will be indebted to him for the perspective on the scope and depth of the exciting and challenging dialogue which he here chronicles.

Eugene J. Fisher
August, 1987

PREFACE

One can barely imagine the quantity of people it is necessary to acknowledge in a work such as this. I will attempt to name a few, and for those that I do not mention, please realize your help has been very much appreciated. This book is dedicated to my father, who has co-authored the first chapter with me. The education he helped give me has had a profound influence on my life. His help with this work has been invaluable, and without his sympathetic ear and critical eye it would never have been accomplished. I must express my appreciation to Larry Axel, my teacher, mentor, and friend, whom I hold in high regard; he has always been there to give me advice. Without him I also would not have been able to complete this work. Art Zannoni and Joe Haberer have proven instrumental in my religious development and were always sources of support and encouragement. They were the primary forces that motivated me to become involved in Jewish-Christian relations. Their editorial skills were most helpful as well. I asked Eugene Fisher to aid me in my efforts to locate many resources and he always complied quickly and efficiently. I appreciate his help and wish to thank him for writing the foreword. Alice Eckardt, John Pawlikowski, Philip Culbertson, Judith Banki, Michael Cook, John Roth, and Eugene Borowitz have been very helpful with all that I have requested of them. Alice especially went above and beyond call with many useful suggestions. I wish to thank all those that agreed to be listed in the speakers bureau for providing the information that was necessary to compile a resource such as this. I am most grateful to Kari Norborg, Mary Westrick, and Lulla Shermis who helped with the proofreading. I am extremely appreciative of Kathy Garner, Ruth Rothenberg, and the rest of the staff at the Interlibrary Loan Department at Purdue University Library, for the patience they showed while I repeatedly requested large quantities of books. I would like to give credit to Alice Eckardt, Michael McGarry, Herman Blumberg, Warren Jacobs, Solomon Bernards, John Koenig, Carl Evans, Jon Stein, Clark Williamson, Jacob Petuchowski, and Meyer Feldblum, who were kind enough to let me present their syllabi. Thanks to Julie and Andy McGuire, who provided me with access to the computer that made the printing of the manuscript a much easier project and for their steady friendship throughout this project. I wish to thank Lauren

Bryant at Indiana University Press for her continued guidance and support. She always made herself available for advice and encouragement; it was a pleasure to work with her. To all other friends and acquaintances who have suffered my importunity in my quest for information, thanks so much. I hope the realized product will have made it all worthwhile.

Thanks to all organizations who supplied me with their description. Other organizations and journals that I wish to acknowledge are: the Anti-Defamation League of B'nai B'rith, who consented to let me use the annotations for their films; the Center for Jewish-Christian Learning at the College of St. Thomas in St. Paul, Minnesota, who published a bibliography on Christology in their Proceedings, parts of which have been included in this work; the American Journal of Theology & Philosophy and Shofar published bibliographic articles from which portions have also been included.

What is helpful and useful in this work is the product of the Jewish-Christian dialogue community; errors and mistakes are my own.

INTRODUCTION

Over the past twenty-five years there has been a veritable explosion of materials developed for and about the Jewish-Christian dialogue and Jewish-Christian relations. Although Jews and Christians have been talking in one form or another since the inception of Christianity, the dialogue has usually been polemical or exploitative. Only in the last twenty-five years has a new spirit emerged. The dialogue has taken on a positive nature as attitudes and statements have become more affirmative, flexible, and open. Such changes in attitude have generated a wealth of new activities and resource materials. This resource book has been compiled to make the newly published, immense quantity of materials more manageable and to help scholars, beginning dialoguers, and those somewhere in between, use available references more effectively. It is a guide for use by beginning dialoguers to start, maintain, and bring their own dialogue to fruition. At the same time this reference will enable scholars and serious students to locate the most often used research literature with greater ease.

There are several different perspectives for those who study the relationship between Jews and Christians. These include the disciplines of archaeology, history, psychology, sociology, and theology. Those employing these perspectives have many different concerns. In some cases, the interest seems to be pragmatic: the prevention of future anti-Judaism.* In others, one detects a desire to atone for an anti-Jewish past. Some writers seem motivated by the implications of their theology. One also sees an attempt to set a confused record straight. Occasionally there are hidden agendas, i.e., some works seem to be aimed at proselytizing and some appear to wish to demonstrate the theological superiority of their religion. Some works open new paths while others tread relatively well worn ones. In some cases, one sees an extensive citation of mainstream research, and in others references are made to works that have only recently been unearthed.

Many shared themes are present in this array of impressive literature and media. Frequently the belief in the commonalities of the two faiths and the importance of research in order to reduce the potency of anti-Judaism is expressed. It is also evident that many authors believe there is a need for updating a Christian understanding of Judaism as well as of Christianity and the "inter-Testamental period." The most poignant of the works express the need to address difficult and sensitive questions in the dialogue. Some of the other themes include: the concern for proselytism, the State of Israel, the Holocaust, the concept of messiah and savior, and the understanding of the natural or supernatural status of Jesus. There are also many novel themes—novel in that they have not yet become an issue to those involved in the dialogue. Some of these issues have only recently emerged, e.g., Jewish-Christian-Muslim, Black-Jewish, or Polish-Jewish relations. There are also themes that appeal to specialists with an historical perspective; for instance, the status of the Samaritans in Israel or the historical formation of authority in Catholic and Jewish institutions.

What follows in this reference work is the largest known published list of materials dealing with these perspectives, concerns, problems, issues, and themes in as many different modes as was possible to compile. "Modes," in this case, means books, pamphlets, important articles, journals, congresses, media, syllabi, organizations, and speakers. There is an essay on the educational resources in the dialogue. There are over 550 books separated into eighteen categories and over sixty pamphlets and booklets listed. Each book has been annotated, many with a qualitative evaluation. Religious scholars in the field were informally surveyed to determine the most important articles. This resulted in a list of twenty-five articles sufficiently up-to-date and inclusive to enable one to keep current in the field. A list of journals has been separated into categories that will help readers choose those most appropriate for their needs. Congresses, conferences, symposia, forums, seminars, encounters, meetings, dialogues, colloquia, consultations, and workshops on and about Jewish-Christian relations held since 1965 have been listed. A catalogue of media has been included for those who wish to supplement their studies, classes, or dialogue groups with audio, visual, or audio/visual media. A small sample of syllabi from classes taught by rabbis, priests, ministers, and professors is made available to help guide teachers and professors in their search for books and topics appropriate for their classes. There is a directory, arranged alphabetically and geographically, of organizations that are concerned with the Jewish-Christian dialogue or specific areas within the dialogue. A list of speakers who are willing and able to address dialogue issues has been compiled. This list includes addresses and phone numbers so that speakers can be contacted personally. Finally there are indexes for subjects, names, titles, and media to enable this reference work to be as valuable as possible.

This book is intended for several different groups of readers and organizations. Writers and editors of religious education and scholarly texts should find this reference work most helpful. Faculty and students of theological seminaries and university departments of religion, Semitic, and Jewish studies will be able to utilize this resource guide for classroom and individual study. It should improve religious studies holdings in public, church, public school, college, university, seminary, synagogue, and community organization libraries and media centers. Last and perhaps most important, this reference is for Christian and Jewish laypersons who have developed an interest in the field of interreligious dialogue. It is they who have the greatest and, ironically, the most unfulfilled need to know.

*   The dictionary refers to a "Semite" as loosely meaning a "Jew." It originally referred to a person using languages spoken by Arabs and Jews, e.g., Arabic and Hebrew. In contemporary usage, when we refer to a Jew as a Semite it is only done in the pejorative sense, i.e., anti-Semitism.

Anti-Semitism is a neologism coined in the nineteenth century and thus can be considered historically inaccurate as a descriptive term. Even though "anti-Semitism" has come to mean the hatred of the Jews, in this work the more precise phrases, "anti-Judaism" and "anti-Jewish," will in most cases be utilized.

I.
Educational Aspects of
the Jewish-Christian Dialogue
by S. Samuel and Michael Shermis

This chapter will offer an introduction to what is available educationally in the field of Jewish-Christian dialogue. The objectives of the people who enter into the dialogue, from both academia and the general populace, will be discussed. An examination of the different levels of knowledge and understanding as well as the varied motivations of participants in the Jewish-Christian dialogue will also be presented. In addition, this chapter will include 1) issues for discussion in the dialogue, 2) specific educational resources on how to begin a dialogue group, and 3) information regarding the higher education programs available in Judaeo-Christian studies.

Introduction

Paradoxically, the ones who have the most need for the Jewish-Christian dialogue are probably not reading this chapter and have virtually no knowledge that such a dialogue has been taking place for the last twenty years. The rapprochement that began between Catholics and Jews after Vatican II now includes many sects within Protestantism and has clearly grown in both numbers and importance. However, in view of many terroristic acts directed against Jews throughout the world and in light of the certain knowledge that for many centuries we have witnessed orchestrated violence and genocide stemming from religious motives, we have just cause to regret that those who have the most to gain by holding a dialogue are almost totally unaware that a dialogue exists.

Unfortunately we cannot alter our past, but we can learn from tragedies and change our future. And indeed a desire for amelioration is one of the most noteworthy incentives for the Jewish-Christian dialogue. The better informed and more motivated people seek to help their faith grow through the dialogue by scholarship, research, and speaking. The ideas cited in these works have helped many find respect for other religious traditions. There has not only been an improvement in Jewish-Christian relations but people are becoming aware that Eastern and Western religions are also beginning the same dialogue process. As we engage in these theological and religious encounters, we help our own tradition reach a maturity heretofore unattained. This process of learning has opened up new avenues of growth that religious traditions can begin to travel.

Thus, the path to improvement through the dialogue is not only to increase the numbers of those who are talking to each other but, qualitatively to improve the effectiveness of the discussions that are now taking place. Hence, this chapter on education and the dialogue. By paying attention to some basic ideas about reading, understanding, listening, talking, and leading discussions, all dialogue participants can gain much more from their efforts.

To Whom Is the Dialogue Important?

Let us make a distinction. We can say that the dialogue is important to all Christians and Jews. However, in fact, the Jewish–Christian dialogue is, as we have said, scarcely perceived by many Jews and Christians. Many are unaware that such a dialogue has taken place, nor do they know why, nor do they understand that the course of future Christianity is very likely to be changed by the dialogue and by published research on the origins of Christianity. Jews who are indifferent to the dialogue, on the other hand, may not recognize that their peace and security in this country depend, to a large measure, on the goodwill of non–Jews, most especially Christians. Thus the paradox: many Jews and Christians do not perceive the existence of the dialogue, let alone see it as important; but the dialogue has important implications for both Christians and Jews. It ought to be considered important.

The Jewish–Christian dialogue is important to well–intentioned theologians, both Christian and Jewish, leaving aside for the moment whether we can speak of a "Jewish theology." We think that the dialogue has been taking place on a serious level since Vatican II in 1964. Indeed, the argument which preceded Vatican II—that there ought to be a dialogue—brought about the climate in which Christians and Jews could begin to say, "Despite our differences, despite the past, despite our essentially negative perceptions of each other, we really need to talk." Of course, simply talking, while it is necessary, is not sufficient; the dialoguers obviously need to learn from each other.

The dialogue is important to religious professionals: rabbis, cantors, Jewish and Christian educators and administrators, Christians ordained as ministers, priests, and teaching brothers and sisters. These persons have historically been intermediaries between the scholars and the laity. Through the years they have been the ones who have translated to the faithful the formative ideas within their religions. To be sure, to the extent that Christian teachers and preachers have transmitted the deicide accusation, to that extent they have created insurmountable obstacles to their own message of love, forgiveness, and redemption. To the extent that Jews have refused to deal with Christian theology—as can be verified in an examination of Jewish religious school textbooks—to that extent, they have been ignorant of the origin of negative attitudes and also of the true nature of Christianity as it relates to Judaism, positively as well as negatively.

The dialogue is important to those who are neither Christian nor Jewish but who wish to examine a model of a dialogue for their own purpose. At this moment, one can read and hear hostile stereotypes in which the terms "Arab," "Muslim," and "terrorist" are equated. One can also hear Muslims and Arabs express anger, fear, and resentment at being unfairly linked with those whose business it is to spread hatred and terror. Jewish and Black leaders lament the erosion of the historical cooperations between them. Indeed, it is possible to identify a good many groups who feel threatened and who wish that they could somehow "get their story across" to others. What they are really talking about, of course, is a dialogue.

What is now taking place between some Christians and Jews, with emphasis on peaceful, open, honest communication, provides a model for problem resolution. This model should be of considerable practical interest to many others.

What Dialogue Is and What It Is Not

A dialogue is not a debate. Nor is it an argument. It is not a veiled attempt to convert others to the right point of view. Finally, it is not an opportunity to "prove" that one's religion is superior to the other. Instead, the dialogue is an attempt to engage in an honest, open, sensitive process of exchanging views on those matters that we take to be supremely important—our religious convictions—with no other agenda than dialogue.

Objectives

The most important objective of the dialogue is also the means: to dialogue, i.e., to communicate with one another. In a sense, the dialogue is both end and means. The rationale for the Jewish-Christian dialogue is that Jews and Christians allow themselves to talk to one another. What can be discussed in a proposed dialogue?

What individuals can learn from talking to one another is a good deal more about their own religion and that of others. The two are inseparable: the more I learn about your point of view, the more I understand what mine means to me. This process—called "concept development" in educational terminology—suggests that as I learn what you understand by, e.g., "God the Creator" or "biblical faith," the more I learn about what these terms signify for me.

For Christians, there is increasingly a special agenda: learning about the roots of their religion. That Christianity evolved from a parent religion in the first century is beyond dispute. By the same token, for Jews, learning about historical events during the first century means not only learning how Christianity and Rabbinic Judaism emerged from Second Temple Judaism, it is also a lesson in how Jews in this era conceived of the meaning of "law," "messiah," "savior," and other extremely important concepts that define some of the differences between Judaism and Christianity.

Christians ordinarily refer to the Bible as "Old Testament" to distinguish it from the "New Testament." But this is not simply a matter of nomenclature. For Jews, it is the Hebrew Scriptures or Jewish Bible and they do not signify simply that which preceded fulfillment in the New Testament. It is a complete text of and by itself. For some Christians the Bible is the inerrant word of God, as it also is to some Jews. For others in both religions it is an account and interpretation of events, persons, and God's plan. In short, the Bible has different meanings for Jews and Christians but its meanings can only be determined through inquiry and discussion. For Christians and Jews, there are many different understandings of the nature of God. The tendency for some Christians is to contrast their God of love with what they perceive as the Hebrew God of vengeance, the one who says "revenge is mine" and who punishes transgressing Israel. But this is only part of the truth. Jews can point to numerous instances in their Bible of a God which, like the Christian God, is a creator, but also a God of love, of forgiveness, and of redemption.

The origin and similarities of rite and ritual are sometimes of interest to those in the Jewish-Christian dialogue. Jews who visit a Catholic mass or Protestant service for the first time sometimes express surprise at how many words, terms, and prayers are identical. And, of course, the reverse is also true. On the other hand, given centuries-old Jewish aversion to blood, the rite of transubstantiation—in which the wine and wafer become the blood and flesh of Christ—may appear incomprehensible. Rite and ritual can only be understood in terms of the meaning of the symbolic referents to the entire history of a religion. And this, at least in some measure, may be discussed in a dialogue.

There are differences and similarities in the ethical and moral structure of the two religions. Christians tend at times to simplify the issue by contrasting their ethic of love, peace, and forgiveness with what they assume to be a Jewish insistence on following the letter of the law. Jews, on the other hand, contrast the superiority of their ethical position, in which one does good for its own sake, with a vulgar caricature of Christians who do good only to get a "star in their crown" in an afterlife. What Jews and Christians believe about the meaning of good—and the good life—can only be discovered in a sympathetic exchange of views on the subject.

There are, of course, theological differences that cannot be bridged no matter how long or intensive the efforts. The meaning of "savior" and "messiah"—by no means the same thing—is a case in point. So, too, with the notion of "sin" and the concept of "afterlife." However, there is no necessity of bridging these differences for, to repeat, the goal is not to persuade. Simply understanding what the ideas signify to the other is its own rationale, its own justification.

Given the similarity in social justice between different emphases within Judaism and Christianity, identifying areas of commonality can serve as the basis for cooperation. Cooperation toward social and economic justice may be manifested by establishing a food bank, rebuilding slum dwellings, feeding the hungry, or serving on local Human Relations committees. Within the political arena both Christians and Jews may cooperate by working to pass or defeat legislation, elect candidates, and publicize policies considered of transcending importance: for instance, many in both faith communities are extremely sensitive to global ecological suicide and to disarmament proposals and civil rights. Indeed during the 1960s, cooperation between Jewish and Christian clergy was a hallmark of the civil rights movement.

There are many reasons for identifying some of the ancient and more recent historical barriers that separate the two faiths. These involve putting first-century Judaism and emergent Christianity in perspective, exploring the origins of theological anti-Judaism and of the Jewish response to it, grappling with what has been called the "absolute evil" of the Holocaust, and understanding the place of the State of Israel in Jewish and Christian belief structures.

Another prime objective involves breaking through the veil of misconceptions and stereotypes through which we have tended to see one another. Offensive anti-Jewish stereotypes which have been reinforced in literature—e.g., Shylock in Shakespeare and Fagan in Dickens—have permeated Western civilization until many equate Jews with avarice and unethical business practices. Jews have their own quota of stereotypes, tending to see all Christians through a lens consisting of upper-class "WASPs" enforcing restricted covenants and excluding Jews from country clubs, rural Protestants harping on the deicide charge, and Catholics busily disseminating that dreadful forgery known as The Protocols of the Elders of Zion. These stereotypes have served to distort the perceptions that Jews and Christians have of one another, functioning as a rationale for negative and hostile treatment and inhumane behavior.

Motivation

Individuals enter the Jewish-Christian dialogue with a variety of motivations. Personal growth is certainly an important one. John Dewey pointed out frequently that growth is a means to which the end is growth. Growth is its own reason for being. His complex theory suggested that growth was a process of deepening and widening one's insights and appreciations. First there is a simple awareness that you have different holidays from mine. Much later one may grow to understand the differences between your metaphysical assumptions and the ones which I employ. In this case, growth is not simply learning quantitatively more about one's assumptions; it also includes bringing one's assumptions to conscious awareness and seeing subtle distinctions between one position and another.

Curiosity is an amazingly powerful motivator. It means simply the desire to know more for no other reason than to satisfy one's curiosity. It is likely that such curiosity arises out of a recognized problem, e.g., you become aware that others have different holidays that you know nothing about, or you sense that individuals whom you consider as behaving ethically do so for reasons that seem quite obscure. It is nearly impossible for a problem to arise without an individual making an attempt to deal with it—"solve" is perhaps too powerful a term. Those in the Jewish-Christian dialogue are uniquely fortunate: it is virtually impossible entirely to satisfy one's curiosity about anything. New issues, new challenges, new ways of perceiving or stating a problem constantly arise; for this reason a particular Jewish-Christian dialogue group may roll on with considerable momentum month after month.

In recent years, individuals—both Jews and Christians—have talked increasingly about "discovering their roots," meaning that they wish to know more about the relationship between one's present and the past, often the distant past. This phrase was popularized by the phenomenally popular Roots, which revealed how deeply the author, Alex Haley, wished to know of the buried chronicles of his distant ancestors. Given the popularization of archaeology, many Jews and Christians are becoming simultaneously more knowledgeable about the biblical era and about the complex connections between them—connections which have not been satisfied by the New Testament. Having glimpsed the parallels between their religion and Judaism, many Christians wish to know more about the Pharisaic roots of Jesus, of the role of the Roman Empire in his crucifixion, or of the difference between Judaism, first-century Christianity, and Platonism.

Another motivation is the validation of one's own religious beliefs. This is scarcely surprising; one's belief structure is constantly under attack and it has become a challenge for individuals to know what to believe under the relentless battering of conflicting beliefs in a pluralistic society. Were it possible for an individual to remain completely isolated within one's physical and cultural environment—as for instance Mormons in central Idaho—it would not be especially important to validate one's religious beliefs. However, when Catholics, Protestants, Jews, Muslims, nonbelievers, members of Eastern religious faith communities, and adherents to cults—whatever this term may denote—mix daily, belief structures are constantly being questioned, even threatened. Thus, the desire to undergird and inform one's religious beliefs is, for some, a powerful motivation.

As negative as it may be, we must consider conversion as a motivation. Christians may join a Jewish-Christian dialogue with a hidden agenda: to convert the marginal. Deeply observant Jews may join a dialogue with a similar motivation: to show those people just how superior Judaism is. Under these conditions, there is not likely to be the open, frank, honest discussion we described above, for this is not dialogue and we argue that it is not an appropriate motivation for entering a dialogue.

A desire to understand the religious belief of one's girlfriend or boyfriend, fiance, or spouse has proven to be a motivator for some. In a sense, this motivation is instrumental: it is, unlike curiosity, based upon a desire to understand religious differences as a means to further a personal relationship. However, it is also the case that such a motivation may change and deepen as the individual becomes engaged in a dialogue; what was glimpsed only as a means can become an end in itself, for the newly discovered information takes on a life of its own.

Academics may have their own agenda in the Jewish-Christian dialogue. Some are motivated to become conversant with the latest developments in theology and religious philosophy. Historians, anthropologists, literature teachers, philosophers, to name only a few, may perceive the Jewish-Christian dialogue as touching upon their research interests. Historians, especially, may be professionally interested in the dialogue because recent discussions by some historians have distinguished between intellectually defensible and spurious history. That is, some publications in the Jewish-Christian dialogue employ questionable research procedures, make unwarranted generalizations from too limited data, for instance, to teach conclusions about the New Testament based upon irrelevant sources. Other academics may wish to learn more about some of the amazingly numerous discoveries in biblical archaeology. There are as many motivations for academics to become interested in the dialogue as there are for any other group.

Educational Issues

The following questions represent issues that people in the Jewish-Christian dialogue often discuss. These certainly are not exhaustive, but they will give your dialogue group hours of thoughtful, probing, and controversy-generating conversation. The beginning questions can serve as a springboard for a new dialogue group. The rest of the questions are organized thematically and reflect most of the issues that have for many years divided Judaism and Christianity.

BEGINNING QUESTIONS

How do you react to the statement that Jesus Christ was a Jew?

What reasons cause Christians and Jews to engage in dialogue?

As a Jew, something I've always wondered about Christians is . . .

As a Christian, something I've always wondered about Jews is . . .

Are there any misconceptions/misunderstandings you feel Christians have about Jews, or Jews have about Christians? What do we in the two traditions have to learn from each other?

A subject of much debate among some Jews and some Christians is mission/proselytization/making converts. What are the issues? Where are the issues? Where do the tensions arise between the two groups and also within each group?

Do "I" really know who "you" are? As I see it, what is of central importance to your belief and practice is . . . Am I correct?

What are your personal reasons for becoming involved in a Jewish-Christian dialogue and what is the extent of your involvement?

List and explain some of the reasons you think that Jews and Christians should be getting together.

Describe the person or event that made you want to know more about Christians and Christianity or about Jews and Judaism.

ANTI-JUDAISM

Some research—by no means accepted by all scholars—has strongly suggested that the prime source of anti-Judaism in the U.S. comes from the training of fundamentalist Protestant clergy. What implications does this have? For whom? When? (For instance, would believing Christians have to reassess the New Testament and attempt to expunge presumptive anti-Judaism?)

Describe that point in time at which you became aware that Christians routinely employ negative stereotypes in thinking and talking about Jews.

Explain the dangers of using stereotypes. Describe how they have stood between you and some friendships. Do you think that the teaching of contempt for Jews is destructive of Christian biblical understanding of Christianity and how to live with people?

In view of the historical connection between certain Christian teachings and anti-Judaism, what do you think Christians should say to Jews before inviting them to engage in a dialogue?

Although most American Christians might be willing to assert that any religious minority has a right to exist, do you think that some Christians have mental reservations about the right of Jews and Judaism to exist? What reservations? Who holds them? With what effect?

How do you account for anti-Judaism and its persistence over the centuries as well as its virulence?

How do you feel about contemporary anti-Catholicism in America today? About stereotypes of evangelicals and fundamentalist Christians? About Muslims and Arabs?

It is often held that the Wandering Jew—the Jew who is condemned to wander, homeless and friendless through the earth—is a natural unfoldment of the original sin of deicide. In view of 2,000 years of continuous anti-Judaism, do you think that there is perhaps some validity to this belief? Do you think that anti-Judaism is the same as any other racial or religious prejudice? Or is it different? If so, how is it different? If not, then what does anti-Judaism have in common with other forms of prejudice?

For Christians in what sense can anti-Judaism be seen as a rebellion against God and Christ?

BIBLE

Describe how your views of Torah and/or the Christian Bible have changed over the years.

Do you have certain favorite passages from the Torah (from Tanach, from the Christian Bible)? What are they? What do you find meaningful about them?

If the Hebrew Scriptures were to be removed from the Bible, would the New Testament make sense of and by itself?

COMPARING THE TWO TRADITIONS

Are Jewish ethics "the same" as those of Christianity? If not, what are the differences? If so, how—other than that one historically precedes the other—are they alike?

Does the issue of officially composed or approved prayer in public schools possibly threaten Jewish-Christian relations in this country? Or is it an ephemeral issue that will, like prohibition, vanish as soon as we come to our senses?

Describe and explain struggles that you are having with Christianity. With Judaism.

Describe your early understanding of Christians and Christianity and Jews and Judaism. Can you identify what, if anything, has changed over the years? What accounts for these changes?

[For Christians] What images and impressions do we have of Jews? Of ourselves as Christians? Do these square with Judaism and Christianity as they actually are? Or are they twisted? And if so, how and why did they get twisted?

[For Jews] What images and impressions do we have of Christians? Of ourselves as Jews? Do these square with Judaism and Christianity?

Has the de-Judaizing of Christianity been carried to an extreme by the churches? What form does it take? Has the denial of religious legitimacy to Christianity been carried to an extreme by the Jewish community? What form does it take?

Are the basic statements of the churches on Judaism since 1948 well known in your denomination? If so, what are they? If not, how can they become well known? What points might a hypothetical comparable Jewish statement on Christianity make?

[For Jews] Christian identity rests on faith in God. Can you explain to Christians why a nonpracticing Jew who expresses doubt in the existence of God is still a Jew?

Many Jews feel that Catholics tend to locate authority in what is taken to be a divine institution while Protestants tend to locate authority in what is taken to be a book of divine revelation. Where do Jews locate authority? All Jews? Some Jews? Is the characterization above concerning the Protestant and Catholic stance toward authority accurate? Partly accurate?

There are a number of beliefs about covenant. One is that there was one covenant for Christians and one for Jews. Another is that there was one covenant in two parts. Which one do you accept? Neither? Is there another covenant belief that you do accept? What is it?

THE CRUCIFIXION

Why are many Christians so unwilling to admit the active role of Pontius Pilate in crucifying Jesus and so willing to indict the Jews?

Christians have often characterized Jewish concern with the way Christians teach the crucifixion story as unwarranted. Would you agree or disagree with the statement that Jews have realistic historical reasons for their anxiety? If so, what are they?

Is the sin or crime of deicide possible? That is, can human beings kill God? Discuss why or why not.

It may be helpful to examine Jewish and Christian approaches to the crucifixion from a perspective that is neither Christian nor Jewish, but skeptical of both traditions. A thoroughgoing naturalistic position would raise questions about both Jewish and Christian theological suppositions. From a naturalistic position, we are asked to believe that God sent Her/His only son, that is, someone who was of the same (or like) substance, to earth to perform a mission and then sacrificed him, which is to say, sacrificed Her/Himself.

What trends within the Christian church led to the gradual elimination of Roman and Gentile complicity in the crucifixion and to the idea that only Jews were responsible?

Why would the idea that the Jews killed Christ be a denial of the central elements of the Christian church? What are these elements and why are they essential?

Even if all Jews living in Jerusalem were in fact guilty of killing Jesus, what is the responsibility of succeeding generations of Jews? What are the implications of your conclusion?

What precisely is the difference between Jews and Christians concerning the person of Jesus as human? As divine?

DIALOGUE

What specifically does Christianity have to offer Judaism? What specifically does Judaism have to offer Christianity?

Assuming that you could talk directly to God, who must then respond to you, what would you say? What would you ask? Assuming you were God what would you respond?

What do you believe an interfaith dialogue will accomplish that is important and meaningful?

In what way can the dialogue with Jews help bring Christians together ecumenically?

What are the hopes and fears that Christians bring into the dialogue with Jews? And what do you think are the hopes and fears of Jews in approaching the dialogue?

To which one, if any, of the following objections to the dialogue do you subscribe?

[For Jews]

Christian religious teaching, beliefs, and proselytizing activities demonstrate contempt for Jews and the Jewish people.

Christian teaching contributed to and resulted in the Holocaust. Thus, it is too soon to engage in dialogue. Jews should rebuild in isolation.

Christian apathy concerning Israel's survival reflects Christian antipathy concerning Jews, even after Auschwitz.

Dialogue is a tool for Christian proselytizing disguised in a friendly form.

[For Christians]

The Jewish-Christian dialogue was invented by Jews, who stand to benefit most from it.

[For Christians and Jews]

Dialogue may stimulate anti-Judaism by causing differences to surface. Or it may encourage participants to downplay important distinctions between Judaism and Christianity.

Christianity has nothing of interest to say to Jews. Judaism has nothing of interest to say to Christianity.

In any dialogue between Jews and Christians, religious language and concepts may be diluted and distorted.

Interreligious cooperation should be limited to those areas of social action that both can accept.

The more successful Jewish-Christian dialogue is, the more likely it is to lead to assimilation and intermarriage.

Why is dialogue even necessary in a secular age?

ISRAEL

What is a "proper" Christian attitude toward the State of Israel today?

Where was the Christian community in 1948? In 1956? In 1967? In 1973? What are the significances of these dates?

How can the Jews of Israel, who began a country of, by, and for refugees, then deliberately create another large class of refugees?

Some very vocal supporters of Israel are fundamentalist Christians, whose support seems to be motivated by their interpretations of parts of Scripture as predictions of the end of time. How do Jews feel about this? Does this color Jewish attitudes towards liberal Christians?

MISSION

If we grant that missionizing is a legitimate Christian attempt to share the benefits of the Gospel, can you understand the fears of Jews in the face of Christian attempts to convert them?

Is it proper for Christians to engage in a dialogue in the hope that dialogue will soften up the Jews for conversion? Or to regard the dialogue as a subtle means of converting them?

React to the statement that Nazis sought to destroy Jews in the gas chambers and Christians seek to annihilate Jews by conversion.

RELIGIOUS HISTORY

Are there misconceptions that have kept Christians from appreciating the richness of their own heritage? If so, what are they?

Are there misconceptions that have kept Judaism from appreciating the richness of the Christian heritage as a development of key aspects of biblical Judaism? If so, what are they?

From a Christian perspective, what do you think created the split between Christianity and Judaism? Conversely, from a Jewish perspective, what do you think created the split between Christianity and Judaism?

As a Jew or a Christian does the existence today of a viable Jewish community alongside the Christian church signify that God has some intention for Jews that the Christians must discern?

The term "supercessionism" refers to the belief that one religion has superseded, that is, has taken the place of, another. The term "triumphalism" means that the coming of Jesus marked the triumph and the victory of Christianity and that Christianity has triumphed over all other world religions. Some Jews and Christians feel that their tradition is superior philosophically to others. Do you subscribe to any of these concepts? Do you think others in your tradition subscribe to them? Do these concepts create problems for the Jewish-Christian dialogue?

RITUAL

Describe the religious practices of your family when you were growing up. Have they changed since you became an adult?

Explain why certain practices seem especially meaningful to you now.

Within your own religion, what pleases you about certain observances and what disturbs you?

These questions are meant as suggestions which you may wish to elaborate on, ignore, combine, or modify. None of these questions has a "right" answer but adequate answers may result from discussion. Some questions are designed to draw upon participants' experience and some necessarily draw upon a body of knowledge. These questions are meant to bridge—not minimize—the differences between Jews and Christians. Some of these questions may cut to the root of long-held feelings, but this means only that they are the ones that need to be discussed.

Educational Resources Available

There are a number of excellent educational resources to utilize when beginning a dialogue group. Consider the following:

1.   Interfaith Circles

This is a series of six programs, each with four sessions, for bringing Christians and Jews together in small groups. Groups are formed as members of a Jewish congregation and members of a Christian congregation meet together. Reverend Martin Marty and Reverend Edward H. Flannery, from the Christian perspectives, and Rabbi Alan Mittleman, from the Jewish perspective, provide the overview of each topic for the presenters' materials.

The first three programs seek to build personal friendships, eliminate stereotypical thinking, provide Christians with insight regarding their Jewish roots, and develop new understandings between the two faith communities.

The following programs are meant to deepen friendships and encourage boldness to speak and act against intolerance and bigotry. They expose and confront harmful presuppositions and develop a means of approaching mutual problems together.

Programs include:
A.   Getting Acquainted
      1.   First Steps for Dialogue
      2.   Our Religious Observances
      3.   What the Bible Means to Us
      4.   Knowing "Others"
B.   Celebrations of Faith
      1.   Christmas and Hanukkah
      2.   Easter and Passover
      3.   Pentecost and Shavuot
      4.   Good Friday and Rosh Hashana, Yom Kippur
C.   God and Everyday Life
      1.   Primary Patterns of Worship

      2. The Place of Righteous Acts
      3. Life's Major Decisions
      4. Life's Certainties/Uncertainties
D. Main Concepts
      1. Sacred Literature
      2. Creation, Election, Covenant
      3. Prophecy, Redemption, and Salvation
      4. Holiness, Sanctification, Messiahship
E. Historical Realities
      1. Peoplehood/Church
      2. Anti-Semitism/Philo-Semitism
      3. Holocaust and Remembrance
      4. The Land of Israel
F. Social Challenges
      1. Pluralism
      2. Intermarriage
      3. Mutual Concerns
      4. Solving Problems Together

The printed materials for each program include: host/hostess pages, facilitator folder, presenters' guides, response sheets, evaluation form, and supplementary helps. For information on an Interfaith Circles workshop in your area, phone Robert and Lois Blewett (612) 421-1596 or write Interfaith Resources, Inc., 1328 Oakwood Drive, Anoka, Minnesota 55303.

2. A Jewish-Christian Resource Packet: Exploring a Theological Relationship between Christianity and Judaism

The contents of this packet are intended to enlarge the spirit and mind, pointing to further study and appropriate responses in the interest of clarified and strengthened Jewish-Christian relationships.
Printed materials include:
An Introduction.
A Selected Bibliography.
The Meaning and Conduct of Dialogue, by Dean M. Kelley and Bernhard E. Olson.
Homework for Christians: Preparing for Christian-Jewish Dialogue, rev. ed. by Eugene J. Fisher.
Homework for Jews: Preparing for Jewish-Christian Dialogue, second ed. by Janet Sternfeld.
A Study Discussion Guide (divided into six sessions with a purpose, background, and other resources section).
Course Outline for Living-Room Dialogue Groups.
"The Root and the Wild Olive" (worship booklet containing six worship services), prepared by Donald C. Lacy.
"The Church's False Witness Against Jews," by Carl D. Evans.
"A Jewish Perspective: This Moment in Jewish-Christian Relations," by Daniel F. Polish.
"The Holocaust and Christian Responsibility," by Eugene J. Fisher.
Use Report (evaluation form).
Prepared by: Jewish-Christian Resource Packet Task Force, Department of Ecumenical Concerns, Indiana Council of Churches. Distributed by: Indiana Council of Churches, 1100 West 42nd Street, Room 225, Indianapolis, Indiana 46208
Price: $7.50 pre-paid.

3. A Guide to Interreligious Dialogue. By Judith Hershcopf and Morris Fine.

    This pamphlet explains some of the reasons for the growing popularity of interreligious dialogue and offers a number of guidelines for such discussions involving lay members of churches, synagogues, or other organizations. Available through the American Jewish Committee, Institute of Human Relations, 165 East 56 Street, New York, New York 10022.
Price: Single copy, $0.50, quantity prices on request.

4. Guidelines on Dialogue with People of Living Faiths and Ideologies.

    Prepared by the World Council of Churches, and using the theme of "Dialogue in Community," this pamphlet contains the concerns, questions, and experiences of the member churches of the WCC. Designed for Christians. Available through the World Council of Churches, 150 Route de Ferney, 1211 Geneva 20, Switzerland.
Price: $1.75.

5. The Process of Dialogue. Developed by Ellen Charry.

    Divided into three sections.
Part I. "Introduction to Dialogue" presents three models for explaining the purpose and scope of dialogue to participants. Group leaders in the prologue to dialogue stage will likely want to select one model for initial presentation.
Part II. "Introduction to Leadership" contains guidelines for leading and planning dialogue groups.
Part III. "Bibliography" covers the organization, management, and group process of dialogue.
    Available through the National Conference of Christians and Jews, Inc., 71 Fifth Avenue, New York, New York 10003.

6. Interreligious Interaction: A Program Guide

    This booklet is provided as a source of ideas which are taken from successful programs sponsored and conducted by Reform congregations in the local community. It has been designed to help encourage the development of interreligious programs.
Programs include: Worship, Holidays, Adult Education, Religious Education, Social Service, Social Action, and Dialogue. Designed for Jews.
    Available through the Department of Interreligious Affairs, Union of American Hebrew Congregations, 838 Fifth Avenue, New York, New York 10021.

Educational Programs

    The institutions of higher learning listed below hold special programs, classes, or other such events that make them worth mentioning for those who might be interested in furthering their education in Jewish-Christian relations. Please write to these institutions for more information.

American Institute for the Study of Religious Cooperation
401 Broad Street

Philadelphia, Pennsylvania 19108
Irving J. Borowsky, President

Boston Theological Institute
Interreligious Dialogue Program
140 Commonwealth Drive
Chestnut Hill, Massachusetts 02167
(Member schools include Andover Newton Theological School, Boston College,
Episcopal Divinity School, Gordon Conwell Theological Seminary, Harvard
University Divinity School, Holy Cross Greek Orthodox School of Theology,
St. John's Seminary, and West School of Theology.)

Center for Jewish-Christian Learning
College of St. Thomas
2115 Summit Avenue
St. Paul, Minnesota 55105
Rabbi Max Shapiro, Director

Center for Jewish-Christian Studies
Chicago Theological Seminary
5757 South University Avenue
Chicago, Illinois 60637
Dr. Andre Lacocque, Director

Center for Jewish-Christian Studies and Relations
General Theological Seminary
New York, New York 10011
Dr. James Carpenter, Director

Ecumenical Institute of Theology
St. Mary's Seminary and University
5400 Roland Avenue
Baltimore, Maryland 21210

Hebrew Union College-Jewish Institute of Religion
Judaeo-Christian Studies
3101 Clifton Avenue
Cincinnati, Ohio 45220
(513) 221-1875

Hebrew Union College-Jewish Institute of Religion
Judaeo-Christian Studies
3077 University Avenue
Los Angeles, California 90007
(213) 749-3424

Hebrew Union College-Jewish Institute of Religion
Brookdale Center
One West 4th Street
New York, New York 10221
(212) 674-5300

Institute of Judaeo-Christian Studies
Seton Hall University

South Orange, New Jersey 07079
Monsignor John M. Oesterreicher, Director

Intersem
635 South Harvard Boulevard
Los Angeles, California 90005
(Member schools include American Baptist Seminary of the West, Fuller
Theological Seminary, San Francisco Theological Seminary, California
School of Theology at Claremont, and University of Judaism.)

Conclusion

   We began this chapter with the observation that those who are most
in need of a Jewish-Christian dialogue are probably not reading this
reference work. However, for those who are reading it because they are
motivated to begin a dialogue with friends and colleagues, we hope we
have presented some useful ideas for embarking on a dialogue.
   Those who are deeply interested in the Jewish-Christian dialogue
entertain, as we have already noted, a variety of motivations. The
motivation for this work is to help disseminate important information.
Through this resource we further justify and define the field—making
it a more legitimate enterprise with which Christians and Jews will want
to be involved. If you believe that it is time to begin a better chapter
in human relations in this country and throughout the world, then you
are ready to begin a Jewish-Christian dialogue.

II.
Annotated Bibliography

Book-length works obtained from bibliographies, syllabi, articles, books, etc., have been included in this selected, annotated bibliography. These works were selected for their relevance to Jewish-Christian relations. Several scholars surveyed sections of the bibliography in their particular areas to ensure that each section included a representative selection. There are no claims made to total inclusiveness, for this bibliography is not meant to be comprehensive or definitive. If there seems to be a title missing, please see the title index, which should help in locating the book in another section.

Books have been annotated with a short description. Descriptions may contain the theme, goal, aim, or purpose of the book. Some will utilize an illustrative quote, others will list chapters or topics. Anthologies will have a list of the essays or contributors. When possible, a qualitative evaluation was made. For the few works that do not have annotations, it is because the works were not available.

A. Judaism and Christianity

Most books presented in this section are comparative. Many will serve as helpful introductions to the two faiths.

Ayers, Robert H. Judaism and Christianity: Origins, Developments, and Recent Trends. Lanham, Md.: University Press of America, 1983.

A quality presentation of the major beliefs of the two traditions; suitable as an introductory textbook for college or seminary courses. However, the growing body of literature showing the interconnectedness of Judaism and Christianity has not been fully utilized.

Baeck, Leo. Judaism and Christianity. Trans. Walter Kaufman. Philadelphia: Jewish Publication Society, 1958.

Although polemical in nature--for Baeck sees Judaism as superior to Christianity--this book can serve a purpose for those studying the dialogue. Baeck's criticisms can be utilized by the serious Christian who is searching for an understanding of the essence of her or his faith. Helpful to anyone reflecting on the dimensions of Christianity and Judaism.

Berthold, Fred, Jr., et al., eds. Basic Sources of the Judaeo-Christian Tradition. Englewood Cliffs, N.J.: Prentice-Hall, 1962.

Primary sources have been assembled in a large volume on the Judaeo-Christian tradition. Meant for undergraduate use, this work features introductions, summaries, and vignettes of the Hebrew and Christian Scriptures. It also contains representative and influential Jewish and Christian authors from the medieval to modern period.

Blue, Lionel. To Heaven, with Scribes and Pharisees: The Jewish Path to God. New York: Oxford University Press, 1976.

An explanation--by a Jew to non-Jews--about Jewish spirituality and being a Jew in the modern world. Written in a popular, story-telling style.

Brod, Max. Paganism—Christianity—Judaism: A Confession of Faith. Trans. William Wolf. University, Ala.: University of Alabama Press, 1970.

This English translation of the original German work, published in 1921, has its faults; and the author admits as much in the foreword to this revised edition. He feels that classical antiquity has not been done justice, the book needs a more detailed discussion of great Christian authors, and the forces that determine world history have changed. Regardless, this book does present some interesting perspectives on ultimate concepts in the world from the viewpoints of Christianity, Judaism, and paganism.

Buber, Martin. Two Types of Faith: The Interpretation of Judaism and Christianity. Trans. Norman Goldhawk. New York: Harper Torchbook, 1961.

One of the most important statements on faith today. Buber, an eminent Jewish thinker in the history of Jewish-Christian relations, has given the Jewish reader much to think about in terms of Jesus' place in Judaism. He also presents the Christian reader with an understanding of the New Testament that differs from the Pauline version of Christianity.

Corneille, Roland de. Christians and Jews: The Tragic Past and the Hopeful Future. New York: Harper and Row, 1966.

An able attempt to lay bare the tragedy that has occurred in the history of the Church and the Synagogue. This historical survey also touches upon the dialogue by exploring the motivations of those who come to dialogue and by reflecting on the events in the early sixties. Several good questions with practical suggestions are included, along with a ceremony for the Passover seder meal.

Davies, W. D. Christian Origins & Judaism. Philadelphia: Westminster, 1962.

Ten essays previously published have been collected in a single volume. These studies concentrate on the interaction of Christianity and Judaism in the first century. Scholarly investigations are evidenced by the extensive footnotes.

Eckstein, Yechiel. What Christians Should Know about Jews and Judaism. Chicago: Word Books, 1984.

Christians will find this popular introduction useful in understanding Judaism and the common elements that the two faiths share. The chapter "Christian Missions and the Jews" is imperative reading for evangelicals.

Heyer, Robert, ed. Jewish-Christian Relations. New York: Paulist, 1974.

A set of short essays by Jewish and Christian scholars presented in a popularized fashion for the beginning dialoguer. Also included are the relevant passages from the Declaration on Non-Christian Religions and the Guidelines and Suggestions for Implementing the Conciliar Declaration 'In Our Times'.

Kirsch, Paul J. We Christians and Jews. Philadelphia: Fortress, 1975.

A useful introduction for the college classroom. Kirsch deals with the issues in an honest and frank manner. The book is divided into seven sections: 1) "Estrangement," 2) "Messiah," 3) "Passion," 4) "Holocaust," 5) "Covenant," 6) "Israel," and 7) "Agenda."

Kung, Hans, and Walter Kasper. Christians and Jews. New York: Seabury, 1974.

A short volume of helpful essays on the significance of the law, liturgy, religiousness, messianic hope, Jesus, and the future of Christian-Jewish dialogue. Each theme is analyzed from the perspective of a well-known Jewish scholar and well-known Christian scholar.

Parkes, James W. The Foundations of Judaism and Christianity. Chicago: Quadrangle, 1960.

The title of this book is an accurate description as Parkes traces the historical foundations of the two religions from the Exile through the rise of Christianity to the emergence of Rabbinic Judaism.

————. Judaism and Christianity. Chicago: University of Chicago Press, 1948.

A scholarly work that has become a classic in the field. Parkes's compassionate understanding of Judaism is evident as he traces the origins and historical developments of the relationship between the two traditions and looks at future tasks. This work makes evident the accuracy with which he foresaw many later developments.

Pawlikowski, John T. <u>Sinai and Calvary</u>: <u>A Meeting of Two Peoples</u>. New
    York: Benziger, 1976.

In this work, Pawlikowski writes for two audiences, beginning dialoguers
and scholars. Many works do not succeed at such an attempt; this
one does because it explains complex issues on a basic level. Contents
are divided into three parts: 1) "The Basis of Judaism in the Bible,"
2) "The Intertestamental and New Testament Periods," and 3) "Judaism
and Christianity in the Post-Biblical Period."

Rosenberg, Stuart E. <u>Christians and Jews</u>: <u>The Eternal Bond</u>. New York:
    Ungar, 1985. rev. ed. of <u>Bridge to Brotherhood</u>: <u>Judaism's Dialogue</u>
    <u>with Christianity</u>, 1961.

A capable attempt to bridge and not minimize the differences between
the two faiths. This work can serve as a guide for an enhanced
understanding of Judaism and Christianity. Rosenberg organizes
the material into four categories: "Sacred Places," "Sacred Moments,"
"Sacred Times and Seasons," and "Sacred Ideas."

Rosenstock-Huessy, Eugen, ed. <u>Judaism despite Christianity</u>: <u>The "Letters</u>
    <u>on Christianity and Judaism" between Eugen Rosenstock-Huessy and</u>
    <u>Franz Rosenzweig</u>. University, Ala.: University of Alabama Press,
    1969.

A true dialogue by two important figures in the history of the
Jewish-Christian dialogue. The informal and personal character of
the letters offer the reader a look at the very human side of dialogue.
They present to the Jew a Christianity not diluted by paganism, and
to the Christian a Judaism that is not merely incomplete Christianity.

Sandmel, Samuel. <u>Two Living Traditions</u>. Detroit: Wayne State University
    Press, 1972.

A collection of essays by the late rabbi who dedicated his professional
career to helping Christians understand Judaism. The value of this
work—for these essays have appeared in a variety of places—is that
one may look at the breadth and depth of his writings. Sandmel
explores many different issues; a sampling includes crime, modern
theology, biblical scholarship, methods of scholarly research, myth
and genealogy, world history, ethics, and communication.

Schoeps, Hans Joachin. <u>The Jewish-Christian Argument</u>: <u>A History of</u>
    <u>Theologies in Conflict</u>. Trans. David E. Green. New York: Holt,
    Rinehart, and Winston, 1963.

This third edition of the original (printed in 1937) does not deal with
the Holocaust or the State of Israel, major events which constitute
an important part of any dialogue on theology between Christians
and Jews. Of value is Schoeps's examination of the after-emancipation
period, from Moses Mendelssohn until Franz Rosenzweig and Martin
Buber.

Silver, Samuel H. Explaining Judaism to Jews and Christians. Reprint ed. New York: Arco, 1974.

A short, straightforward book on the major concepts of Judaism. Should be used as an introduction for someone who is not familiar with Judaism. Many of the sections are done in a question-answer style.

Weiss-Rosmarin, Trude. Judaism and Christianity: The Differences. Middle Village, N.Y.: Jonathan David, 1965.

As the title indicates, this short and popular book sets forth the distinctions between Jewish and Christian perspectives on several topics. The two traditions' views on God, miracles, Jesus, free will vs. original sin, faith vs. law, sin and atonement—as well as attitudes toward asceticism and interpretations of Judaism—are all examined.

Zerin, Edward. What Catholics and Other Christians Should Know about Jews. Dubuque, Iowa: Wm. C. Brown, 1980.

The basic fundamentals of the Jewish faith are presented in a comprehensible style. Helpful to those Christians who know little or nothing about Judaism.

B.   First-Century Judaism and the Emergence of Christianity

Although there is some overlap with the next section, most of the works in this section are concerned with events, people, and places in the first century.

Abrahams, Israel. Studies in Pharisaism and the Gospels. New York: Ktav, 1967.

This edition is a reprint of a famous study of the Gospels done between the years 1917 and 1924. Abrahams portrays the Gospels against the Jewish background in which they developed. He relies on rabbinic sources to enlighten his readers on the dynamics and evolution of the Pharisaic movement. Originally developed as an appendix to C. G. Montefiore's commentary on the Gospels.

Aron, Robert. Jesus of Nazareth: The Hidden Years. Trans. Frances Frenaye. London: H. Hamilton, 1962.

Aron's intentions are to remind Jews of aspects of their heritage; to help Christians understand the beginning of their religion; and to highlight the conflict of Judaism in the pagan world. He suggests that Jesus was a product of his environment and that his growing years were filled with everyday events that a normal Jewish boy of this era would experience, i.e. holidays, school, work, etc. This is a thoughtful and valuable portrayal of Jesus in the context of his Jewish faith.

————. The Jewish Jesus. Trans. Agnes H. Forsyth and Anne-Marie de Commaille in collaboration with Horace T. Allen, Jr. Maryknoll, N.Y.: Orbis, 1971.

An attempt is made to place Jesus in his socio-religious context by looking at his faith and participation in Jewish worship. Lack of references and too much conjecture make this book less valuable than others of this genre.

Baeck, Leo. The Pharisees and Other Essays. Introduction by Krister Stendahl. New York: Schocken, 1966.

One of the better known writers in the Jewish-Christian dialogue has selected essays on the Pharisees, tradition in Judaism, Judaism in the Church, origins of Jewish mysticism, Greek and Jewish preaching, two world views compared, and the character of Judaism.

Bammel, Ernst, ed. The Trial of Jesus: Cambridge Studies in Honour of C. F. D. Moule. Naperville, Ill.: A. Allenson, 1970.

These scholarly expositions consider several features of the New Testament account of the trial of Jesus. Their investigations are detailed, perceptive, and well-written.

Blanch, Stuart. The Trumpet in the Morning: Law and Freedom Today in the Light of the Hebraeo-Christian Tradition. New York: Oxford University Press, 1979.

A perceptive discussion on the place of law in society and how the Hebrew and Christian Scriptures, Paul, and Jesus should play a part in determining how we live by the law.

Boadt, Lawrence, Helga Croner, and Leon Klenicki, eds. Biblical Studies: Meeting Ground of Jews and Christians. New York: Paulist, 1980.

After the introductory essay by Boadt, there are eight essays in three areas: 1) "Trends in Biblical Research," 2) "The Relationship of Hebrew Bible and New Testament," and 3) "The Bible as Record and Revelation." Contributors include S. David Sperling, Jorge Mejia, Leonard S. Kravitz, Joseph Blenkinsopp, Andre LaCocque, Martin A. Cohen, Monika K. Hellwig, and Leon Klenicki.

Bonsirvin, Joseph. Palestinian Judaism in the Time of Jesus Christ. Trans. William Worl. New York: Holt, Rinehart, and Winston, 1964.

Although this book was published in 1964, most of its work was done in 1934, when Bonsirvin published Le Judaisme Palestinien au temps de Jesus-Christ. Thus recent scholarship in the last fifty years, including the discovery of the Dead Sea Scrolls, makes this work outdated. It is useful to see how much the image of Palestinian Judaism has changed with the writings of scholars such as E. R. Goodenough.

Bowker, John. Jesus and the Pharisees. Cambridge, Eng.: Cambridge University Press, 1973.

An enlightening study of original sources pertaining to the Pharisees. Bowker precedes his translation of 183 selections from Josephus, the Talmuds, the Dead Sea Scrolls, and Apocryphal works with a helpful introductory essay on the difficulties of studying the Pharisees.

Bowman, John. The Samaritan Problem: Studies in the Relationship of Samaritanism, Judaism, and Early Christianity. Trans. Alfred M. Johnson, Jr. Pittsburgh: Pickwick, 1975.

From the Pittsburgh Theological Monograph Series, this work is divided into four sections: 1) "The History of the Samaritans," 2) "The Religion of the Samaritans," 3) "The Samaritans and the Gospel," and 4) "The Samaritans and the Sect of Qumran." Includes a selected bibliography and indexes for biblical passages and noncanonical literature.

Brandon, Samuel George F. The Fall of Jerusalem and the Christian Church: A Study of the Effects of the Jewish Overthrow of A.D. 70 on Christianity. London: SPCK, 1981. Originally published in 1948.

Against the backdrop of Jewish history and the war in 70 C.E., Brandon analyzes the origins of primitive Christianity and the early Church. This is a classic piece of scholarship concerning the effects the Jewish catastrophe of 70 C.E. had on the formation of Christianity and its writings.

————. Jesus and the Zealots: A Study of the Political Factor in Primitive Christianity. New York: Scribner, 1967.

Brandon contends that Jesus was a kind of Jewish nationalist, similar in ideology to the Zealots. This theory has not found much acceptance; however, there are many points that he has made that deserve notice in any discussion of the political aspects of Jesus' life.

————. The Trial of Jesus of Nazareth. New York: Stein and Day, 1968.

Along with Paul Winter's examination of the trial of Jesus, this assessment has also been lauded as central to an understanding of the historical aspects of Jesus' trial. Although he presents an historical study, Brandon is also sympathetic to the theological issues that are raised when interpreting sacred beliefs.

Branscomb, Bennett Harvie. Jesus and the Law of Moses. New York: Richard R. Smith, 1930.

In this insightful examination of Christian origins, the relationship of the New Testament and the Church to the Hebrew Scriptures and the Synagogue is examined. Particular attention is paid to how the teachings of Jesus bear on the rejection of Jewish law.

Cadbury, Henry J. The Peril of Modernizing Jesus. New York: Macmillan, 1937.

An appeal to view Jesus in the first century rather than in a twentieth-century framework. Cadbury looks at the Jewishness of the Gospels and suggests ways of viewing them and Jesus that are more appropriate in the first-century context.

Callan, Terrance. Forgetting the Past: The Emergence of Christianity from Judaism. New York: Paulist, 1986.

This aptly titled book surveys the events that led to the separation of Christianity from Judaism. The author concentrates on how the developing Church emerged from Judaism in the first four centuries.

Catchpole, David R. The Trial of Jesus: A Study in the Gospels and Jewish Historiography from 1770 to the Present Day. Leiden: Brill, 1971.

Catchpole presents a scholarly treatment of the subject matter. Divided into five sections: 1) "The Influence of Rabbinic Sources," 2) "The Question of the Charge against Jesus in the Sanhedrin," 3) "The Problem of the Sanhedrin Hearing in Luke," 4) "The Legal Setting of the Trial of Jesus," and a conclusion. Also includes a Jewish bibliography, reviews of Paul Winter's book, On the Trial of Jesus, a non-Jewish bibliography, and indexes.

Cohn, Haim. The Trial and Death of Jesus. New York: Ktav, 1977.

Written by an Israeli Supreme Court justice, this book considers the trial of Jesus in light of Jewish legal practice in Jesus' day. Done in a dramatic style, Cohn takes issue with the New Testament account and contends that the trial could not have taken place as described.

Cook, Michael J. Mark's Treatment of the Jewish Leaders. Leiden: Brill, 1978.

A scholarly examination of the Jewish leadership portrayed in Mark. Cook contends that the Evangelists were unclear about the identity of Jewish leaders and asserts that the group titles were literary devices. This work will assist those who wish to thoroughly explore the relationship of Jesus to his contemporary Jewish authorities.

Dalman, Gustaf. Jesus-Jeshua: Studies in the Gospels. Trans. Paul P. Levertaff. New York: Ktav, 1971.

First published in 1929, this study of Jesus' environment looks at the part Palestinian languages, the Synagogue, the fulfillment of the law, the Passover meal, and the cross played in his life. Valuable to scholars because of the research done in the original Aramaic, Greek, and Hebrew, and the helpful appendixes and indexes.

Danielou, Jean. The Theology of Jewish Christianity. Vol. 1 of The Development of Christian Doctrine before the Council of Nicaea. Trans. and ed. John A. Baker. Chicago: H. Regnery, 1964.

Danielou considers Jewish Christianity that expressed itself "in forms borrowed from Judaism," which included the Jerusalem Christian community and Jews who accept Christ as the messiah. This work will be of help to those attempting to understand the primitive Church and to those who wish to examine an historical study of Christian doctrine.

Danniel, Benjamin. Jesus, Jews, and Gentiles: The True Story of Their Relationship as Recorded in the Bible. New York: Arco, 1948.

A sharp and controversial evaluation of the New Testament. The author argues that the teaching of Christian anti-Judaism is based on misunderstanding and misinterpretation of the New Testament.

Daube, David. The New Testament and Rabbinic Judaism. Reprint ed. New York: Arno, 1973.

The rabbinic background of the New Testament is reviewed by examining parallel passages from Hebrew Scriptures and rabbinic literature. Sections include: 1) "Messianic Types," 2) "Legislative and Narrative Forms," and 3) "Concepts and Conventions."

Davies, W. D. Jewish and Pauline Studies. Philadelphia: Fortress, 1984.

A collection of Davies's essays. In them, he highlights Paul's Judaic background. Sections are on "Judaica," "Pauline Studies," and "New Testament Miscellanea."

——————. Paul and Rabbinic Judaism: Some Rabbinic Elements in Pauline Theology. Philadelphia: Fortress, 1980.

First published in 1948, this fourth edition contains yet another new preface by the author and more additions to bring this work up to date with Pauline scholarship. He frames the thesis of this work as "an attempt to set certain pivotal aspects of Paul's life and thought against the background of the contemporary Rabbinic Judaism, so as to reveal how, despite his apostleship to the Gentiles, he remained, as far as was possible, a Hebrew of the Hebrews, and baptized his rabbinic heritage into Christ."

Eller, Meredith Freeman. The Beginnings of the Christian Religion: A Guide to the History and Literature of Judaism and Christianity. New York: Bookman Associates, 1958.

Meant as a textbook for an introduction to biblical studies, this work thoroughly covers the period in which Christianity emerged. Helpful suggestions for further reading at the end of each chapter.

Enslin, Morton Scott. Christian Beginnings. New York: Harper and Brothers, 1938.

For a student, this work will ably cover the range of topics necessary to understand the origins of Christianity. Divided into three sections: 1) "The Jewish Background of Christianity," 2) The Beginnings of the Gospel Story," and 3) "Commentary and the Twenty-seven Books that Comprise the Literature of the Christian Movement."

Falk, Harvey. Jesus the Pharisee: A New Look at the Jewishness of Jesus. New York: Paulist, 1985.

Falk's thesis is that Jesus' criticism of his fellow Jews was directed principally at an opposing school, the School of Shammai. This kind of intra-Jewish criticism was common; regardless, it does not clearly support Falk's thesis. He makes extensive use of talmudic literature, but he has not thoroughly researched the several critical studies that have been published lately.

Finkel, Asher. The Pharisees and the Teacher of Nazareth: A Study of Their Background, Their Halachic and Midrashic Teachings, the Similarities and Differences. Leiden: Brill, 1974.

Thorough footnoting makes this work on the origins and teachings of the Pharisees useful to those who wish to understand this movement and its relationship to Jesus (who is frequently claimed to have been a Pharisee).

Fiorenza, Elisabeth Schussler, ed. Aspects of Religious Propaganda in Judaism and Early Christianity. Notre Dame, Ind.: University of Notre Dame Press, 1976.

From the lectures in a series on "Apologetics and Mission in Judaism and Early Christianity," these essays "attempt to elucidate in various ways and approaches the interdependence of Jewish and early Christian missionary activity and apologetics with the culture of the time." Contributors include Dieter Georgi, Wayne A. Meeks, Louis H. Feldman, Hans Dieter Betz, Judah Goldin, and Paul J. Achtemeier.

Fitzmyer, Joseph A. Essays on the Semitic Background of the New Testament. Missoula, Mont.: Scholars Press, 1974.

A scholarly presentation of the factors and conditions of the Semitic worlds of the eastern Mediterranean that pertain to the New Testament. Several of the essays analyze the relevance of various Aramaic and Qumran texts and fragments of passages in the New Testament.

Flusser, David. Jesus. Trans. Ronald Walls. New York: Herder and Herder, 1969.

Using New Testament scholarship and an understanding of Rabbinic Judaism, Flusser presents an absorbing account of "the story of Jesus' life."

Freyne, Sean. The World of the New Testament. Wilmington, Del.: Glazier, 1980.

An attempt to place in context—historically, sociologically, and theologically—the events of New Testament times. This introductory volume is meant for "the Christian who is eager to learn but is not a specialist." Contains a time chart and sections on the Greek inheritance, the Roman world, the Jewish religion, and early Christians.

Friedlander, Gerald. The Jewish Sources of the Sermon on the Mount. Prolegomenon by Solomon Zeitlin. New York: Ktav, 1969.

Originally published in 1911, this polemical work shows the connection of the Sermon on the Mount to its Jewish background. The author analyzes the different components of the Sermon on the Mount, i.e., the anti-Pharisaic elements, the aspects in opposition to Jewish teachings, and the antecedents of Hebrew Scripture and rabbinic literature.

Fruchtenbaum, Arnold G. Hebrew Christianity: Its Theology, History, and Philosophy. Washington, D.C.: Canon, 1974.

Those who wish to explore the ·fundamental beliefs and historical foundations of the Hebrew Christianity (also known as Jewish Christianity) movement will find this book helpful. The author broaches a controversial topic among Christians and Jews, that is: What are the qualifications to be a Jew? and Can you still be a Jew and believe in Jesus Christ? Also covers modern theology on the subject.

Fujita, Neil S. A Crack in the Jar: What Ancient Jewish Documents Tell Us about the New Testament. New York: Paulist, 1986.

In a very readable style, meant for the interested layperson, an introduction is offered to discoveries in the Judaean wilderness (chiefly the Dead Sea Scrolls). The impact of these findings on Hebrew Scripture and New Testament studies is then examined. The conclusion is that these findings are invaluable to our understanding of first-century Judaism and the emergence of Christianity.

Gartenhaus, Jacob. The "Christ-Killers": Past and Present. Chattanooga, Tenn.: Hebrew Christian Press, 1975.

A Hebrew Christian's version of the relationship of Jesus to the Jews, both in the first and the twentieth century.

Goldberg, Michael. Jews and Christians Getting Our Stories Straight: The Exodus and the Passion-Resurrection. Nashville: Abingdon, 1985.

Goldberg suggests that "the age-old doctrinal dispute between Jews and Christians has its source in a clash of interpretations centered around two specific stories." These "master stories," as the title indicates, are the Exodus from Egypt and the Resurrection of Jesus.

Goldstein, Morris. Jesus in the Jewish Tradition. New York: Macmillan, 1950.

Looking at Jesus in the Tannaitic period, the Amoraic period, and the post-Talmudic period, the author endeavors to tell the story of Jesus in Jewish life and literature. He states four reasons why this should be done: 1) it will give a clearer understanding of Judaism, past and present, 2) it is likewise of value to the student of Christianity, 3) it is important for the relationship of Christian and Jew, and 4) it gives a continuous historic account of the Jewish viewpoint on Jesus. Although slightly dated, this is a well-done and objective piece of historical research.

Goodman, Paul. The Synagogue and the Church: Being a Contribution to the Apologetics of Judaism. New York: Dutton, 1908.

The author feels that "to point to the imperishable import of the truths embodied in Judaism" it is "necessary to controvert the historic attitude and teachings of the Christian faith."

Goppelt, Leonhard. Jesus, Paul, and Judaism: An Introduction to New Testament Theology. Trans. and ed. Edward Schraeder. New York: Thomas Nelson, 1964.

Jesus' ministry and the primitive Church's controversy with Judaism are discussed. With the use of historical biblical scholarship, this introduction to New Testament theology attempts to understand Jesus and Paul in the context of the Judaism of their day. For the author, Jesus completes God's covenant with Israel.

Grant, Frederick C. Ancient Judaism and the New Testament. New York: Macmillan, 1959.

The author examines the Jewish background of the New Testament. He feels that "one cannot truly understand the New Testament or the religion it enshrines without a deep and sympathetic understanding of Judaism." His writing is indicative of this sympathetic outlook.

Greenspahn, Frederick E., ed. Scripture in the Jewish and Christian Traditions: Authority, Interpretation, Relevance. Nashville: Abingdon, 1982.

From a series of symposia given by the University of Denver's Center for Judaic Studies, these lectures discuss fundamental interpretations of Scripture from the perspective of Catholic, Jewish, and Protestant scholars. Contributors include Avery Dulles, John H. Gerstner, Jacob Neusner, Michael Fishbane, Bruce Vawter, David H. Kelsey, Sheldon H. Blank, Richard P. McBrien, and Krister Stendahl. The editor precedes each section with a helpful introduction.

Guignebert, Charles. The Jewish World in the Time of Jesus. Introduction by Charles Francis Potter. New York: University Books, 1959.

Originally published in French in 1935, this is another Christian work that puts Jesus into the Jewish milieu in which he was born. It discusses the political nature of Palestine, foreign influences, and Jewish religious life, all in the time of Jesus. Bibliography includes 340 works.

Hagner, Donald A. The Jewish Reclamation of Jesus: An Analysis and Critique of Modern Jewish Study of Jesus. Grand Rapids: Zondervan, 1984.

This evangelical perspective has its merits. Specifically, it is well-written and a fairly accurate assessment. However, there could be a wider selection of Jewish scholars treated, and Hagner's contention—that Jews have been unsuccessful in dealing with the Gospels because they have not accepted Jesus as the Messiah—will be problematic for Jews.

Harvey, A. E. Jesus and the Constraints of History. Philadelphia: Westminster, 1982.

Utilizing the best in New Testament scholarship, Harvey examines the historical, political, and legal constraints that existed in Jesus' lifetime. Well-written perspectives on the crucifixion, miracles, and monotheism.

Harvey, A. E., ed. Alternative Approaches to New Testament Study. London: SPCK, 1985.

The authors of these essays suggest that anthropological, linguistic, literary, and sociological developments should be utilized in the study of the New Testament. These suggested methods, designed to examine the New Testament in light of Judaism and the Graeco-Roman environment, are useful, but not particularly new.

Hengel, Martin. The Son of God: The Origin of Christology and the History of Jewish-Hellenistic Religion. Trans. John Bowden. Philadelphia: Fortress, 1976.

This short, critical discussion of New Testament Christology attempts to unite historical and theological scholarship and examines the idea of "the Son of God" in Graeco-Roman and Jewish thought.

Herford, R. Travers. Judaism in the New Testament Period. London: Lindsey, 1928.

Intended for New Testament readers who have no knowledge of rabbinic literature. Although the book is quite readable, it is dated and lacks accounts of recent discoveries and modern scholarship.

Jewett, Robert. Christian Tolerance: Paul's Message to the Modern Church. Philadelphia: Westminster, 1982.

Using Paul as a promoter of tolerance is not the norm. However, Jewett suggests that the passages considered intolerant are later interpolations, and that we should instead concentrate on his message of tolerance offered in Romans 15:7. This provocative work is dependent upon the historical-critical method.

Jocz, Jakob. The Jewish People and Jesus Christ: A Study in the Relationship between the Jewish People and Jesus Christ. London: SPCK, 1949.

An examination of the divisions created in Judaism when Jesus was proclaimed the Christ. Jocz also looks at primitive and contemporary Hebrew Christianity and other theological issues in the dialogue between Judaism and Christianity.

Kee, Howard Clark. Christian Origins in Sociological Perspective: Methods and Resources. Philadelphia: Westminster, 1980.

A lack of sociological concepts normally utilized for evaluating a community in a sociological perspective render the title an inaccurate description of this work.

Klausner, Joseph. From Jesus to Paul. Trans. William Stinespring. New York: Macmillan, 1943.

This work continues Klausner's examination of Christian origins. In it he attempts to understand Paul's role in early Christianity and why most Jews rejected Pauline Christianity.

————. Jesus of Nazareth: His Life, Times, and Teaching. Trans. Herbert Danby. New York: Macmillan, 1925.

Klausner, an eminent Jewish scholar, approaches the life of Jesus from an historical-critical perspective. He suggests that Jesus was basically a nationalist who did not achieve the goal of redeeming his people, and that this is the reason the Jews did not accept him as the Messiah.

Koenig, John. Jews and Christians in Dialogue: New Testament Foundations. Philadelphia: Westminster, 1979.

An exploration of the anti-Jewish polemic in the New Testament. The author suggests that there is much about the New Testament that is pro-Jewish and that can render it useful as a resource in Jewish-Christian dialogue.

Lachs, Samuel Tobias. A Rabbinic Commentary on the New Testament: The Gospels of Matthew, Mark, and Luke. New York: Ktav, 1987.

Lapide, Pinchas E. Israelis, Jews, and Jesus. Trans. Peter Heinegg. New York: Doubleday, 1979.

Jewish images of Jesus are explored in Hebrew literature, Israeli schoolbooks, and rabbinic literature. The section on the Israeli educational system is worth reading but the other two essays are superficial compared to studies done by Sandmel, Sanders, and Vermes on the same subject.

————. The Resurrection of Jesus: A Jewish Perspective. Minneapolis, Minn.: Augsburg, 1983.

One of the most controversial books included in this bibliography. Lapide, an Orthodox Jew, takes a positive view on Jesus' resurrection without accepting the Christian claim that Jesus was the Messiah. Carl E. Braaten, in the introduction, discusses the place of this book in the Jewish-Christian dialogue.

Lapide, Pinchas E., and Ulrich Luz. Jesus in Two Perspectives: A Jewish-Christian Dialog. Minneapolis, Minn.: Augsburg, 1985.

These two distinguished scholars discuss three questions: 1) "Did Jesus identify himself as the Messiah?" 2) "How did the people of Israel respond to Jesus?" and 3) "Did Jesus repudiate his own people?"

Lapide, Pinchas E., and Peter Stuhlmacher. Paul: Rabbi and Apostle. Trans.
    Lawrence W. Denef. Minneapolis, Minn.: Augsburg, 1984.

A Jewish and Christian theologian dialogue on Paul. Stuhlmacher's
essay is entitled "Paul: Apostate or Apostle?" and Lapide's is "The
Rabbi from Tarsus."

Leaney, A. R. C. The Jewish and Christian World 200 B.C. to A.D. 200.
    New York: Cambridge University Press, 1984.

This book, meant as an introductory text for college students, is an
account of Jewish and early Christian literature in the period of 200
B.C.E. to 200 C.E., and an outline of the history of the Jewish people
and the other nations with whom they came into contact. It serves
as a companion volume in the Cambridge Bible Commentary series.

Maccoby, Hyam. The Mythmaker: Paul and the Invention of Christianity.
    New York: Harper and Row, 1986.

Unorthodox theories are the norm in this work. Maccoby offers a
radical interpretation of the New Testament in which Paul was a
Sadducee--not a Pharisee--and the founder of Christianity.

————. Revolution in Judaea: Jesus and the Jewish Resistance. New
    York: Taplinger, 1981.

A dramatic revisionist reading of the Gospel that posits Jesus as the
leader of a revolutionary movement. Even if one could not possibly
entertain these fascinating theories (i.e., Jesus and Barabbas were
the same person, Judas Iscariot was Jesus' brother, etc.), it is valuable
to be exposed to them.

————. The Sacred Executioner: Human Sacrifice and the Legacy of
    Guilt. New York: Thames and Hudson, 1982.

Myths involving sacrificial rites, i.e., those surrounding Cain, Lamech,
Abraham and Isaac, Judas Iscariot, are analyzed in this absorbing and
well-written work. Maccoby argues that myth is the medium that
disguises the brutality of these events by which they have become
acceptable to human reason. There is also a chapter on the sacred
executioner in the modern world.

McNamara, Martin. Palestinian Judaism and the New Testament.
    Wilmington, Del.: Glazier, 1983.

This work is designed to be utilized by the New Testament student
who has little or no familiarity with first-century Judaism. McNamara
attempts to make understandable the diversity and variety of Judaism
in New Testament times by treating the relation of the New Testament
to Jewish apocalyptic literature, the Essenes, the Dead Sea Scrolls,
rabbinic tradition, and Arabic Targums.

Meyers, Eric M. and James F. Strange. Archaeology, the Rabbis, and Early
    Christianity. Nashville: Abingdon, 1981.

The authors integrate historical literature and current archaeological findings as they concentrate upon non-literary sources, archaeological discoveries in Galilee, languages of Roman Palestine, Jewish burial practices, and ancient churches and synagogues.

Modras, Ronald. Jesus of Nazareth: A Life Worth Living. Minneapolis, Minn.: Winston, 1983.

An attempt to bring what modern scholarship has discovered about Jesus to a wider readership. Written for those people who are "frightened off by footnotes."

Montefiore, C. G. Judaism and St. Paul: Two Essays. Reprint ed. New York: Arno, 1973.

In this work, originally published in 1914, Montefiore has composed two essays. The first is entitled, "The Genesis of the Religion of St. Paul," and the second, "The Relation of St. Paul to Liberal Judaism."

──────. Rabbinic Literature and Gospel Teachings. Prolegomenon by Eugene Mihaly. New York: Ktav, 1970.

A supplement to Montefiore's study on the Synoptic Gospels, this work examines rabbinic parallels to the gospels.

──────. The Synoptic Gospels. Two vols. Prolegomenon by Lou H. Silberman. New York: Ktav, 1968.

Recent scholarship makes this study somewhat dated. However, Montefiore's perspective (that of liberal Judaism) is presented in a thorough manner useful for someone who wishes to look at secondary literature, to which he refers frequently.

Moore, George Foot. Judaism in the First Centuries of the Christian Era: The Age of the Tannaim. Cambridge: Harvard University Press, 1958.

Moore, one of the first Christian writers to do justice to rabbinic theology, presents to the Christian reader an examination of "the religious conception and moral principles of Judaism, its modes of worship and observance, and its distinctive piety, in the form in which, by the end of the second century, they attained general acceptance and authority."

Neusner, Jacob. Christian Faith and the Bible of Judaism: The Judaic Encounter with Scripture. Grand Rapids: Eerdmans, 1987.

──────. First-Century Judaism in Crisis: Yohanan ben Zakkai and the Renaissance of Torah. New York: Ktav, 1982.

Will serve as a worthwhile introduction to the general chaos and confusion in the world of the Jews in the first century of the common era. Neusner has divided the book into three parts: 1) "Chaos and Routine," 2) "Society and Scripture," and 3) "Death and Rebirth."

————. From Politics to Piety: The Emergence of Pharisaic Judaism. Englewood Cliffs: Prentice Hall, 1973.

In this most readable work on the Pharisees, Neusner assesses and criticizes the problem of the historical Pharisees, the picture of the best-known Pharisee, Hillel, the depiction of the Pharisees by Josephus and the Gospels, and the rabbinical traditions about the Pharisees.

————. Judaism in the Beginning of Christianity. Philadelphia: Fortress, 1984.

Written as a textbook, this is another work that places the development of Christianity into its Jewish milieu and its formative influences. Several topics are discussed, including historical context, Jewish piety, the Pharisees, Hillel, and post-Temple Judaism.

————. Judaism in the Matrix of Christianity. Philadelphia: Fortress, 1986.

A companion volume to Neusner's earlier book, Judaism in the Beginning of Christianity. Whereas the first book examined the emergence of Christianity from Judaism, the second looks at the response of Judaism to emerging Christianity. The emphasis is on the part fourth-century rabbis played in developing concepts such as the outsider, the city, the meaning of Scripture, the Torah, and the messiah. The conclusion is that the study of these two religions should be done in the context of their formation together.

Neusner, Jacob., ed. Christianity, Judaism, and Other Graeco-Roman Cults: Studies for Morton Smith at Sixty. Leiden: Brill, 1975.

An impressive volume of essays by distinguished scholars in the areas of New Testament, early Christianity, Judaism before 70 C.E., Judaism after 70 C.E., and other Graeco-Roman cults.

Oesterley, W. O. E. The Gospel Parables in the Light of Jewish Background. New York: Macmillan, 1936.

Oesterley presents a set of lectures (in revised and amplified form) on the significance of understanding the Hebrew Scriptures to comprehend the meaning and nature of the Gospel Parables. He utilizes the scholarship of Abrahams, Loewe, and Montefiore.

————. The Jews and Judaism during the Greek Period: The Background of Christianity. Port Washington, N.Y.: Kennikat, 1970.

Originally published in 1941, the author intended this work as preparation necessary for understanding the New Testament and its origins. The six sections include 1) "Historical introduction," 2) "The Sources," 3) "The Theology of Early Judaism," 4) "Worship," 5) "Teachers," and 6) "Belief in Intermediate Supernatural Beings."

Oesterley, W. O. E., H. Loewe, and Erwin I. J. Rosenthal, eds. Judaism and Christianity. Three vols. in one. New York: Ktav, 1969.

A dense opus comprised of essays on the age of transition, the contact of Pharisaism with other cultures, and law and religion. Excellent for scholars and students doing a serious examination of the subject matter.

Rhyne, C. Thomas. Faith Establishes the Law. Chico, Calif.: Scholars, 1981.

Dissertation that concentrates on "the question of the continuity between Judaism and Christianity as it relates to Paul's understanding of the law." Well-argued exegesis on Paul's letter to the Romans.

Riches, John. Jesus and the Transformation of Jesus. London: Darton, Longman, and Todd, 1980.

This work's central concern is a response to the question "What was Jesus' purpose?" Riches attempts to answer this question by presenting an historical appreciation of Jesus and the cultural and political background in which he lived. He also examined Jesus' relationship to the "Kingdom of God."

Rivkin, Ellis. A Hidden Revolution. Nashville: Abingdon, 1978.

Rivkin is known for his scholarly work on the Pharisees, and this book substantiates his fame. His thorough research helps the reader to understand that the stereotyped image of the Pharisees has no valid place in history. Analyzing several resources and building upon past insights, he presents a clearer and more detailed picture of the Pharisees and their movement.

—————. What Crucified Jesus? Nashville: Abingdon, 1984.

The answer to the question is, the imperial system of Rome. Rivkin believes that the Romans were responsible for the political execution of a charismatic, Jesus. This brief religious, social, and political history of life in Jesus' time is stimulating and thoughtful reading.

Russell, D. S. From Early Judaism to Early Church. Philadelphia: Fortress, 1986.

Writing with the student in mind, Russell traces the impact of Judaism on early Christianity and the New Testament. Useful as a supplement to a course on the New Testament.

Safrai, S., et al., eds. The Jewish People in the First Century: Historical Geography, Political History, Social, Cultural and Religious Life, and Institutions. 2 vols. Philadelphia: Fortress, 1974-76.

Chapters include 1) "Sources," 2) "Historical Geography of Palestine," 3) "The Jewish Diaspora," 4) "Relations between the Diaspora and the Land of Israel," 5) "The Reign of Herod and the Herodian Dynasty," 6) "The Province of Judaea," 7) "Jewish Self-Government," 8) "The Legal Status of the Jewish Communities in the Diaspora," 9) "The Organization of the Jewish Communities in the Diaspora," 10) "Private Law," 11) "Aspects of Jewish Society: The Priesthood and Other

Classes," 12) "Economic Life in Palestine," 13) "The Social and Economic Status of the Jews in the Diaspora," 14) "Home and Family," 15) "Religion in Everyday Life," 16) "The Calendar," 17) "The Temple," 18) "The Synagogue," 19) "Education and the Study of the Torah," 20) "Art and Architecture in Palestine," 21) "Hebrew and Aramaic in the First Century," 22) "Greek in Palestine and the Diaspora," 23) "Paganism in Palestine," and 24) "The Jews in Greek and Latin Literature."

Sanders, E. P. Jesus and Judaism. Philadelphia: Fortress, 1985.

Sanders, whose previous works have shown a good grasp of Jewish literature and history, has turned his skills to the life, work, and death of Jesus in his Jewish environment. This work, which does not use doctrinal biases as do many others on this subject, is one of the best tools for understanding the "facts" about Jesus and for gaining an awareness of his relationship to Judaism.

──────. Paul, the Law, and the Jewish People. Philadelphia: Fortress, 1983.

Sander's second scholarly volume on Paul clarifies earlier positions and tackles issues not considered in his first book. It is divided into two essays, "Paul and the Law" and "Paul and the Jewish People."

──────. Paul and Palestinian Judaism: A Comparison of Patterns of Religion. Philadelphia: Fortress, 1977.

This comparative study on Palestinian Judaism and the most important New Testament writer offers a new perspective on the Jewish context of Pauline thought. Applying his usual careful and thorough scholarship, Sanders uses a holistic approach to studying first-century Judaism by analyzing apocrypha, the Dead Sea Scrolls, rabbinic sources, pseudepigraphs, and the New Testament.

Sandmel, Samuel. The First Christian Century in Judaism and Christianity: Certainties and Uncertainties. New York: Oxford University Press, 1969.

Sandmel, a Jewish New Testament scholar, considers the variety of thought in the Judaism and Christianity of the first century from the perspective of a religious historian. Important questions are raised in this study.

──────. The Genius of Paul: A Study in History. New York: Farrar, Straus, and Cudahy, 1958.

Paul is seen as a religious genius who transformed a sect of Judaism into a world religion. Sandmel uses this as the basis for interpreting the Jewish background of Paul's teachings. As usual, he argues his interpretations forcefully.

──────. A Jewish Understanding of the New Testament. Augmented ed. New York: Ktav, 1974.

Although written for Jews who know little or nothing about Christian
Scriptures, it would still be good reading for Christians who wonder
what Jews think about the New Testament. Sandmel examines the
Jewish background and places the New Testament in the Hellenistic
world by using an historical approach.

————. Judaism and Christian Beginnings. New York: Oxford University
Press, 1978.

This "non-technical" book has been written with the purpose of relating
scholarship in the areas of Hebrew Scriptures, Palestinian Judaism,
Hellenistic Judaism, Dead Sea Scrolls, New Testament, and rabbinic
literature. Sandmel has provided a helpful perspective by showing
how different aspects of this scholarship can illuminate each other.

————. We Jews and Jesus. New York: Oxford University Press, 1965.

This book was written for Jews with the specific purpose of explaining
the relationship of the "Jewish Jesus" and the "Christian Christ" to
Jews. There are chapters on Judaism's relationship to early
Christianity, to the Gospels, and its attitude toward Christianity.
Sandmel also provides a discerning survey of nineteenth-century and
twentieth-century New Testament scholarship.

Schoeps, Hans-Joachin. Jewish Christianity: Factional Disputes in the
Early Church. Trans. Douglas R. A. Hare. Philadelphia: Fortress,
1969.

Those who wish to know more about early sects of primitive
Christianity, such as the Ebionites, will wish to consult this book.
It is fairly clear that some of the earliest followers of Jesus were
involved in the Jewish Christian movement. Schoeps discusses in
depth the literature, organization, and attitudes of this movement.

————. Paul: The Theology of the Apostle in the Light of Jewish
Religious History. Trans. Harold Knight. Philadelphia: Westminster,
1961.

A perceptive look at the Apostle Paul against the background of
Judaism. Schoeps looks at problems in Pauline research, Paul in
primitive Christianity, the eschatology and soteriology of Paul, and
his relationship to law and grace.

Schurer, Emil. The Literature of the Jewish People in the Time of Jesus.
Ed. with an introduction by Nahum N. Glatzer. New York: Schocken,
1972.

A classic study on the Palestinian-Jewish and Graeco-Jewish literature
in the era of Judaism in the centuries preceding the rise of Christianity
through the Bar Kokhba rebellion.

Segal, Alan F. Rebecca's Children: Judaism and Christianity in the Roman
World. Cambridge, Mass.: Harvard University Press, 1986.

Using social science theories, Segal offers insights into the common heritage Rabbinic Judaism and Christianity shared in the first century of the common era.

————. Two Powers in Heaven: Early Rabbinic Reports about Christianity and Gnosticism. Leiden: Brill, 1977.

An exploration of the relationships between Rabbinic Judaism, Merkabah mysticism, early Christianity, and their views on "two powers in heaven." Insightful scholarship on how the rabbis perceived emerging Christianity.

Shires, Henry M. Finding the Old Testament in the New. Philadelphia: Westminster, 1974.

An example of fulfillment theology. This work emphasizes one's need to understand the Hebrew Scriptures before one can make sense of the New Testament.

Simon, Marcel. Jewish Sects at the Time of Jesus. Trans. James H. Farley. Philadelphia: Fortress, 1967.

It is well known that there were several movements in Judaism in the first century. Simon has presented these movements in a clear readable manner that will throw light on this lively era.

Sloyan, Gerard S. Is Christ the End of the Law? Philadelphia: Westminster, 1978.

The law-grace dichotomy is explored in this work by a reknowned Catholic scholar. Starting with the Torah, he traces the implications of this division through the Gospels, Paul, Graeco-Roman influences, the Church Fathers, and far contemporary faith.

————. Jesus in Focus: A Life in Its Setting. Mystic, Conn.: Twenty-Third Publications, 1983.

Meant for a general readership, this book attempts to show the significance of Jesus and at the same time place him in his historical context. A readable work with aptly chosen examples that illustrate the author's theses.

————. Jesus on Trial: The Development of the Passion Narratives and Their Historical and Ecumenical Implications. Ed. with an introduction by John Reumann. Philadelphia: Fortress, 1973.

Drawing upon evidence from the Gospels, Sloyan contends that even though Jewish leadership was aware of the consequences of the trial, the Romans are the ones who bear responsibility for the death of Jesus. Concludes with a selected bibliography on the passion and trial of Jesus.

Spong, John Shelby. This Hebrew Lord. New York: Seabury, 1974.

The Christian story of Jesus is investigated and found lacking. The author instead calls for an understanding of Jesus through the eyes and minds of the Hebrews. For Christians who are searching to understand what Christ can mean for them in the modern world.

Stendahl, Krister. Paul among Jews and Gentiles and Other Essays. Philadelphia: Fortress, 1976.

This short work has challenged many scholars and others to rethink their understanding of Paul. Useful as a college-level introduction to Paul's thought.

Toynbee, Arnold, ed. The Crucible of Christianity: Judaism, Hellenism, and the Historical Background of the Christian Faith. New York: World, 1969.

An excellent volume which places Christianity in its historical context. Just a few of the subjects covered in this encyclopedic work include historical antecedents of the Mediterranean world, Palestine under the Seleucids and Romans, Jewish religious parties and sects, Christianity as a Jewish sect, and Gnosticism. Also contains a select bibliography and a list and sources of illustrations, drawings, maps, and plans.

Trattner, Ernest R. As a Jew Sees Jesus. New York: Scribner, 1931.

This book is easy reading about the relationship of Jesus to Judaism, the Pharisees, and the modern Jew. Useful even though it is over fifty years old. There is an extensive bibliography of materials on Jesus produced by Jewish writers.

Vermes, Geza. Jesus and the World of Judaism. Philadelphia: Fortress, 1983.

A set of lectures, given by the author and previously published elsewhere, has been compiled and newly revised. The subject matter, Vermes contends, is more suitably described as Jesus within the world of early Judaism.

————. Jesus the Jew: A Historian's Reading of the Gospels. New York: Macmillan, 1973.

Although the book takes advantage of "specialized knowledge of the history, institutions, languages, culture and literature of Israel both in Palestine and the Diaspora," it depends too much on Talmud and Midrash for its understanding of first-century Judaism. Still this is a first-rate contribution that adds much to the growing literature of the field.

Walker, Thomas. Jewish Views of Jesus. London: Allen and Unwin, 1931.

Although several Jewish scholars have published significant works on Jesus since this book was written, the author ably articulates the representative positions of six earlier Jewish scholars who have deliberated on Jesus. For Jewish orthodoxy he cites Paul Goodman and Gerald Friedlander, and for Jewish liberalism he presents C.

G. Montefiore and Israel Abrahams. There are also portraits of Jesus by Joseph Jacobs and Joseph Klausner.

Watson, Francis. Paul, Judaism, and the Gentiles: A Sociological Approach. New York: Cambridge University Press, 1986.

This scholarly work, which grew from a doctoral thesis, examines the problems one is faced with when attempting to interpret Paul's writings with an exclusively theological understanding. The author utilizes a sociological perspective to demonstrate "that the view of Paul's controversy with Judaism and Jewish Christianity which derives from the Reformation is seriously misleading, and that the Pauline texts become much more readily comprehensible when one abandons this overtly theological approach."

Weiss-Rosmarin, Trude, ed. Jewish Expressions on Jesus. New York: Ktav, 1977.

Essays by Jewish scholars that concentrate on the rediscovery of the historical Jesus. Contributors include Jacob Z. Lauterbach, Samuel Sandmel, Solomon Zeitlin, Joseph Klausner, Hans Joachin Schoeps, Ben Zion Bokser, Martin Buber, Jules Isaac, Haim Cohn, Abba Hillel Silver, Walter Kaufmann, and Franz Rosenzweig.

Whittaker, Molly. Jews and Christians: Graeco-Roman Views. New York: Cambridge University Press, 1984.

Ancient pagan literature is used to illuminate Christianity, Judaism, and pagan religions. Helpful commentaries and a good organization make this a convenient resource for students and general readers alike.

Wilkinson, John. Jerusalem as Jesus Knew It: Archaeology as Evidence. London: Thames and Hudson, 1978.

Although it is always important to consider archaeological evidence, the connections drawn between the evidence and the New Testament are frequently conjecture in this presentation.

Wilson, William Riley. The Execution of Jesus: A Judicial, Literary, and Historical Investigation. New York: Scribner, 1970.

A readable analysis of the events surrounding Jesus' crucifixion. Chapters cover the Jewish legal system, Pontius Pilate, the trial in the Gospels, the Roman condemnation, and the execution.

Winter, Paul. On the Trial of Jesus. Second ed. rev. and ed. T. A. Burkill and Geza Vermes. New York: Walter De Gruyter, 1974.

This critical evaluation of the Gospel accounts of Jesus' trial and crucifixion combines literary and historical analysis, resulting in a complex and scholarly treatment. Winter, a European Jewish scholar, separates certain and probable facts from questions which will have to remain unanswered. This revised edition utilizes some of Winter's supplementary notes.

Wolfson, Harry Austryn. Philo: Foundations of Religious Philosophy in Judaism, Christianity, and Islam. 2 vols. Cambridge: Harvard University Press, 1947.

A detailed treatment of the effects of Philonic philosophy on the religious philosophies of Judaism, Christianity, and Islam.

Zeitlin, Solomon. Who Crucified Jesus? New York: Harper and Brothers, 1942.

In this classic on the crucifixion of Jesus, Zeitlin proposes the two-Sanhedrin theory, which claims that one body dealt with religious matters and the other took care of problems of a political nature. This theory and its relevance to the crucifixion of Jesus are explained along with an attempt to reconstruct the historical background of Judaism in Jesus' life.

C. Patristic/Talmudic Period

This section considers works dealing with the period from approximately the second to the fifth century.

Dalman, Gustaf. Jesus Christ in the Talmud, Midrash, Zohar, and the Liturgy of the Synagogue. Reprint ed. New York: Arno Press, 1973.

A short scholarly work on censorship in the Talmud concerning the designations of Jesus, his origins, works, and death. Originally published in 1893, this work includes the original texts and their translations.

De Lange, N. R. M. Origen and the Jews: Studies in Jewish-Christian Relations in Third-Century Palestine. New York: Cambridge University Press, 1976.

Origen and his place in the history of Jewish-Christian relations are assessed against his Jewish background by examining his contact with living Jews. A well-written work with complete indexes, a helpful bibliography, and thorough endnotes.

Grant, Robert M. Early Christianity and Society: Seven Studies. San Francisco: Harper and Row, 1977.

The early Christian church's relationship to Roman society is analyzed in essays on taxation, work, property, charity, and other social themes. A commendable use of sources.

————. Gods and the One God. Philadelphia: Westminster, 1986.

Early Christian identity is examined and placed in its Graeco-Roman context. The Christian and pagan concepts of God are also analyzed.

Herford, R. Travers. Christianity in Talmud and Midrash. New York: Ktav, 1975.

Relevant references to Jesus, New Testament figures, and Christians have been thoroughly compiled, translated, and annotated. This work makes available to scholars rabbinic literature that is useful in understanding the relationship of Judaism to developing Christianity.

Himmelfarb, Martha. Tours of Hell: An Apocalyptic Form in Jewish and Christian Literature. Philadelphia: Fortress, 1983.

Seventeen "tours through hell" are examined in Jewish and Christian texts from late antiquity and the early middle ages. Himmelfarb has produced a well-documented study that will find an audience among those interested in this fascinating aspect of apocalyptic literature.

Klijn, A. F. J., and G. J. Reinink. Patristic Evidence for Jewish-Christian Sects. Leiden: Brill, 1973.

The authors have amassed a collection of passages from early Christian sources for scholars interested in studying the development and origins of Jewish Christian sects in the first centuries of the common era.

Meeks, Wayne A., and Robert L. Wilken. Jews and Christians in Antioch in the First Four Centuries of the Common Era. Missoula, Mont.: Scholars, 1978.

The authors provide resources for the study of early Christianity in the Roman Empire and suggest that in this study it is necessary to understand the Judaism of the same era. Would be a useful textbook for graduate study on the subject because of the variety of content, which includes archaeological sources, letters of Libanius concerning the Jews and his oration on systems of patronage, and John Chrysostum's Homilia Adversus Judaeos.

Meyer, Ben F., and E. P. Sanders. Jewish and Christian Self-Definition Volume 3. Self-Definition in the Graeco-Roman World. Philadelphia: Fortress, 1982.

The third volume in a series of essays on the interpretation of religious institutions in the patristic period. Topics include Graeco-Roman philosophical and medical schools, religious cults, magic, and other defining aspects of Christianity and Judaism in the second and third century.

Neusner, Jacob. Aphrahat and Judaism: The Christian-Jewish Argument in Fourth-Century Iran. Leiden: Brill, 1971.

Neusner has translated the relevant polemical works of Aphrahat, the Christian monk and father of the Syriac-speaking church in Iran. Aphrahat's Demonstrations and other studies of pertinent issues are helpful in understanding Jewish-Christian relations of this era.

————. Judaism and Christianity in the Age of Constantine: History, Messiah, Israel, and the Initial Confrontation. Chicago: University of Chicago Press, 1987.

Richardson, Peter. Israel in the Apostolic Church. Cambridge, Mass.: Cambridge University Press, 1969.

From Justin's claim in 160 C.E. that the Church equals the "true Israel" through the patristic writings and the New Testament itself, this doctoral dissertation examines the estrangement of the early Church from Judaism. This is a worthwhile tool for the study of this problem because of the skilled exegesis, the consideration of the problem historically, sociologically, and theologically, and the inclusion of appendixes and indexes.

Sanders, E. P., ed. Jewish and Christian Self-Definition. Vol. 1 The Shaping of Christianity in the Second and Third Centuries. Philadelphia: Fortress, 1980.

The first of three volumes of papers presented at symposia held at McMaster University in 1978, 1979, and 1980. It concentrates on Christianity's self-definition during its infancy, paying particular attention to the social setting and rejection of Gnosticism. The papers, given by scholars with established expertise in the field, are worthwhile for those interested in further investigation of the patristic period.

Sanders, E. P., ed. with A. I. Baumgarten and Alan Mendelsohn. Jewish and Christian Self-Definition. Vol. 2. Aspects of Judaism in the Graeco-Roman Period. Philadelphia: Fortress, 1981.

Internationally prominent scholars focus on Judaism's rejection of Christianity and the questions this issue raises. This volume recognizes the effects Christianity, Hellenism, the process of canonization, and other factors exerted on normative Judaism in this era.

Simon, Marcel. Verus Israel: A Study of the Relations between Christians and Jews in the Roman Empire, 5135-4252. Trans. by H. McKeating. New York: Oxford University Press, 1986.

Originally published over forty years ago, this work—on the relationship of Judaism and Christianity during its formative period in the Roman Empire—is of central importance to the study of the patristic/talmudic period. Part 1: "The Religious and Political Setting" includes chapters on Palestinian Judaism, the Diaspora, the Church and Israel, Rome, Judaism, and Christianity; Part 2: "The Conflict of Orthodoxies" includes the topics of anti-Jewish polemic, Christians in the Talmud, and Christian anti-Judaism; and Part 3: "Contact and Assimilation" covers the fate of Jewish Christianity, Jewish proselytism, Judaizers within the Church, and superstition and magic.

Wilde, Robert. The Treatment of the Jews in the Christian Writers of the First Three Centuries. Cleveland: Zubal, 1984.

A comprehensive presentation of the treatment of the Jews from pagan writings during the Babylonian exile to Greek ecclesiastical authors at the end of the third century.

Wilken, Robert L. John Chrysostom and the Jews: Rhetoric and Reality
in the Late Fourth Century. Berkeley: University of California Press,
1983.

Wilken's purpose is to use John Chrysostom's homilies "as a window
on the fourth century through which to view the relations between
Jews and Christians in the later Roman Empire." He accomplishes
this from a fresh perspective that makes for interesting reading.

—————. Judaism and the Early Christian Mind: A Study of Cyril of
Alexandria's Exegesis and Theology. New Haven, Conn.: Yale University
Press, 1971.

Examining the nature of Jewish-Christian relations in the patristic
era reveals that polemical works against Judaism had a great influence
in shaping Cyril's exegetical and theological reflection. This book
is a good starting point for understanding not only Cyril but also the
development of Christian thought in this era. Wilken has included
a helpful bibliography of the works of Cyril and secondary sources.

Wilken, Robert L., ed. Aspects of Wisdom in Judaism and Early Christianity.
Notre Dame, Ind: University of Notre Dame Press, 1975.

These essays, originally presented at a seminar on wisdom in late
antiquity at the University of Notre Dame, show the development
of the wisdom tradition in both Christianity and Judaism and its relation
to Graeco-Roman thought. Contributors include James M. Robinson,
Elisabeth Schussler Fiorenza, Birger A. Pearson, Henry A. Fischel,
Jean Laporte, William R. Schoedel, and the editor.

Williams, A. Lukyn. Talmudic Judaism and Christianity. London: Society
for Promoting Christian Knowledge, 1933.

In this short work, the Talmud is considered both apart from and in
relation to the New Testament. Herford's work on the same subject
is far more thorough.

D. From the Middle Ages to the Enlightenment

Includes works covering the period from approximately the sixth century
to the nineteenth century.

Baer, Yitzhak. A History of the Jews in Christian Spain. 2 vols. Trans.
Louis Schoffman. Philadelphia: Jewish Publication Society, 1961.

Volume one covers the age of reconquest to the fourteenth century
and volume two from the fourteenth century to the expulsion. A
definitive study of the subject matter.

Berger, David. The Jewish-Christian Debate in the High Middle Ages:
A Critical Edition of the Nizzahon Vetus. Philadelphia: Jewish
Publication Society, 1979.

The Nizzahon Vetus or Old Book of Polemic is an aggressive piece
of Jewish polemical literature that is filled with insights on the nature
of Jewish-Christian relations in the medieval era. Berger presents
a lucid translation with commentary and the original Hebrew text.

Berman, Lawrence et al., contributors. Bibliographical Essays in Medieval
Jewish Studies. New York: Ktav/Anti-Defamation League of B'nai
B'rith, 1976.

The second volume in the Study of Judaism series, this work contains
essays on Jews in Western Europe, the Church and the Jews, Jews
under Islam, medieval Jewish religious philosophy, medieval Jewish
mysticism, and minor midrashim. Contributors include Lawrence
V. Berman, Mark R. Cohen, Ivan G. Marcus, Kenneth R. Stow, John
T. Townsend, Jochanan H. A. Wijnhoven, and Yosef H. Yerushalmi.

Chazan, Robert, ed. Church, State, and Jews in the Middle Ages. New
York: Behrman House, 1980.

Letters, narratives, official pronouncements, and perceptive
commentary are divided into six parts: 1) "The Formal Position of
the Church," 2) "The Charters of the State," 3) Protection of the
Jews," 4) "Ecclesiastical Limitations," 5) "Missionizing among the
Jews," and 6) "Governmental Persecution."

Eidelberg, Shlomo, trans. and ed. The Jews and the Crusaders: The Hebrew
Chronicles of the First and Second Crusades. Madison, Wis.: University
of Wisconsin Press, 1977.

This historical account of medieval Jewish-Christian hostility contains
The Chronicle of Solomon bar Simson, The Chronicle of Rabbi Eliezer
bar Nathan, Mainz Anonymous, and Sefer Zekhirah.

Friedman, Jerome. The Most Ancient Testimony: Sixteenth-Century
Christian-Hebraica in the Age of Renaissance Nostalgia. Athens,
Ohio: Ohio University Press, 1983.

For a better understanding of Christianity, Protestant scholars in
the sixteenth century had to "return" to the sources and utilize the
abilities of Jewish scholars to understand these sources. In this light,
the author's purpose in this well-written study is to "present some
reasons why Christians used Jewish sources and how they were used,
which sources were the most popular and why, and how this new
learning fit into the framework of Renaissance and Reformation
intellectual and theological contexts."

Grayzel, Solomon. The Church and the Jews in the Thirteenth Century:
A Study of Their Relations during the Years 1198-1254, Based on
the Papal Letters and the Conciliar Decrees of the Period. Rev.
ed. New York: Hermon, 1966.

Authoritative study of references to Jews in official Church documents
in the first half of the thirteenth century. The Latin text and English
translation are provided.

Hailperin, Herman. Rashi and the Christian Scholars. Pittsburgh: University of Pittsburgh Press, 1963.

Over 1,100 notes support the judgment that this is a scholarly treatment of the French rabbi, Rashi (1030-1105), and his impact on Christian scholars, particularly the Franciscan, Nicholas De Lyra. Also contains general, biblical, rabbinic, and other sources indexes.

Hertzberg, Arthur. The French Enlightenment and the Jews. New York: Columbia University Press, 1968.

A major scholarly study of the effects of the French Jews' emancipation in the late 1700s and the resulting cultural and social problems.

Katz, David S. Philo-Semitism and the Readmission of the Jews to England 1603-1655. New York: Oxford University Press, 1982.

In a well-written work, Katz describes the events that led to the Whitehall Conference held in 1655, during which a petition was received to readmit the Jews to England.

Katz, Jacob. Exclusiveness and Tolerance: Studies in Jewish-Gentile Relations in Medieval and Modern Times. Westport, Conn.: Greenwood, 1980.

From the middle ages to the Enlightenment, this work attempts to shed light on Jewish attitudes towards non-Jews. Particular emphasis is placed on Ashkenazi Jewry.

Lasker, Daniel J. Jewish Philosophical Polemics against Christianity in the Middle Ages. New York: Ktav/Anti-Defamation League of B'nai B'rith, 1977.

An excellent addition to the study of medieval Jewish-Christian religious polemics. Jewish philosophical arguments against the doctrines of the incarnation, transubstantiation, the Trinity, and the virgin birth are presented and discussed at length.

Maccoby, Hyam, ed. and trans. Judaism on Trial: Jewish-Christian Disputations in the Middle Ages. Rutherford, N.J.: Fairleigh Dickinson University Press, 1982.

Maccoby, in his usual readable style, presents three disputations and Christian accounts of the Paris Disputations of 1240, the Tortosa Disputation of 1413-14, and the Barcelona Disputation of 1263 (specifically the classic narrative of Nachmanides).

Marcus, Jacob R. The Jew in the Medieval World: A Source Book, 315-1791. New York: Atheneum, 1969.

Marcus presents advertisements, book prefaces, codes, commentaries, communal statutes, epitaphs, ethical and pedagogical writings, folk tales, historical narratives, legal opinions, martyrologies, memoirs, and polemics in an attempt "to reflect the life of the medieval Jew as seen through the eyes of contemporaries." The book is divided into three sections: 1) "The State and the Jew," 2) "The Church and the Jew," and 3) "Jewry and the Individual Jew."

Newman, Louis Israel. Jewish Influences on Christian Reform Movements. New York: Columbia University Press, 1925.

The study of medieval religious thought has been improved by the addition of this encyclopedic volume on the contribution of Judaism to Christian reform movements. Covers the major movements between the eleventh and sixteenth centuries, the Inquisition, and American Puritanism.

Parkes, James. The Jew in the Medieval Community: A Study of His Political and Economic Situation. Foreword by Morton C. Fierman. Second ed. New York: Hermon, 1976.

First published in 1938, this reprint celebrates Parkes's eightieth birthday. One of his many contributions to improving the understanding of the history of Jewish-Christian relations, this work examines the economic and political factors of medieval European Jewry, such as the First Crusades, legal restrictions against the Jews, Christian anti-Judaism, and the origins and role of the Jewish usurer.

Schiffman, Lawrence H. Who Was a Jew? Rabbinic and Halakhic Perspectives on the Jewish Christian Schism. New York: Ktav, 1985.

Utilizing Talmudic sources, Schiffman presents a scholarly look at the issue of Jewish identity by examining the topics of Jew by birth, conversion to Judaism, heretics and apostates, Tannaitic Judaism and the early Christians, and the Jewish Christians in Tannaitic narrative.

Seiferth, Wolfgang S. Synagogue and Church in the Middle Ages: Two Symbols in Art and Literature. Trans. Lee Chadeayne and Paul Gottwald. New York: Ungar, 1970.

An historical study of symbolism in the middle ages, this articulate work concentrates on Jewish and Christian approaches to life. Includes sixty-five illustrations.

Synan, Edward A. The Popes and the Jews in the Middle Ages. New York: Macmillan, 1965.

New translations of documents that are concerned with Jewish-papal relations and thoughtful reflections on their significance for today's Christian.

Trachtenberg, Joshua. The Devil and the Jew: The Medieval Conception of the Jew and Its Relation to Modern Anti-Semitism. Philadelphia: Jewish Publication Society, 1983.

Originally published in 1943. A companion volume to Jewish Magic and Superstition, this insightful work looks at Christian material on the perception of the Jew in the middle ages. The volume is divided into three sections: "The 'Demonic' Jew," "The Jew as Sorcerer," and "The Jew as Heretic."

Williams, A. Lukyn. <u>Adversus Judaeos</u>: <u>A Bird's Eye View of Christian Apologiae until the Renaissance</u>. London: Cambridge University Press, 1935.

Christian apologetics are traced through the Ante-Nicene Fathers, and the Syriac, Greek, Spanish, and Latin writers. The author has intended, as one of the reasons for the study of these treatises, to "supply arguments likely to be of assistance in their presentation of the Faith." However, he concludes they will be of little use as "weapons in our spiritual warfare" because there are modern ones which are much better.

E. Holocaust

There are obviously many more books on the Holocaust than are presented in this section. This selection is, however, representative of works that deal with Jewish-Christian relations in light of the Holocaust, and conversely the Holocaust in light of Jewish-Christian relations. For a more thorough list of books in this area, please refer to the Bibliographies section.

Bauer, Yehuda. <u>A History of the Holocaust</u>. New York: Franklin Watts, 1982.

An eminent Israeli authority on the Holocaust, Bauer has written one of the best works available on the history of the Holocaust. This comprehensive work is a synthesis of the historical conditions that led to the Holocaust, Jewish resistance, Nazi policy, excerpts from diaries and memoirs, modern anti-Judaism, Hitler's rise, the Ghettos, the Weimar Republic, the aftermath, and much more.

----------. <u>The Jewish Emergence from Powerlessness</u>. Toronto: University of Toronto Press, 1979.

Short historical study on the rise of the Jewish people from political powerlessness and its necessity after the Holocaust. Essays include "Jewish Attempts to Negotiate with the Nazis," "Jewish Resistance," and "The Road to Israel."

Berkovits, Eliezer. <u>Faith after the Holocaust</u>. New York: Ktav, 1973.

One of the most controversial works written on religious belief after the Holocaust, Berkovits provides thought-provoking stances on the relationships of the Holocaust to Christianity, Israel, and Judaism's role in the world.

Cargas, Harry James. <u>A Christian Response to the Holocaust</u>. Denver: Stonehenge, 1981.

Meaningful presentation of the implications of the Holocaust for Christians. Elie Wiesel, who wrote the foreword, feels Cargas has explored painful questions that his Christian brothers and sisters need to ask.

Cargas, Harry James, ed. <u>When God and Man Failed</u>: <u>Non-Jewish Views</u>
<u>of the Holocaust</u>. New York: Macmillan, 1981.

Cargas accurately describes this book in the preface when he says,
"This collection of essays on the Holocaust is an attempt to bring
together some of the most eloquent insights by some of the finest
Christian students of the Holocaust in the United States." The
distinguished list of Christian commentators who have wrestled with
the horrors of the Holocaust is Frank S. Parker, Robert F. Drinan,
Eva Fleischner, Franklin H. Littell, John K. Roth, William Heyen,
Robert McAfee Brown, Edward H. Flannery, Bernard Lee, W. Robert
McClelland, Jack S. Boozer, Robert E. Willis, John T. Pawlikowski,
Thomas A. Idinopulos, Alice and Roy Eckardt, and the editor himself.
Belongs in every Holocaust library.

Carr, Joseph J. <u>Christian Heroes of the Holocaust</u>: <u>The Righteous Gentiles</u>.
South Plainfield, N.J.: Bridge, 1984.

Stories about those individual Christians who risked their lives to
save Jews during the Holocaust.

Cohen, Arthur A. <u>The Tremendum</u>: <u>A Theological Interpretation of the</u>
<u>Holocaust</u>. New York: Crossroad, 1981.

One of the most significant theological statements about the Holocaust.
For Jews and others, this book forces one to rethink theologically
the implications of the Jews as a chosen people, the evil resulting
from the Holocaust, and the relation of God to humanity and the
world.

Cohen, Arthur A., ed. <u>Arguments and Doctrines</u>: <u>A Reader of Jewish</u>
<u>Thinking in the Aftermath of the Holocaust</u>. New York: Harper
and Row, 1970.

Twenty-eight essays divided into four sections: 1) "The Foreground
of Jewish Existence," 2) "The Renewal of Theology," 3) "Challenges
to Jewish Belief," and 4) "The Expectation and the Trust." Challenging,
meaningful, and stimulating, these essays present a variety of Jewish
thinking about life after the Holocaust.

Conway, J. S. <u>The Nazi Persecution of the Churches 1933-45</u>. New York:
Basic, 1968.

A detailed treatment "of the methods by which Hitler and his followers
sought to deal with the Christian Churches." An excellent examination
of German documents from the Nazi archives relating to church affairs.
The author concludes with several interesting appendixes, a thorough
set of notes, and a useful bibliography.

Davidowicz, Lucy. <u>The War against the Jews</u>. New York: Holt, Rinehart,
and Winston, 1975.

The Nazi envisionment of a Jew-free Europe is recounted in this
powerful work on the Holocaust. Davidowicz attempts to answer

the difficult question of how the near-total annihilation of Jews could happen.

Des Pres, Terrence. The Survivor: An Anatomy of Life in the Death Camps. New York: Oxford University Press, 1976.

Literary, moral, and psychological analyses of the horrors of life in death camps. Presented in heart-wrenching detail, this is one of the most brutal examinations of the survivors "who suffered . . . who endured all that evil and returned to bear witness."

Donat, Alexander. The Holocaust Kingdom: A Memoir. New York: Holt, Rinehart, and Winston, 1965.

A dramatic and moving account of a Polish family's survival of the Holocaust.

Eckardt, A. Roy, and Alice L. Eckardt. Long Night's Journey into Day: Life and Faith after the Holocaust. Detroit: Wayne State University Press, 1982.

In this outspoken, controversial, and penetrating study, the Eckardts view the Holocaust as a Christian event. They suggest that an examination of Christian history and theology will show that Christian triumphalism is the major source of anti-Judaism, a decisive factor in bringing about the Holocaust.

Fackenheim, Emil L. The Jewish Return into History: Reflections in the Age of Auschwitz and a New Jerusalem. New York: Schocken, 1978.

In this collection of essays, Fackenheim explores the implications of the Holocaust for Judaism, the founding of the modern State of Israel, and the connection between the two.

----------. To Mend the World: Foundations of Future Jewish Thought. New York: Schocken, 1982.

Fackenheim, a Jewish theologian with a great sensitivity to the Holocaust, asks--and attempts to answer the question--how can we mend the rupture in Jewish thought since the Holocaust? He also poses some significant questions for Christians.

Fiorenza, Elisabeth Schussler, and David Tracy, eds. The Holocaust as Interruption. Edinburgh: T. and T. Clark, 1984.

An attempt by theologians to face the issue of the Holocaust theologically. The five sections and their authors include "Jewish Reflections" by Susan Shapiro and Arthur Cohen; "Christian Reflections" by Rebecca Chopp, Johann-Baptist Metz, Gregory Baum, and John Pawlikowski; "Biblical Studies" by Louise Schattroff and Leonore Siegele-Wenschkewitz; "Inter-disciplinary Reflections" by Mary Knutsen and Mary Gerhart; and "Editorial Reflections" by Elisabeth Schussler Fiorenza and David Tracy.

Fleischner, Eva, ed. Auschwitz: Beginning of a New Era? New York:
   Ktav, 1977.

   A probing, thoughtful, and well-organized collection of essays. Of
   particular substance is a well-written paper by Irving Greenberg,
   "Clouds of Smoke, Pillar of Fire." This anthology also includes essays
   by Emil L. Fackenheim and Rosemary Radford Ruether that have
   come to be classic statements on the Holocaust and anti-Judaism;
   Gregory Baum discussing the Church's mission; an important piece
   on liturgy by John T. Pawlikowski; and other studies and responses
   by historians, philosophers, and theologians.

Frank, Anne. The Diary of a Young Girl. Trans. B. M. Moogaart. New
   York: Doubleday, 1952.

   One of the best-known diaries ever written; a young German-Jewish
   girl tells the tale of her family's two years spent in hiding while the
   war raged around them.

Friedlander, Albert H., ed. Out of the Whirlwind: A Reader of Holocaust
   Literature. New York: Schocken, 1976.

   A useful anthology for the classroom. It contains excerpts from diaries,
   memoirs, and novels of literature on the Holocaust. Selections from
   the writings of Leo Baeck, Salo Baron, Alexander Donat, Emil L.
   Fackenheim, Harold Flender, Anne Frank, Abraham J. Heschel, Rolf
   Hochhuth, Primo Levi, and Elie Wiesel, among others.

Friedlander, Henry and Sybil Milton, eds. The Holocaust: Ideology,
   Bureaucracy and Genocide, The San Jose Papers. Milwood, N.Y.:
   Kraus International, 1980.

   The National Conference of Christians and Jews sponsored two
   conferences on the significance of the Holocaust. This book is a
   proceedings volume from these conferences. Topics have been divided
   into six sections: 1) "Before the Holocaust," 2) "The Setting of the
   Holocaust," 3) "The Professions in Nazi Germany and the Holocaust,"
   4) "Anti-Nazi Elites in Occupied Europe, 1933-45," 5) "The United
   States and the Holocaust," and 6) "After the Holocaust."

Friedman, Philip. Their Brother's Keeper. New York: Holocaust Library,
   1978.

   Documentation of those Christians who risked their lives to help
   Jews escape the Nazi regime. Moving tales of these heroes and
   heroines are recounted in detail, showing that there were those with
   courage who gave hope to the few refugees surviving the horror.

Genizi, Haim. American Apathy: The Plight of Christian Refugees from
   Nazism. Ramat Gan, Israel: Bar-Ilan University, 1983

   A survey of the efforts of organizations which helped Christian
   refugees. Scholarly work that includes a useful bibliography of primary
   and secondary sources.

Gilbert, Martin. The Holocaust: The History of the Jews of Europe during the Second World War. New York: Holt, Rinehart, and Winston, 1985.

This tome of over 950 pages "is an attempt to draw on the nearest of the witnesses, those closest to the destruction, and through their testimony to tell something of the suffering of those who perished, and are forever silent." A methodically detailed record of the annihilation of the Jews in World War II.

Gutteridge, Richard. The German Evangelical Church and the Jews 1879-1950. Oxford: Basil Blackwell, 1976.

The author presents the unfortunate history of the relation of German Protestantism to the Jews. Chapters include 1) "The Roots of 'Christian' Anti-Semitism, 1879-1918," 2) "Anti-Jewish Sentiment in the Weimar Period," 3) "Hitler, the Church and the Jews, January-April 1933," 4) "The Aryan Clause, 1933-35," 5) "The Nuremberg Laws and Their Effect upon the Evangelical Church, 1935-38," 6) "The Pogrom of November 1938, Its Aftermath, and Succor for the Afflicted, 1938-41," 7) "The Final Solution, 1941-45." The book ends with a conclusion, several appendixes, and a bibliography.

Hallie, Philip P. Lest Innocent Blood Be Shed: The Story of the Village of Le Chambon and How Goodness Happened There. New York: Harper and Row, 1979.

Hallie tells a moving, true tale of a small French village that lived its Christianity by truly caring about other human beings. At a great risk to their own lives, the village people—led by Andre Trocme, a dedicated minister—saved hundreds of Jews from certain death.

Hellman, Peter. Avenue of the Righteous. New York: Atheneum, 1980.

The author tells the stories of four of the Righteous Gentiles who have trees planted in their names at Yad Vashem in Israel. These stories of Christians who saved Jews are eloquently told.

Helmreich, Ernst Christian. The German Churches under Hitler: Background Struggle and Epilogue. Detroit: Wayne State University Press, 1979.

A thoroughly detailed account of the Protestant and Catholic churches from before 1918 to postwar Germany. Includes analyses of the Weimar Republic, the first confessing synods, the Concordat, wartime restrictions, and other topics central to church resistance.

Hilberg, Raul. The Destruction of the European Jews. Rev. and definitive ed. New York: Homes and Meier, 1985.

This massive three-volume work is considered to be the most comprehensive study ever done on the Nazi's systematic extermination of the European Jews. A detailed and precise presentation that concentrates on the perpetrators. The topics in volume one include precedents, antecedents, the structure of destruction, definition by decree, expropriation, concentration, and mobile killing operations.

Volume two focuses on deportations, while volume three covers the killing center operations, reflections, consequences, and implications. Includes appendixes on German ranks, statistics of Jewish dead, and notations on sources. The publisher has also prepared a student edition of 360 pages.

Kenneally, Thomas. Schindler's List. New York: Simon and Schuster, 1982.

A novelized biography on the life of Oskar Schindler, the righteous Gentile factory operator who helped save hundreds of Jews from sure death. A moving story.

Lapide, Pinchas E. Three Popes and the Jews. New York: Hawthorne, 1967.

This book is primarily a defense of Pope Pius XI, Pope Pius XII, and Pope John XXIII and their efforts to help defend the Jews from the Nazi Holocaust. Despite the lack of strong disclaimers against the slaughter, Lapide provides actual proof of the Church's part in saving 860,000 lives.

Levi, Primo. Survival in Auschwitz: The Nazi Assault on Humanity. New York: Macmillan, 1961.

The late Levi presents a witness account of the human suffering of the Holocaust and the atrocities the Nazis committed.

Levin, Nora. The Holocaust: The Destruction of European Jewry 1933-1945. New York: Schocken, 1973.

A popular history that chronicles the destruction, rescue, and resistance of the Jews of Europe. Detailed research written in dramatic style.

Lewy, Guenter. The Catholic Church and Nazi Germany. New York: McGraw-Hill, 1964.

This work looks at the historical relationship of German National Socialism and the Catholic Church.

Littell, Franklin H. The Crucifixion of the Jews. New York: Harper and Row, 1975.

An important contribution to the field of Holocaust Studies, this work also touches upon Christian anti-Judaism and Israel. Littell's impassioned plea for Christians to confront the betrayal of the Jews during the Holocaust is intense, controversial, and valuable reading for all.

Littell, Franklin H. and Hubert G. Locke, eds. The German Church Struggle and the Holocaust. Detroit: Wayne State University Press, 1974.

This book contains papers from the conference, The Church Struggle and the Holocaust. It is organized thematically with sections on historical background, political considerations, theological implications, and personal reflections. The essay "Talking and Writing and Keeping Silent," by Elie Wiesel, is profound and deeply meaningful with far-reaching ramifications.

Morley, John F. Vatican Diplomacy and the Jews during the Holocaust 1939-1943. New York: Ktav, 1980.

Morley investigates, in a country-by-country analysis, the lack of involvement by the Pope and the Vatican diplomatic corps in the Holocaust. Using documents from the Vatican archives, he has found that the Vatican believed it more important to maintain diplomatic relations than to fulfill its obligation to stand up for what was morally correct. Includes over fifty pages of appendixes and a well-compiled bibliography.

Oesterreicher, John M. Auschwitz, the Christian, and the Council. Montreal: Palm, 1965.

Short commentaries on the horror of the Holocaust, on Vatican Council II, and their ramifications for the Christian.

Rabinowitz, Dorothy. About the Holocaust: . . . What We Know and How We Know It. New York: American Jewish Committee, 1979.

The subtitle is appropriate. This is short documentation of the Holocaust that stresses the importance of remembering the evil and those who perished because of it.

Ramati, Alexander. The Assisi Underground: Priests Who Rescued Jews. New York: Stein and Day, 1978.

Ramati tells the moving story of Father Rufino Niccacci, a Franciscan priest in the village of Assisi. Niccacci, along with his fellow monks and nuns, sheltered and protected three hundred Jews.

Rausch, David A. A Legacy of Hatred: Why Christians Must Not Forget the Holocaust. Chicago: Moody, 1984.

Rausch presents an eloquent plea on the need for Christians to come to grips with the Holocaust. Although we must never forget the horror of the Holocaust—since this increases the chance that it could happen again (and there still are those who spread the "Holocaust was a lie" theory)—Rausch perhaps exaggerates his fear that the United States is similar to pre-Nazi Germany.

Rittner, Carol, and Sondra Myers, eds. The Courage to Care: Rescuers of Jews during the Holocaust. New York: New York University Press, 1986.

A celebration of the "Righteous Gentiles" who risked their lives to save Jews. Includes photos, maps, stories of the rescuers, a section on Le Chambon, and reflections by Elie Wiesel, Moshe Bejski, Pierre Sauvage, Robert McAfee Brown, and Shlomo Breznitz. Now an Academy Award-nominated documentary.

Ross, Robert W. So It Was True: The American Protestant Press and
    the Nazi Persecution of the Jews. Minneapolis: University of
    Minnesota Press, 1980.

    This work attempts to explain why the American churches—though
    clearly aware of the Nazi atrocities to the Jews—protested so little.
    It examines Protestant religious periodicals between 1933-1945. There
    are two sections, the first on the years of persecution and the second
    on Christianity and the Holocaust.

Rubenstein, Richard L. After Auschwitz: Radical Theology and
    Contemporary Judaism. Indianapolis: Bobbs-Merrill, 1966.

    A probing set of essays written by a man who attempts to grasp the
    meaning of the Holocaust for Jews and Gentiles alike. Rubenstein
    looks at the problem of evil, Israel, the Protestant establishment,
    the Death-of-God movement, and other issues in a post-Holocaust
    light.

Rubenstein, Richard L. and John K. Roth. Approaches to Auschwitz:
    The Holocaust and Its Legacy. Atlanta: John Knox, 1987.

    Interdisciplinary in focus, this large book goes a long way toward
    evaluating the Nazi's efforts to eradicate Jews. It will be particularly
    useful for those who teach about the Holocaust and its historical
    roots and consequences.

Ryan, Michael D., ed. Human Responses to the Holocaust: Perpetrators
    and Victims, Bystanders and Resisters. New York: E. Mellen, 1981.

    Papers from the 1979 Bernhard E. Olson Scholars' Conference on
    The Church Struggle and the Holocaust sponsored by the National
    Conference of Christians and Jews. Besides essays on the subtitle,
    there are also post-Holocaust theological and ethical reflections
    and an extensive bibliography of journal articles.

Tec, Nechama. When Light Pierced the Darkness: Christian Rescue of
    Jews in Nazi-Occupied Poland. New York: Oxford University Press,
    1986.

    The author, a Jew who passed as a Catholic girl during the war, draws
    upon her own experiences and those of other Holocaust survivors
    and investigates the underlying reasons behind Christian efforts to
    save Jews. Her narrative is portrayed in a gripping style.

Trunk, Isaiah. Jewish Responses to Nazi Persecution: Collective and
    Individual Behavior in Extremis. New York: Stein and Day, 1979.

    This book is divided into two parts. Part one contains the historical
    antecedents and responses to the Nazis. Part two lets the reader
    relive the brutality of the Nazis by presenting sixty-two eyewitness
    accounts of "the day-to-day life and struggle of the Jewish victims."

Wiesel, Elie. Night. Trans. Stella Rodway. New York: Farrar, Straus,
    and Giroux, 1960.

In Elie Wiesel's words, he tells "a tale directly, as though face to face with the experience." This is a deeply moving personal account of the sheer terror of the Holocaust. A powerful story that tells of the events of the Holocaust and the moral dilemmas Wiesel faced.

Wytwycky, Bohdan. The Other Holocaust: Many Circles of Hell. Washington, D. C.: Novak Report, 1980.

A short, penetrating, and readable chronicle of the many who suffered the same cruel fate as the Jews in the Holocaust. The author tells the story of the Gypsies, Slavs, etc., while still preserving the uniqueness of the attempted destruction of all Jews.

Zimmels, H. J. The Echo of the Nazi Holocaust in Rabbinic Literature. New York: Ktav, 1977.

Rabbinic response to Nazi persecution is organized chronologically: 1) "Beginning Nazi Rule, 1933-38," 2) "1938 to Beginning of World War II," 3) "World War II, 1939-45," and 4) "Aftermath and Reconstruction." Zimmel's work also contains useful sections on Nazi laws and an anthology of responses.

F. Israel

Representative books about Israel, specifically those that are useful to Jewish-Christian relations.

Aharoni, Yohanan. The Archaeology of the Land of Israel: From the Prehistoric Beginnings to the End of the First Temple Period. Trans. Anson F. Rainey. Philadelphia: Westminster, 1982.

This book is a useful introduction to the study of archaeology in Israel. It is filled with resources such as figures, plates, photographs, chronological tables and maps, lists of flint tools and pottery, and a selected bibliography. Sections cover the prehistoric era, the Chalcolithic period, the Canaanite period, and the Israelite period.

Brueggemann, Walter. The Land: Place as Gift, Promise, and Challenge in Biblical Faith. Philadelphia: Fortress, 1977.

One of the important works in the Overtures to Biblical Theology series, containing fresh definitions in biblical theology. Brueggemann has organized the study "around three histories of the land: (a) the history of promise into the land, (b) the history of the management into exile, and (c) the new history of promise which begins in exile and culminates in kingdom."

Davies, W. D. The Gospel and the Land: Early Christianity and Jewish Territorial Doctrine. Berkeley: University of California Press, 1974.

A thorough examination of the role Israel plays in the history of ancient Judaism and early Christianity. Includes extensive footnotes, several appendixes, and a large bibliography.

Davis, Moshe, ed. With Eyes toward Zion: Scholars' Colloquium on American-Holy Land Studies. Reprint ed. New York: Arno, 1977.

Four major aspects of the historical relationship between the United States and Palestine are considered: "Christian Devotion," "Cultural Aspects," "Diplomatic Policy," and "Jewish Attachment."

Drinan, Robert F. Honor the Promise: America's Commitment to Israel. Garden City, N.Y.: Doubleday, 1977.

Drinan, a champion of Israel, believes Christians should support and defend Israel on historical and moral grounds. Notably pro-Israeli, the book examines Israel's creation, Zionism, Christian reaction to the emergence of Israel, the Palestinian refugees, the PLO, Arab hostility, Israel's economic future, and more.

Eckardt, A. Roy, and Alice L. Eckardt Encounter with Israel: A Challenge to Conscience. New York: Association, 1970.

This challenge that the Eckardts offer—Christians must see that they have a moral responsibility towards Israel—confronts the central moral and political questions that must be faced in a discussion of the State of Israel. Although they take a pro-Israel stand, there is a balanced appraisal of the Arab-Israeli conflict. Such a balanced appraisal, they conclude, should be part of any Jewish-Christian understanding.

Eckardt, Alice L., ed. Jerusalem: City of the Ages. Lanham, Md.: University Press of America, 1987.

Epstein, Lawrence J. Zion's Call: Christian Contributions to the Origins and Development of Israel. Lanham, Md.: University Press of America, 1984.

The author's purpose for writing this book is stated as: "because too few people know how much Christians have contributed to the Zionist movement and to the nation of Israel." The Christian Zionist movement is presented chronologically with chapters on: 1) "What is Christian Zionism?" 2) "The Beginnings of the Movement," 3) "From Religion to Politics," 4) "The Emergence of the Zionist Movement," 5) "Christian Zionism in England: The Twentieth Century," 6) "Christian Restorations in America: The Nineteenth Century," 7) "Christian Zionism in America: The Twentieth Century."

Feldblum, Esther Yolles. The American Catholic Press and the Jewish State 1917-1959. New York: Ktav, 1977.

An admirable piece of research on the role of the American Catholic press in shaping the attitudes and opinions of the Catholic community. Feldblum's examination of Catholic publications in this time period is an aid to understanding how opinion towards the State of Israel specifically, and Jews generally, has developed.

Fishman, Hertzel. American Protestantism and a Jewish State. Detroit: Wayne State University Press, 1973.

Not a particularly broad representation of American Protestant attitudes towards Israel since it focuses primarily on liberal Christianity and The Christian Century. Yet it does contain a useful analysis of the negative attitudes of American Protestants towards Zionism.

Hertzberg, Arthur, ed. The Zionist Ideal: A Historical Analysis and Reader. New York: Harper and Row, 1959.

This "intellectual history of the Zionist Revolution" examines the great figures in the history of Zionism.

Heschel, Abraham Joshua. Israel: An Echo of Eternity. New York: Farrar, Straus, and Giroux, 1967.

Heschel applies his thoughtful analysis to the role of Israel in the history of humankind. He ably integrates his text with many verses from the Hebrew Scriptures.

Jaeger, D. M. A., ed. Christianity in the Holy Land: Papers Read at the 1979 Tantur Conference. Jerusalem: Ecumenical Institute for Theological Research, 1981.

These proceedings are described in the foreword by Walter Harrelson as the "first fruits of collaboration among many institutions and individuals on the history and significance of the Christian presence in the Holy Land." Topics of the essays include theology, spirituality, history, ecumenism, interreligious relations, and evangelization and acculturation. Some essays are in German or French.

Littell, Franklin. A Pilgrim's Interfaith Guide to the Holy Land. Jerusalem: Carta, 1981.

A very useful and practical guidebook to the major sites in Israel. The sites, each with a map and description, were selected for the traveler of any religious faith. Littell lists places sacred to the faiths of Baha'i, Christianity, Islam, and Judaism.

Malachy, Yona. American Fundamentalism and Israel: The Relation of Fundamentalist Churches to Zionism and the State of Israel. Jerusalem: Hebrew University Press, 1978.

Important study on the relationship of American evangelical-fundamentalist Protestantism to the State of Israel. Examines the modern Adventist movement, Jehovah's Witnesses, the Pentecostal movement, and American Dispensationalism.

Parkes, James. End of an Exile: Israel, the Jews, and the Gentile World. Marblehead, Mass.: Micah, 1982.

Parkes's astute and sensitive perspectives on the State of Israel and its relations with other peoples and nations are presented. The book also includes in the appendix previously published relevant articles by Robert A. Everett, Carl Hermann Voss, Reinhold Niebuhr, Rose G. Lewis, and A. Roy Eckardt.

————. Whose Land? A History of the People of Palestine. New York: Taplinger, 1970.

Based on A History of Palestine from 135 A.D. to Modern Times, this book examines the people who have lived in "the Land" and "the Land's" effect on Jewish, Christian, and Muslim traditions. Contains four parts, entitled "The Makers of its History," "Its Meaning to Three Religions," "Modern Re-adjustment," and "The Restoration of the Balance."

Peters, F. E. Jerusalem: The Holy City in the Eyes of Chroniclers, Visitors, Pilgrims, and Prophets from the Days of Abraham to the Beginnings of Modern Time. New Jersey: Princeton University Press, 1985.

A wonderful, diverse selection of first-hand accounts of adventurers, chroniclers, crusaders, monks, merchants, novelists, pilgrims, priests, rulers, scholars, soldiers, and tourists who have visited the holy city of Jerusalem. Almost all of these people were touched by their visits and this is reflected in their accounts. Peters connects these texts with an informative narrative.

Pragai, Michael. Faith and Fulfillment: Christians and the Return to the Promised Land. London: Vallentine, Mitchell, 1985.

A chronicle of Christian support for the Holy Land and for its return to the Jewish people.

Rausch, David A. Zionism within Early American Fundamentalism 1878-1918: A Convergence of Two Traditions. New York: E. Mellen, 1979.

The author contends that the "theory of 'Fundamentalist anti-Semitism' is not only biased—it is totally inaccurate." He traces the historical relationship of Fundamentalism and Zionism by examining Prophecy conferences, the Moody Bible Institute, mission, and the national restoration of the Jews. Includes an extensive bibliography.

Rudin, James. Israel for Christians. Philadelphia: Fortress, 1983.

The author, long active in Jewish-Christian dialogue, has written a book to help Christians in their understanding of modern Israel. Chapters on Zionism, the Holocaust, Arabs, Jerusalem, and the Christian community.

Sachar, Howard M. A History of Israel: From the Rise of Zionism to Our Time. New York: Knopf, 1979.

A comprehensive work (over nine hundred pages) useful for the college classroom. A few of the thoroughly treated topics are Jewish nationalism, political Zionism, the Balfour Declaration, Arab-Jewish confrontation, independence, economic survival, and the Six-Day War.

Safran, Nadav. Israel: The Embattled Ally. Cambridge, Mass.: Beknap, 1981.

The history of modern Israel is traced through the Zionist movement to statehood. The major concern of the book is the relationship of Israel with the United States and Middle Eastern politics. This penetrating and thorough analysis is over 600 pages long.

Sandmel, Samuel. The Several Israels and an Essay: Religion and Modern Man. New York: Ktav, 1971.

In a set of lectures given at Duke University in 1968, Sandmel takes a look at different dimensions of the meaning of Israel. The four lectures are entitled "The Hebrew Israel," "The Christian Israel," "The State of Israel," and "The True Israel?"

Vital, David. The Origins of Zionism. New York: Oxford University Press, 1975.

Vital, using primary sources in several languages, gives a scholarly presentation of the beginnings of the Zionist movement, which he contends were formulated in the pogroms in Russia between 1881-1884.

————. Zionism: The Formative Years. New York: Oxford University Press, 1982.

In this continuation of his research on Zionism, Vital carefully analyzes the onset of the Zionist revolution from 1897 to Theodor Herzl's death.

Williams, Albert N. The Holy City. Boston: Little Brown and Co., 1954.

Thirty centuries of the history of Jerusalem, the city that has played such a central role in the history of Judaism, Christianity, and Islam.

G. Vatican II

Includes books having to do with Vatican II, specifically those that consider the Declaration on the Relation of the Church to Non-Christian Religions.

Anderson, Floyd. Council Daybook: Vatican II. Washington D.C.: National Catholic Welfare Conference, 1966.

The four sessions of Vatican II are included in three volumes that record the day-by-day occurrences. News stories and feature articles from the National Catholic Welfare Conference News Service document the deliberations and discussions of the Council Fathers. Also contains speeches and the texts of documents. Recommended for those who plan extensive study on the history of Vatican II.

Bea, Augustin Cardinal. The Church and the Jewish People: A Commentary on the Second Vatican Council's Declaration on the Relation of the Church to Non-Christian Religions. New York: Harper and Row, 1966.

This commentary, written by one of the chief architects of the document, is meant for "people of ordinary education, since it is

precisely upon them that the practical implementations of the
Declaration will depend."

Gilbert, Arthur. The Vatican Council and the Jews. Cleveland: World,
1968.

The first effort by a member of the Jewish community to expound
upon issues debated at Vatican II that concerned specifically
Jewish-Christian relations. Gilbert examines Jewish criticism of
the document and statements bearing upon the Church's relation
with the Jewish religion.

Laurentin, Rene, and Joseph Neuner, eds. The Declaration on the Relation
of the Church to Non-Christian Religions: Promulgated by Pope
Paul VI October 28, 1965. New York: Paulist, 1966.

Short, readable commentaries on the Declaration. Laurentin challenges
Christians to rethink their prejudices, and Neuner looks at the
implications of the Declaration for the Church.

Oesterreicher, John M. The New Encounter between Christians and Jews.
New York: Philosophical Library, 1986.

Detailed outline of the background and history of the Second Vatican
Council. Oesterreicher provides an eyewitness account of the dramatic
events that led to the Catholic Church's proclamations that God has
not rejected the Jews and that all expressions of contempt towards
the Jewish people are deplorable.

Vorgrimler, Herbert, ed. Commentary on the Documents of Vatican II.
New York: Herder and Herder, 1967.

These commentaries were written by those involved in the Council's
work. Although the organization does not make this book easy to
use, it will still be helpful for in-depth study on the subject matter.

Yzermans, Vincent A., ed. American Participants in the Second Vatican
Council. New York: Sheed and Ward, 1967.

In this large volume, Yzermans has compiled each decree and
constitution of the Council and has written an historical introduction.
It also includes 118 written interventions by the American hierarchy
at Vatican II and commentaries by Catholic authorities.

H.   Anti-Judaism

This section looks at works on anti-Judaism/anti-Semitism, prejudice,
hatred, and totalitarianism in the history of Jewish-Christian relations,
including that found in the New Testament.

Allport, Gordon W. The Nature of Prejudice. Garden City, N.Y.:
Doubleday, 1958.

One of the classic studies of prejudice, this work is divided into eight sections: 1) "Preferential Thinking," 2) "Group Differences," 3) "Perceiving and Thinking about Group Differences," 4) "Sociocultural Factors," 5) "Acquiring Prejudice," 6) "The Dynamics of Prejudice," 7) "Character Structure," and 8) "Reducing Group Tensions."

Arendt, Hannah. The Origins of Totalitarianism. New York: Harcourt, Brace, Jovanovich, 1966.

An important and lengthy work by a distinguished author on anti-Judaism, imperialism, and totalitarianism.

Baum, Gregory. Is the New Testament Anti-Semitic? A Re-examination of the New Testament. Rev. ed. New York: Paulist, 1965.

Even though the author believes that many New Testament passages that are "read out of context do seem to express resentment against the Jews," he argues here that the New Testament is without anti-Jewish elements. He has since changed his mind. See his foreword to Rosemary Radford Ruether's book Faith and Fratricide.

Beck, Norman A. Mature Christianity: The Recognition and Repudiation of the Anti-Jewish Polemic of the New Testament. Cranbury, N.J.: Susquehanna University Press, 1985.

This is one of the most thorough attempts to repudiate the anti-Jewish polemic of the New Testament. The author has identified three forms of anti-Jewish polemic: christological, supersessionistic, and defamatory. He then identifies these polemics in each book of the New Testament. His claim that Christianity has attained maturity and should now be ready to confront these issues is welcomed by many involved in the dialogue.

Braham, Randolph, L., ed. The Origins of the Holocaust: Christian Anti-Semitism. Social Science Monographs/Institute for Holocaust Studies of the City University of New York. New York: Columbia University Press, 1986.

This work is a volume of proceedings from a major Holocaust conference. The conference centered around Hyam Maccoby's controversial theory that anti-Judaism "forms an essential ingredient in the Christian myth of redemption." His presentation brought several important responses from distinguished Jewish and Christian Holocaust scholars, Eugene J. Fisher, Robert A. Everett, A. James Rudin, Marc Tanenbaum, and Alan T. Davies.

Bratton, Fred Gladstone. The Crime of Christendom: The Theological Sources of Christian Anti-Semitism. Boston: Beacon, 1969.

The author feels that "traditional theology of Christianity . . . is the ultimate source of Jew-hating." With this in mind, he contends that the churches must make fundamental changes or abandon their creeds if they are really to change attitudes.

Cohen, Jeremy. The Friars and the Jews: The Evolution of Medieval Anti-Judaism. Ithaca, N.Y.: Cornell University Press, 1982.

Cohen convincingly contends that the friars' activities in developing anti-Jewish polemic and undermining the religious freedom of the Jews were all part of an attempt "to implement a new Christian theology with regard to the Jews, one that allotted the Jews no legitimate right to exist in European society." He has ably presented both the attacks against the Jews by leading Dominican and Franciscan friars and the Jewish response to these attacks.

Cohn, Norman. Warrant for Genocide: The Myth of Jewish World Conspiracy and the Protocols of the Elders of Zion. Chico, Calif.: Scholars, 1981.

A look at how the notorious forgery, the Protocols, was used as justification for mass genocide from Russia's civil war to Hitler's Germany.

Cutler, Allan Harris, and Hellen Elmquist Cutler. The Jew as Ally of the Muslim: Medieval Roots of Anti-Semitism. Notre Dame, Ind.: University of Notre Dame Press, 1986.

The Cutlers challenge the normative account of the roots of anti-Judaism in the middle ages. Rather than use socioeconomic rivalry between Christians and Jews or the deicide charge as an explanation, they instead contend that Jewish-Christian relations cannot be understood apart from the study of Christian-Islamic relations. This connection is made by medieval Christians because of the association of Jew with Muslim and in turn the close relationship between anti-Islamic feelings and anti-Judaism. To validate this claim the authors utilize a good deal of medieval Christian documents and Hebrew texts.

Davies, Alan T. Antisemitism and the Christian Mind: The Crisis of Conscience after Auschwitz. New York: Herder and Herder, 1969.

Davies, a well-known Christian theologian, takes a penetrating and critical look at Christian theology and the challenges it faces in its history of anti-Judaism and the tragedy of the Holocaust. The last chapter provides a thoughtful set of theological guidelines for Jewish-Christian relations.

Davies, Alan T., ed. Antisemitism and the Foundations of Christianity. New York: Paulist, 1979.

An anthology of profound essays that are crucial to an understanding of the role anti-Judaism has played in the formulation of christology. Of particular importance is Rosemary Radford Ruether's essay, "The Faith and Fratricide Discussion: Old Problems and New Dimensions," which addresses the other essays, and Douglas John Hall's article, "Rethinking Christ."

Epstein, Benjamin R., and Arnold Forster. "Some of My Best Friends . . .". New York: Farrar, Straus, and Cudahy, 1962.

A dispassionate examination of discrimination against the Jews in society, in housing, in higher education, and in employment.

Flannery, Edward H. The Anguish of the Jews: Twenty-Three Centuries of Antisemitism. Rev. ed. New York: Paulist, 1985.

Meant for the educated reader, this work is a concise and well-written classic that traces the history of anti-Judaism in a century-by-century chronological arrangement.

Forster, Arnold, and Benjamin R. Epstein. The New Anti-Semitism. New York: McGraw Hill, 1974.

Written in a journalistic style. The authors are concerned with the rise of new forms of anti-Judaism. They examine factors that perpetuate anti-Judaism in groups such as a black teachers' association, the clergy, the media, the radical left, Arabs, the radical right, and the hatemongers.

Friedman, Saul S. The Oberammergau Passion Play: A Lance against Civilization. Carbondale, Ill.: Southern Illinois University Press, 1984.

Considered by many to be the best work on the Oberammergau Passion play, this penetrating analysis explores the play's history, its anti-Jewish content, and the controversy surrounding the attempts to rid it of this content.

Gager, John G. The Origins of Anti-Semitism: Attitudes toward Judaism in Pagan and Christian Antiquity. New York: Oxford University Press, 1983.

This revisionist reading is a well-researched study of anti-Judaism from the third century B.C.E. to the fourth century C.E. Contains several interesting theories on Paul's thoughts about the Jews and a response to Rosemary Radford Ruether's Faith and Fratricide.

Glassman, Bernard. Anti-Semitic Stereotypes without Jews: Images of the Jews in England, 1290-1700. Detroit: Wayne State University Press, 1975.

Superb resource for studying Anglo-Jewish history and the attitude of the Christian community in the centuries after the expulsion. The thorough footnoting and primary and secondary source bibliographies make this a useful tool for Jewish and Christian theologians who are studying anti-Judaism in the medieval period.

Glock, Charles Y., and Rodney Stark. Christian Beliefs and Anti-Semitism. New York: Harper and Row, 1966.

Well-known sociological study on the role contemporary Christian teaching has played in the furtherance of anti-Judaism.

Graeber, Isacque, and Steuart Henderson Britt, eds. Jews in the Gentile World: The Problem of Anti-Semitism. New York: Macmillan, 1942.

Experts in the fields of anthropology, economics, history, philosophy, political science, psychology, and sociology utilize their findings to examine anti-Judaism.

Grosser, Paul E., and Edwin G. Halperin. Anti-Semitism: Causes and Effects, An Analysis and Chronology of 1900 Years of Anti-Semitic Attitudes and Practices. Second ed. New York: Philosophical Library, 1983.

This work will be a great aid to those trying to understand the historical consequences of anti-Judaism. It catalogues, in chronological order, anti-Jewish incidents and analyzes and synthesizes "the causes and theories of anti-Semitism that are apparent from the catalogue."

Hay, Malcolm. Thy Brother's Blood: The Roots of Christian Anti-Semitism. New York: Hart, 1975. Originally published as The Foot of Pride: The Pressure of Christendom on the People of Israel for 1900 Years, 1950 and Europe and the Jews, 1960.

A look at how the Church's unofficial and official policies have perpetuated the persecution of Jews. Hay is concerned with the place of anti-Judaism in Christian teaching and theology and its destructive consequences.

Heer, Friedrich. God's First Love: Christians and Jews over Two Thousand Years. Trans. Geoffrey Skelton. New York: Weybright and Talley, 1970.

Tracing the history of Jewish-Christian relations, this impassioned work concentrates on Christian anti-Judaism. The dedication reads: "This book, by an Austrian Catholic, is dedicated to the Jewish, Christian, and non-Christian victims of the Austrian Catholic, Adolph Hitler."

Isaac, Jules. Has Anti-Semitism Roots in Christianity? New York: National Conference of Christians and Jews, 1961.

The famous French historian's goal is "the reappraisal of the position of Israel in Christian education." In this short work, Isaac affirmatively answers the question the title proposes and sets forth eighteen points to remedy Christian anti-Judaism by reforming Christian education.

—————. Jesus and Israel. Ed. with a foreword by Claire Huchet Bishop. Trans. Sally Gran. New York: Holt, Rinehart, and Winston, 1971.

Originally published in 1948, Isaac wrote this volume in response to the Holocaust and the anti-Judaism Christendom has fostered over the centuries. In a provocative format, he presents twenty-one propositions on Jesus and his relationship to Judaism.

—————. The Teaching of Contempt. Trans. Helen Weaver. New York: Holt, Rinehart, and Winston, 1964.

This shorter work, which summarizes much of Jesus and Israel, has been lauded as an incisive examination of the part the Christian Church has played in perpetuating anti-Judaism. Isaac considers three main themes in the teaching of contempt: 1) "the dispersion of the Jews: providential punishment for the crucifixion," 2) "the degenerate state of Judaism at the time of Jesus," and 3) "the crime of deicide."

Katz, Jacob. From Prejudice to Destruction: Anti-Semitism, 1700-1933. Cambridge, Mass.: Harvard University Press, 1980.

Written by a Jewish social historian, this is an extensive study of Austrian, French, German, and Hungarian literary and political figures and their contributions to secular anti-Judaism.

Klein, Charlotte. Anti-Judaism in Christian Theology. Philadelphia: Fortress, 1978.

The author criticizes German biblical scholarship and textbooks by Gentiles. She also suggests that a revision is needed in New Testament scholarship that utilizes a literal rendering (instead of an historical approach) of such a subject as the Jews' guilt in the execution of Jesus.

Loewenstein, Rudolph M. Christians and Jews: A Psychoanalytic Study. New York: International Universities Press, 1951.

A psychiatrist interprets the roots of anti-Judaism by reflecting on its motives, its character traits, and other factors. He develops the theory that Christians and Jews have formed a "cultural pair" which has separated and united them.

Maritain, Jacques. A Christian Looks at the Jewish Question. Reprint ed. New York: Arno, 1973. Originally published in 1939.

This lecture, given in Paris and New York in 1938, speaks about countries where anti-Judaism is gaining a foothold, the dispersion of Israel, and the situation of the Jews in Europe. An impassioned plea to find a solution to the problem of anti-Judaism.

Moehlman, Conrad H. The Christian-Jewish Tragedy: A Study in Religious Prejudice. Rochester, N.Y.: Printing House of Leo Hart, 1933.

An apologetical work whose author believes that there are "millions of Christians who desire to know what really transpired at Calvary rather than to go on believing the fiction of Oberammergau." Moehlman is a Christian who wishes to recognize the nineteen centuries of prejudice promulgated by Christians against the Jews.

Monti, Joseph. Who Do You Say That I Am? The Christian Understanding of Christ and Antisemitism. New York: Paulist, 1984.

A short, but notable, study on Christology with helpful suggestions on the reconstruction of a Christology that does not supersede Judaism or other religions. Good for the dialogue beginner ready to explore her/his Christology.

Oberman, Heiko A. The Roots of Anti-Semitism: In the Age of Renaissance and Reformation. Trans. James I. Porter. Philadelphia: Fortress, 1984.

This heavily documented work is divided into three sections: 1) "The Jews at the Threshold of the Modern Age," 2) "From Agitation to Reformation: The Spirit of the Times Reflected in the 'Jews' Mirror,'" and 3) "Martin Luther: The Jews as Benefactors and Malefactors."

Oesterreicher, John M. Anatomy of Contempt: A Critique of R. R. Ruether's "Faith and Fratricide". New Jersey: Seton Hall University Press, 1975.

A thorough, detailed, and perhaps overly critical review of Ruether's attempt to repudiate theological anti-Judaism. This is an illustration of how much controversy her book has created.

Parkes, James. Antisemitism. London: Valentine Mitchell, 1963.

Parkes is considered by many a pioneer in Jewish-Christian relations. Here he turns his talents toward analyzing anti-Judaism as he traces its historical roots and looks at it as a modern phenomenon. Significant chapters on anti-Judaism in the Soviet Union and Israel's relations with the Arab world.

----------. The Conflict of the Church and Synagogue: A Study in the Origins of Antisemitism. New York: Atheneum, 1969.

Parkes traces the origins of anti-Judaism from the Roman world and its rise in pagan and Christian civilization through the middle ages. A well-documented examination of a troubled relationship.

Perlmutter, Nathan, and Ruth Ann Perlmutter. The Real Anti-Semitism in America. New York: Arbor House, 1982.

A frank exposition on the new forms of negative political and social attitudes towards the Jews. The first chapter on "Nazis I Have Known" sets the tone for this readable work.

Pinson, Koppel S., ed. Essays on Anti-Semitism. Second ed., rev. and enl. New York: Conference on Jewish Relations, 1946.

A set of high-quality historical and regional studies presented in a disturbing form. Contributors include such distinguished scholars as Hannah Arendt, Solomon Grayzel, Jacob R. Marcus, and Bernard D. Weinryb. Foreword by Salo W. Baron.

Poliakov, Leon. The History of Anti-Semitism. Four vols. Trans. Richard Howard. New York: Vanguard, 1965.

Anti-Judaism is reviewed from pagan antiquity to the present in a work that is a useful resource for the educated layperson.

Quinley, Harold E. and Charles Y. Glock. <u>Anti-Semitism in America</u>. New York: Free, 1979.

> This is the "wrap-up" volume of nine studies on anti-Semitism conducted between January 1963 and August 1975. Sponsored by the Anti-Defamation League of B'nai B'rith and conducted by the University of California Survey Research Center, this study examines the amount and character of anti-Judaism, Black-Jewish relations, and the role of churches, schools, and the mass media in combating anti-Judaism. It then summarizes these findings with a chapter on their implications.

Richardson, Peter, with David Granskou. <u>Anti-Judaism in Early Christianity</u>. Vol. 1: <u>Paul and the Gospels</u>. Waterloo, Ontario, Canada: Wilfrid Laurier University Press, 1986.

> These essays, written by Canadian professors of New Testament and religious studies, are part of the Studies in Christianity and Judaism series. The purpose of this series is to provide original insight into Judaism and Christianity, especially as the two have related to one another historically. The authors take a critical look at anti-Judaism in the different books of the New Testament by emphasizing the history and context of early Christianity.

Rotenstreich, Nathan. <u>The Recurring Pattern</u>: <u>Studies in Anti-Judaism in Modern Thought</u>. New York: Horizon, 1964.

> A detailed analysis of "the problem of the evaluation of Judaism in some of the representative trends in modern thought, philosophic and historic."

Ruether, Rosemary Radford. <u>Faith and Fratricide</u>: <u>The Theological Roots of Anti-Semitism</u>. New York: Seabury, 1974.

> An explosive treatment on the question of whether anti-Judaism is inherent in the New Testament. Ruether's conviction that "anti-Judaism is the left hand of Christology" has been frequently quoted. This is a controversial study on the theological dilemmas of anti-Judaism in Christianity, asserting that the history of Jewish-Christian relations needs to be viewed in a new light so that Christian theology can be reconstructed. The introduction by Gregory Baum has also received much-deserved attention.

Runes, Dagobert D. <u>The Jew and the Cross</u>. New York: Philosophical Library, 1965.

> The subject of this short book, the author states, is "Jew hatred," particularly the Christian church's (largely Roman Catholic) role in anti-Judaism. Runes is a severe critic of anti-Judaism, whose presentation is harsh and at some points oversimplified.

Sandmel, Samuel. <u>Anti-Semitism in the New Testament?</u> Philadelphia: Fortress, 1978.

> One of the most controversial of Sandmel's books, this work attempts to expose animosity towards the Jews in the New Testament itself.

Sandmel believes it is necessary to understand the first-century milieu, rabbinic polemics, and prophetic rebuke in order to come to terms with the message the New Testament has for people of today.

Seiden, Morton Irving. The Paradox of Hate: A Study in Ritual Murder. Cranbury, N.J.: T. Yoseloff, 1967.

Seiden surveys the backgrounds, foregrounds, documents, and perspectives of anti-Judaism while inquiring "into but one aspect of . . . the psychological origins of irrational hatred and irrational guilt." Historians will note that he is not concerned with the economic, political, and social causes of anti-Judaism.

Sevenster, J. N. The Roots of Pagan Anti-Semitism in the Ancient World. Leiden: Brill, 1975.

Scholarly work on the origins and development of anti-Judaism. Contains an excellent introduction on the history of the concept of anti-Semitism, including the controversy that has developed.

Stark, Rodney, et al. Wayward Shepherds: Prejudice and the Protestant Clergy. New York: Harper and Row, 1971.

This volume of the project on anti-Judaism, sponsored by the Anti-Defamation League of B'nai B'rith and conducted by the University of California Survey Research Center, is a sociological study that concentrates on clerical prejudice. It is divided into five sections complete with tables: 1) "Christian Beliefs and Anti-Semitism —Revisited," 2) "Theological Convictions," 3) "Religious Conceptions of the Jews," 4) "Secular Anti-Semitism," and 5) "Ministers as Moral Guides: The Silent Majority."

Tal, Uriel. Christians and Jews in Germany: Religion, Politics, and Ideology in the Second Reich, 1870-1914. Trans. Noah Jonathan Jacobs. Ithaca, N.Y.: Cornell University Press, 1975.

A distinguished scholar presents a comprehensive analysis of factors that contributed to the growth of anti-Judaism in Germany between the years 1870-1914. At the end of the book, selected sources and studies have been compiled into a valuable bibliographical essay.

Vogt, Hannah. The Jews: A Chronicle for Christian Conscience. New York: Association, 1967.

An historical account of Judaism written to show the wickedness of anti-Judaism and its distasteful association with Christianity. This book is also a plea for Christians to revise their teaching and attitudes to help create a much-needed brother/sisterhood with Jews.

Williamson, Clark M. Has God Rejected His People? Anti-Judaism in the Christian Church. Nashville: Abingdon, 1982.

Williamson tackles the theme "anti-Judaism is anti-Christian" by surveying anti-Judaism from the New Testament to the post-Holocaust period. This well-written introduction to historical anti-Judaism contains specific steps toward correcting a sad chapter in the Church's history by challenging today's Christians to reestablish the bond between the Synagogue and the Church.

I. Christian Perspectives of Judaism

What follows is a list of books that Christians have written in considering Jews and Judaism in Christian theology.

Carlson, Paul R. O Christian! O Jew! Elgin, Ill.: D. Cook, 1974.

An informally written story of one man's attempt to "seek a bridge of reconciliation" with Jews and understand their heritage and mysteries.

Ecclestone, Alan. The Night Sky of the Lord. New York: Schocken, 1980.

Another post-Holocaust attempt, this one by an Anglican clergyman, that wrestles with the implications of the Holocaust for Christian faith. The author writes on a fairly sophisticated level about why and how Judaism and Christianity separated, the Jewishness of Jesus, and the State of Israel.

Eckardt, A. Roy. For Righteousness' Sake: Contemporary Moral Philosophies. Bloomington: Indiana University Press, 1987.

To categorize this book as specifically a Christian perspective on Judaism would perhaps do it an injustice because it is much more. It does take into account the talmudic and rabbinic traditions; however, it also speaks to challenging ethical and moral issues, masters a vast array of literature, and critically treats the views of numerous important figures in theology and philosophy.

Fisher, Eugene J. Faith without Prejudice. New York: Paulist, 1977.

This attempt to "rebuild Christian attitudes toward Judaism" actually belongs in almost all the categories in this bibliography. It would serve well the teacher, the liturgist, and those interested in the history of the dialogue since Vatican II. A useful introduction and re-examination of Christian anti-Jewish attitudes. Contains several helpful appendixes including a proposed future curriculum for Catholic education.

Harrington, Daniel J. God's People in Christ: New Testament Perspectives on the Church and Judaism. Philadelphia: Fortress, 1980.

Although Jewish-Christian dialogue is not the primary concern, this short book is a good primer for the nonspecialist interested in a biblical/ theological study of the early Church and its relation to Judaism and Jesus in the context of his life, death, and resurrection.

Hedensquist, Gote, ed. The Church and the Jewish People. London: Edinburgh House, 1954.

The World Council of Churches asked that this volume be assembled to "bring home to Christians their continuing responsibility in relation to the Jewish people of today." Contains essays on a variety of topics by scholars from the early fifties.

Holmgren, Frederick. The God Who Cares: A Christian Looks at Judaism. Atlanta: John Knox, 1979.

Meant for the student, layperson, and pastor, this introduction is a "nontechnical presentation of some central themes in ancient and modern Judaism." Ideal for Bible study groups.

Knight, George A. F. A Christian Theology of the Old Testament. Richmond, Va.: John Knox, 1959.

The author admittedly presupposes "that the Old Testament is nothing less than Christian Scripture." His goal is to find the significance of the Old Testament for the New, rather than to attempt to bring New Testament principles in line with a comprehension of the Hebrew Scriptures.

Knitter, Paul F. No Other Name? A Critical Survey of Christian Attitudes Toward the World Religions. Maryknoll, N.Y.: Orbis, 1985.

With a creative approach to the study of Christology, this book develops a theocentric Christology that takes into account a pluralistic society and is sensitive to more than just Judaism. This type of Christology —and much of the rest of Knitter's theology—when utilized in dialogue with world religions, is revolutionary.

McGarry, Michael B. Christology after Auschwitz. New York: Paulist, 1977.

The author insists that Christian theologians cannot construct their Christologies without considering today's Judaism. He also presents an overview and analysis of attitudes expressed by Christian documents that discuss relations with the Jews.

Mussner, Franz. Tractate on the Jews: The Significance of Judaism for Christian Faith. Trans. Leonard Swidler. Philadelphia: Fortress, 1984.

Biblical, ecumenical, and theological questions about the Church's relationship to Judaism are posed with answers that present a Christian theology mindful of Judaism. In-depth research makes this an interesting overview of the issues that unite and divide Christians and Jews.

Pawlikowski, John T. Christ in the Light of Christian-Jewish Dialogue.
New York: Paulist, 1982.

This volume, in the excellent Stimulus series on Studies in Judaism
and Christianity, is concerned with the development of a Christology
that takes into account the relationship of Jesus to Judaism. This
is accomplished by looking at Christianity and Judaism in current
systematic theology, Jesus' link with Pharisaic Judaism, and Christology
in the light of the Holocaust.

Piper, Otto, Jakob Jocz, and Harold Floreen. The Church Meets Judaism.
Minneapolis, Minn.: Augsburg, 1960.

Christians looking at Judaism consider basic theological concerns in
this record of a theological consultation on "The Church and Judaism."
Participants in this consultation convened by the National Lutheran
Council are interested in promoting evangelism to the Jews.

Thoma, Clemens. A Christian Theology of Judaism. New York: Paulist,
1980.

Although there are problems with this book, particularly with regard
to organization and methodology, it belongs in the libraries of those
sensitive enough to see the role of Judaism in Christian theology.

Van Buren, Paul M. A Theology of the Jewish-Christian Reality Part 1:
Discerning the Way. New York: Seabury, 1980.

This book, which considers the people Israel and how Jews and Christians
can walk together down the path of history, is essential reading for
the serious student of Christian theology. It is one of the most
thoughtful approaches that a Christian theologian has offered.

————. A Theology of the Jewish-Christian Reality. Part 2: A Christian
Theology of the People Israel: New York: Seabury, 1983.

Second volume of a projected four-part series, this is one of the most
earnest attempts by a Christian theologian to take into account the
Jewish witness to God by reworking his own Christology. Van Buren
eloquently expresses the need for the Christian Church to redefine
and nurture its relationship with Judaism.

————. A Theology of the Jewish-Christian Reality. Part 3: Christ
in Context. New York: Harper and Row, 1987.

J.   Jewish Perspectives of Christianity

Works in which Jews have contemplated Christianity.

Agus, Jacob B., ed. Judaism and Christianity: Selected Accounts, 1892-1962.
Reprinted. New York: Arno, 1973.

A compilation of articles by Jewish scholars of the past century. Their
viewpoints consider different aspects of the emergence of Christianity
out of Judaism.

Berger, David, and Michael Wyschogrod. Jews and "Jewish Christianity."
    New York: Ktav, 1978.

    A short, easy-to-read explanation of why Jews reject Christian
    fundamentalist beliefs. Writing for young Jews who are attracted
    to Christianity, the authors present a lucid statement of the Jewish
    attitude toward Christianity. Also contains an examination of groups
    who claim to be both Jews and Christians, such as the "Jews for Jesus"
    and Jewish-Christians.

Bokser, Ben Zion. Judaism and the Christian Predicament. Foreword
    by Frederick C. Grant. New York: Knopf, 1967.

    The author has done a good critical study of the differences and
    similarities between the two faiths in the areas of Scriptures, rabbinic
    literature, and Jesus. Bokser, like Grant in the foreword, suggests
    we recognize and repudiate the historical distortions that have come
    down through the centuries.

Borowitz, Eugene B. Contemporary Christologies: A Jewish Response.
    New York: Paulist, 1980.

    Borowitz, an eminent Jewish theologian, examines contemporary
    formulations of Christian doctrines on Christ and gives an objective
    and well-written view of whether it is possible for Jews and Christians
    to engage in dialogue on the divisive issue of Christology. This Jewish
    response advances the Jewish-Christian dialogue by challenging
    Christians to investigate their Christologies.

Danby, Herbert. The Jew and Christianity: Some Phases, Ancient and
    Modern, of the Jewish Attitude towards Christianity. London: Sheldon,
    1927.

    Essays on "representative statements at various stages in the history
    of Christian-Jewish relations and . . . the general conditions out of
    which those expressions of opinion arose."

Gilbert, Arthur. A Jew in Christian America. New York: Sheed and
    Ward, 1966.

    Presented in an informal style, these essays are the experiences of
    a rabbi who has long been involved in promoting Jewish-Christian
    relations.

Gordis, Robert. Judaism in a Christian World. New York: McGraw-Hill,
    1966.

    Judaism is viewed in relation to contemporary society. Topics covered
    include: Jewish tradition in the modern world, factors of disintegration
    and regeneration, Jewish learning, existence, identity, community,
    and future, intermarriage, the Judaeo-Christian tradition, and Judaism
    in the Christian world view.

Jacob, Walter. Christianity through Jewish Eyes. New York: Hebrew Union College Press, 1974.

> An introduction to Jewish thinkers from Moses Mendelssohn to Emil Fackenheim who have considered Christian theology in their writings.

Novak, David. The Image of the Non-Jew in Judaism: An Historical and Constructive Study of Noachide Laws. New York: E. Mellen, 1983.

> In the long history of Judaism, the non-Jew's role has had a deeply felt influence in the development of Jewish philosophy. For the Jew and the non-Jew, this treatment will greatly help in a better understanding of their relationship throughout history. Part one of this work deals with each of the Noachide laws and the second part is concerned with the concept of Noachide law in Aggadah and the thought of Jewish philosophers. A conclusion by the author suggests the Noachide laws as a starting point for Jewish philosophical reflection. Includes a noteworthy bibliography.

Rankin, Oliver S. Jewish Religious Polemics of Earlier and Later Centuries. New York: Ktav, 1970.

> Rankin presents the reader with a selection of translated polemical texts, taken from the first to the seventeenth century, which were used for such purposes as discouraging potential apostates and confronting Christian missionaries. He also places these texts in historical context. Sections on polemic in narrative, poetry, letters, and debate.

Rosenberg, Stuart E. The Christian Problem: A Jewish View. New York: Hippocrene, 1986.

> As is true of many Jewish scholars, Rosenberg is looking not for agreement with Christians but rather a response to the issues he raises. Among these issues are the Jewishness of Jesus, the notion of a supernatural messiah, Paul as the "arch-apostate" of the Jews, and popular myths (such as "the Jewish community did not band together to reject Jesus," and "the 'Old Testament' is not the Hebrew Bible") that help perpetuate Christian anti-Judaism.

Rosenzweig, Franz. The Star of Redemption. Trans. William W. Hallo. Boston: Beacon, 1972. Originally published in 1921.

> Considered to be one of the truly great Jewish thinkers, Rosenzweig used his "new thinking" to present an original approach to religious thought. His belief that the thinker is involved in a reality that confronts God, humanity, and the world helped lead him to his famous proposition that Judaism and Christianity are "equally 'true' and valid views of reality." A significant precursor to today's Jewish-Christian dialogue.

Rubenstein, Richard L. My Brother Paul. New York: Harper and Row, 1972.

> A highly personal account of Rubenstein's theological development. He considers Paul to be "one of the greatest theologians the Jewish

world has ever produced." This controversial position, unusual among Jews, is but one of the ideas that makes this book thought-provoking.

Sandmel, Samuel. We Jews and You Christians: An Inquiry into Attitudes. New York: J. P. Lippincott, 1967.

Sandmel responds to the question "What is the attitude of you Jews to us?" In a thoughtful and readable manner he presents the historical background, the formation of attitudes, and the future of the relationship of Jews towards Christians.

Scharper, Philip, ed. American Catholics: A Protestant-Jewish View. New York: Sheed and Ward, 1959.

Well-known Jewish and Christian scholars, including Stringfellow Barr, Martin E. Marty, Robert McAfee Brown, Arthur A. Cohen, Arthur Gilbert, Allyn P. Robinson, and Gustave Weigel, look at the cultural, religious, and social image of American Catholics with the purpose of helping Catholics in the process of self-analysis.

Silver, Abba Hillel. Where Judaism Differed: An Inquiry into the Distinctiveness of Judaism. Philadelphia: Jewish Publication Society, 1956.

Although not specifically examining Christianity, the author does spend a good deal of time considering what Christianity (and other world religions) has to offer that Judaism rejected.

Zurer, Rachel. A Jew Examines Christianity. New York: Jenna, 1985.

Written in a popular style, this book is described on the book jacket as a "scholarly whodunit." It looks at Jesus, Paul, the Crucifixion, the Gospels, anti-Judaism, and other related topics.

K. Jewish-Christian-Muslim Relations

The brevity of this section attests to the lack of published research in this area.

Biggar, Nigel, Jamie S. Scott, and William Schweiker, eds. Cities of Gods: Faith, Politics and Pluralism in Judaism, Christianity and Islam. New York: Greenwood, 1986.

Appropriate only for those familiar with scholarly work in theology and politics because of the high level of abstraction of some of the essays. The authors speak to the "mutual entanglements" of the three faiths' political and religious involvement. Half of the essays were addresses given at the 1982 Spring Conference, "Religious Conviction and Public Action: The Life of Faith in a Pluralistic World," held at The Divinity School of The University of Chicago.

al Faruqi, Isma'il Raji. <u>Trialogue of the Abrahamic Faiths.</u> New York: International Institute of Islamic Thought, 1982.

The papers included in this book were presented to the Islamic Studies Group of the American Academy of Religion in 1979. Nine well-known Jewish, Christian, and Muslim scholars treat one of three topics: 1) "The Other Faiths," 2) "The Nation State as Form of Social Organization," and 3) "The Faith-Community as International Actor for Justice and Peace."

Gremillion, Joseph, ed. <u>Food/Energy and the Major Faiths.</u> New York: Orbis, 1978.

A record of the conversations held by Hindu, Buddhist, Jewish, Muslim, and Christian leaders on the food/energy crisis. The Interreligious Peace Colloquium in Bellagio, Italy, was the setting for discussion of the crisis, its impact on world peace and social justice, and strategies for meeting the crisis.

Gremillion, Joseph, and William Ryan, eds. <u>World Faiths and the New World Order: A Muslim-Jewish-Christian Search Begins.</u> Washington, D.C.: Interreligious Peace Colloquium, 1978.

The subject of the second conference of the Interreligious Peace Colloquium in Lisbon, Portugal was "The Changing World Order: Challenge to Our Faiths." The conference included papers in three areas: 1) "Socio-Economic, Political and Cultural Elements," 2) "The Dimensions of Faith," and 3) "Followup and Future." Helpful summaries, prepared by the editors, follow each section.

Maybaum, Ignaz. <u>Trialogue between Jew, Christian, and Muslim.</u> Boston: Routledge and Kegan Paul, 1973.

Writing about current events in Jewish history and the necessity of the "trialogue" taking place, Maybaum—a Jewish Reform theologian —has divided his topics into three sections: 1) "From Hasidism to Theology," 2) "Franz Rosenzweig—Today's Guide for the Perplexed," and 3) "The Home-coming of the Humanist."

Peters, F. E. <u>Children of Abraham: Judaism/Christianity/Islam.</u> Princeton, N.J.: Princeton University Press, 1982.

The author presents an introduction with the purpose of underlining "both the parallels and the differences" of Judaism, Christianity, and Islam, "to connect them to common origins and to a common spiritual and intellectual environment." Topics deal with Scripture, community, law, tradition, liturgy, asceticism, mysticism, and theology.

Ye'or, Bet. <u>The Dhimmi: Jews and Christians under Islam.</u> Trans. David Maisel, Paul Fenton, and David Littman. Rutherford, N.J.: Fairleigh Dickinson University Press, 1985.

The Dhimmi, which means "protected person," is the minority living under Islamic rule. This comprehensive treatise presents the Koran's tenets for the treatment of religious minorities and documents that deal with this and past political practice towards the Dhimmi.

L.   Biographies

Although this is certainly not a complete list of books that have been written about important figures involved in the Jewish-Christian dialogue, it includes a representative sample of the ones most useful in Jewish-Christian relations.

Balthasar, Hans Urs von. Martin Buber and Christianity: A Dialogue between Israel and the Church. Trans. Alexander Dru. London: Harvill, 1961.

Written by a Roman Catholic, this reply to the works of Martin Buber studies the relationship of Judaism to Christianity and Christianity to Judaism. Chapters include 1) "Author and Work," 2) "The Source and the Living Voice," 3) "The Prophetic Principle," 4) "The Sacramental Principle," 5) "Israel and the Nations," and 6) "Israel's Mission."

Berenbaum, Michael. The Vision of the Void: Theological Reflections on the Works of Elie Wiesel. Middleton, Conn.: Wesleyan University Press, 1979.

Berenbaum presents us with a perceptive look at Wiesel's writings, which he summarizes as "an attempt to come to terms with that marginal experience and to construct a new universe to replace the one that was shattered." Berenbaum contrasts Wiesel's theology with that of contemporary Jewish theologians Emil Fackenheim, Richard Rubenstein, and Eliezer Berkovits.

Berry, Donald L. Mutuality: The Vision of Martin Buber. Albany: State University of New York Press, 1985.

A short, readable work on the nature of Buber's thought. The chapters on "The Brother" and "The Vision" add qualitatively to the discussion of the Jewishness of Jesus and his importance to relations between Judaism and Christianity.

Brown, Robert McAfee. Elie Wiesel: Messenger to All Humanity. Notre Dame, Ind.: University of Notre Dame Press, 1983.

A moving testimony to the moral dilemmas that Wiesel poses, not just for Jews and Christians, but for all humanity. Making no claim to be a critical analysis, this volume is a sympathetic appraisal of Wiesel's works.

Cargas, Harry James. Harry James Cargas in Conversation with Elie Wiesel. New York: Paulist, 1976.

Wiesel responds to Cargas's intense and probing questions on Arab-Israeli relations, Christianity, the Holocaust, literature, personal experience, religion, Soviet Jewry, and other topics. Each interview is preceded by an excerpt from Wiesel's works and concludes with thoughtful commentary by Cargas.

Cargas, Harry James, ed. Responses to Elie Wiesel. New York: Persea, 1978.

A host of well-known Jewish and Christian scholars respond to the writings and vision of Elie Wiesel.

Diamond, Malcolm. Martin Buber: Jewish Existentialist. New York: Harper and Row, 1968.

While the whole book is especially readable, the chapter on "The Jewish Jesus and the Christ of Faith" is outstanding. Diamond carefully weaves Buber's writings together to illuminate his thoughts on the relationship of Jesus to God, to humanity, and to Jews.

Friedlander, Albert H. Leo Baeck: Teacher of Theresienstadt. New York: Holt, Rinehart, and Winston, 1968.

This is a scholarly exposition of Baeck, who is considered by many to be one of the major Jewish theologians in twentieth-century religious thought. Most of Baeck's teachings, including his encounter with Adolph Harnack, his relationship to Christianity, and his theology of the Holocaust, are thoughtfully explored.

Friedman, Maurice S. Martin Buber: The Life of Dialogue. Chicago: University of Chicago Press, 1955.

An introduction and systematic presentation of one of the great forces in contemporary religion and philosophy. Friedman furnishes the reader with insight into several different aspects of Buber's thought.

Glatzer, Nahum N. Franz Rosenzweig: His Life and Thought. Second rev. ed. New York: Schocken, 1961.

Glatzer presents the life and thought of Rosenzweig, considered by many to be one of the few outstanding contemporary Jewish philosophers. Sections include: 1) "The New Thinking: Philosophy and Religion," 2) "Renaissance of Jewish Learning and Living," 3) "On the Scriptures and Their Language," 4) "God and Man," 5) "The Jewish People," and 6) "Zion and the Remnant of Israel."

Merkle, John C., ed. Abraham Joshua Heschel: Exploring His Life and Thought. New York: Macmillan, 1985.

Papers from the Symposium on the Life and Thought of Abraham Joshua Heschel, held in 1983 at the College of Saint Benedict in Minnesota. Discusses Heschel as a person, biblical theologian, philosopher and poet, and social critic and ecumenist. The last section contains a relevant essay by Eva Fleischner on his significance for Jewish-Christian relations.

Moore, Donald J. Martin Buber: Prophet of Religious Secularism. Philadelphia: Jewish Publication Society, 1974.

This is a scholarly exposition sympathetic to Buber's thought. It is divided into three parts, 1) "The Judaic Writings," 2) "The Personalism of Buber," and 3) "The Critique of Religion."

Oesterreicher, John M. The Unfinished Dialogue: Martin Buber and the Christian Way. New York: Philosophical Library, 1986.

Oesterreicher assists the reader in understanding Buber, who can "enlarge the horizons of faith and understanding for biblical believers, whether Jews or Christians." In addition, this book can be used by non-beginners, for it takes issue with Buber's portrayal of Paul and at the same time delves into Buber's special affection for Jesus and the I-Thou relationship.

Rosenfeld, Alvin, and Irving Greenberg, eds. Confronting the Holocaust: The Impact of Elie Wiesel. Bloomington: Indiana University Press, 1978.

Twelve essays and a selected annotated bibliography make up this volume of reflections originally offered at the 1976 conference "The Work of Elie Wiesel and the Holocaust Universe." Also includes a personal statement by Wiesel.

Roth, John K. A Consuming Fire: Encounters with Elie Wiesel and the Holocaust. Atlanta: John Knox, 1979.

Writings, thoughts, and stories of Elie Wiesel and their implications for humanity are recounted in this volume on what Jewish suffering can mean for Christians. This is incisive inquiry at its best. A prologue by Wiesel is included.

M. Education

Although the first chapter of this work discusses available educational resources for the dialogue, that chapter does not list books on the subject. This section is specifically about books that examine teaching materials, catechesis, and other educational aspects of Jewish-Christian relations.

Bishop, Claire Huchet. How Catholics Look at Jews: Inquiries into Italian, Spanish, and French Teaching Materials. New York: Paulist, 1974.

Christian attitudes toward the Jews and Judaism in teaching materials are examined by one of the early promoters of the dialogue. Bishop analyzes historical inaccuracies in parochial textbooks with the hope that the effort will help "replace old enmities with a new amity."

Borowitz, et al. Image of the Jews: Teacher's Guide to Jews and Their Religion. New York: Anti-Defamation League of B'nai B'rith, 1970.

Eugene Borowitz, Irving Greenberg, Jules Harlow, Max J. Rottenberg, Dore Schary, and Michael Wyschogrod are contributors to this volume of instructional materials on Judaism. The largest part of the book is a teachers' guide written by Ruth Seldin. It contains aims and objectives, an overview, suggested classroom activities and discussion topics, and a bibliography on "The American Jew," "What Jews Believe," "Jewish Worship and the Jewish Year," and "The Life of the Jew."

Boys, Mary C. Biblical Interpretation in Religious Education: A Study of the Kerygmatic Era. Birmingham, Ala.: Religous Education Press, 1980.

Meant for both religious educators and biblical scholars, this lucid historical overview of salvation history reflects upon concerns that "reach to the very core of Christianity, and have serious implications as well for its self-understanding vis-a-vis Judaism."

Cunningham, Philip A. Jewish Apostle to the Gentiles: Paul as He Saw Himself. Mystic, Conn.: Twenty-Third Publications, 1986.

The theme, as the title indicates, is not that Paul rejected Judaism but rather that he felt himself "sent" to the Gentiles to save them—with the use of Christ's message—from damnation. Good use is made of recent Pauline scholarship in the ten years since Krister Stendahl's Paul among Jews and Gentiles. The reflective questions at the end of each chapter make this short book especially appropriate for adult education and Bible study groups.

Fasching, Darrell J., ed. The Jewish People in Christian Preaching. New York: E. Mellen, 1984.

Essays from "New Horizons or Old Dilemmas? Judaism in Christian Theology and Preaching," a symposium held in 1979 at Syracuse, New York. Exceptionally well-written essays that serve "to update clergy, religious educators, and interested lay persons on recent developments in Christian theology relating to Judaism." Scholars participating include Michael J. Cook, Paul M. van Buren, Eugene Fisher, Krister Stendahl, and the editor. The final chapter is from We Jews and You Christians by Samuel Sandmel, to whom the book is also dedicated.

Fisher, Eugene J. Homework for Christians: Preparing for Christian-Jewish Dialogue. Rev. ed. from the original by Bernhard C. Olson. New York: National Conference of Christians and Jews, 1985.

The ideal beginning booklet for Christians preparing for Jewish-Christian dialogue. It asks the right questions and is sensitive to proper dialogue procedures.

—————. Seminary Education and Christian-Jewish Relations: A Curriculum and Resource Handbook. Washington, D.C.: National Catholic Educational Association, 1983.

Filled with useful information, this short work should have a place on the shelves of every seminarian. Fisher presents resources and suggestions for sacred Scripture, liturgy and homiletics, Church history, catechetics, systematics, and moral theology. Includes a curriculum outline, a resource bibliography, and important appendixes of official Roman Catholic Church positions on the Jews and Judaism.

Fitzmyer, Joseph A. A Christological Catechism: New Testament Answers. New York: Paulist, 1982.

Useful for Christians exploring their Christology, this catechism reflects modern biblical scholarship. Sensitive to the guidelines of Vatican II.

Kagan, Henry Enoch. Changing the Attitude of Christian toward Jew: A Psychological Approach through Religion. New York: Columbia University Press, 1952.

A psychological experiment that attempts to change anti-Jewish attitudes by using teaching and private conference techniques at Christian summer church camps. Deserving of praise, this study does not deal with highly prejudiced people but rather tries to help Christian teenagers examine the superficiality of their anti-Jewish attitudes.

Kane, Michael. Minorities in Textbooks: A Study of Their Treatment in Social Studies Texts. Chicago: Quadrangle/Anti-Defamation League of B'nai B'rith, 1970.

This study examines textbooks and their treatment of minorities, as did the original ADL report in the 1960s. The suggested changes from the earlier study have not been heeded. One of the author's conclusions is that "material on the Jews continues to suffer from an overemphasis on their ancient past and on the theme of persecution," as well as their stereotyped treatment.

Kaufman, Harriet L. Jews & Judaism since Jesus. Cincinnati: Forward Movement, 1987.

Written as a teaching aid for Christians, this short introduction to Jewish life and the history of Judaism would be best utilized by Bible study groups and Christian education programs.

Littell, Marcia Sachs, ed. Holocaust Education: A Resource Book for Teachers and Professional Leaders. New York: E. Mellen/Anne Frank Institute, 1985.

Essays from the Eighth Conference on Teaching the Holocaust and Its Lessons, which had the theme "Lessons of the Holocaust: Signs of Oppression." This is another valuable resource for Holocaust educators.

Long, J. Bruce, ed. Judaism and the Christian Seminary Curriculum. Chicago: Loyola University Press, 1966.

An outstanding investigation of Judaism in the theological curriculum of Christian seminaries. Scholars such as William D. Davies, Charles

Education

Y. Glock, Jerald C. Brauer, George G. Higgins, J. Coert Rylaarsdam, and Robert Gordis, among others, presented papers at a Catholic-Protestant Conference on Judaism and the Christian Seminary Curriculum, March 24-25, 1966, at the University of Chicago. A clear example of the two traditions' move, in the sixties, away from tea and sympathy towards respect and understanding.

McGinley, John. Catechism for Theologians: The Foundations for Meaningful Jewish-Christian Dialogue. Washington, D.C.: University Press of America, 1981.

The subtitle is inaccurate. The author's position is triumphal, i.e., when Jews accept Jesus as the Messiah, then they will discover their divine nature. Meaningful dialogue does not have this as a foundation.

Olson, Bernhard E. Faith and Prejudice: Intergroup Problems in Protestant Curricula. New Haven, Conn.: Yale University Press, 1963.

This large, penetrating self-study on religious animosity and religious instruction analyzes catechetical literature. Olson, who headed this seven-year study by the Yale Divinity School, examined four basic theological viewpoints, conservative, fundamentalist, liberal, and neo-orthodox, to determine if religious education fosters prejudice.

Pawlikowski, John T. Catechetics and Prejudice: How Catholic Teaching Materials View Jews, Protestants, and Racial Minorities. New York: Paulist, 1973.

Pawlikowski analyzes the St. Louis University Textbook Studies on Catholic teaching materials. The conclusion of the studies is that Jews and Judaism are presented unfavorably and much less objectively than are other religions. Contains suggestions to help change the anti-Jewish attitudes these texts foster.

Sternfield, Janet. Homework for Jews: Preparing for Jewish-Christian Dialogue. Second ed. New York: National Conference of Christians and Jews, 1985.

The most useful "how to" book available; it offers excellent preparation for Jews to enter into the vibrant and exciting world of Jewish-Christian dialogue.

Strober, Gerald S. Portrait of the Elder Brother: Jews and Judaism in Protestant Teaching Materials. New York: American Jewish Committee, 1972.

This short evaluation of texts and teaching materials used in religious education looks at Bernhard E. Olson's Yale study and concludes that many of the suggested changes have not come about. A noteworthy part of this study is the recognition of the lack of reflection in teaching materials on the recent developments in Jewish-Christian relations.

Weinryb, Bernard D., and Daniel Garnick. Jewish School Textbooks and Inter-Group Relations. New York: American Jewish Committee, 1965.

One of the three studies the American Jewish Committee sponsored with the aim of eliminating "prejudice-producing material from religious education."

N. Intermarriage

Resources on the subject of intermarriage are offered with the aim that they will be used by members of the clergy or others who are dealing with Jews and Christians who wish to marry.

Berman, Louis A. Jews and Intermarriage: A Study in Personality and Culture. New York: T. Yoseloff, 1968.

This volume begins with a preface that identifies false assumptions and half-truths. The author then attempts to provide information to clarify these mistaken ideas. This extensive study covers a wide range of psychological and social attitudes regarding intermarriage and is meant for scholars and serious students.

Bossard, James H. S., and Eleanor Stoker Boll. One Marriage Two Faiths: Guidance on Interfaith Marriage. New York: Ronald, 1957.

A balanced appraisal of the issues that those who wish to intermarry must face. A helpful set of case histories with analysis is included.

Cahnan, Werner J., ed. Intermarriage and Jewish Life: A Symposium. New York: Herzl/Jewish Reconstructionist, 1963.

These essays, the proceedings of a conference on intermarriage and Jewish life, look at the demography of intermarriage. They examine the social scientist's point of view on intermarriage in different communities around the world.

Gittelsohn, Roland B. The Extra Dimension: A Jewish View of Marriage. New York: Union of American Hebrew Congregations, 1983.

A well-written summary of marriage in the Jewish tradition. Of particular worth is the chapter on mixed marriage. It discusses in detail a rabbi's point of view on whether to officiate at a mixed marriage.

Gordon, Albert I. Intermarriage: Interfaith, Interracial, Interethnic. Boston: Beacon, 1964.

The most extensive treatment of intermarriage available. Although this is twenty years old, it is a very thorough analysis that covers more than just interfaith marriages, and as a result will come in handy for other purposes. The chapter "The Jew and Intermarriage" includes many statements from Jewish organizations on intermarriage that are helpful in understanding "official" Jewish viewpoints.

Hathorn, Raban, William H. Genne, and Mordecai L. Brill, eds. Marriage: Interfaith Guide for All Couples. New York: Association, 1970.

This book, edited by a Roman Catholic priest, a Protestant minister, and a Jewish rabbi, stresses the spiritual ties that are necessary for a good marriage to work. Along with a joint statement on marriage and family life by the three major religious groups in the United States, there are also chapters by husband and wife counseling teams. Easy and enjoyable reading recommended for those doing premarital counseling.

Kaye, Evelyn. Crosscurrents: Children, Famlies, and Religion. New York: Clarkson N. Potter, 1980.

Although written in an informal style, this work is useful for parents who are experiencing difficulty in raising children of two religions in their household, e.g., remarriages, "blended" families. The author emphasizes the enrichment and opportunities possible for a child in such a family rather than the confusion that may result.

Luka, Ronald. When a Christian and a Jew Marry. New York: Paulist, 1973.

Preparation for the realities of a Jewish-Christian marriage for the couple, parents, and religious leaders. Also included is a Jewish-Christian wedding ceremony which combines the basic features of ceremonies from both faiths.

Mayer, Egon. Children of Intermarriage: A Study in Patterns of Identification and Family Life. New York: American Jewish Committee, 1983.

This pamphlet is the result of a study commissioned by the American Jewish Committee. It looks at the Jewish identity of the children of those who intermarry by asking many questions that are concerned with patterns of Jewish behavior, attitudes regarding Jews and Judaism, exclusiveness and group identity, and feelings about oneself and family relationships.

_____. Love and Tradition: Marriage between Jews and Christians. New York: Plenum, 1985.

A popular and up-to-date sociological study of Christians and Jews who marry. The author has interviewed hundreds of intermarried couples and their children. He analyzes decisions these couples must face by investigating their case histories as well as the results of his survey. An insightful look into the problems of intermarriage.

Mayer, Egon, and Carl Scheingold. Intermarriage and the Jewish Future: A National Study in Summary. New York: American Jewish Committee, 1979.

A booklet concerned with the effects of intermarriage on the partners, on identification with Judaism, on alienation arising out of a troubled marriage, and on the feelings of the non-Jewish spouse about Judaism. These findings are used in Mayer's book Love and Tradition.

Pike, James Albert. If You Marry outside Your Faith: Counsel on Mixed Marriages. New York: Harper, 1954.

Even though this book is over thirty years old, it can still serve as a useful tool for those faced with mixed marriage and those who counsel people facing this situation. The reader is presented with the author's analysis of several cases designed to prepare couples for the problems they may encounter.

Sandmel, Samuel. When a Jew and Christian Marry. Philadelphia: Fortress, 1977.

Because of the religious and cultural problems that are likely to occur, the author counsels against intermarriage. But this work is also meant for those who have already married or have decided to do so. This would be a helpful book for those who do not realize the difficulties involved in an intermarriage because it is more thorough than most that deal with issues that separate Christians and Jews.

Seltzer, Sanford. Jews and Non-Jews: Falling in Love. New York: Union of American Hebrew Congregations, 1976.

This guide, to be used by Jews, non-Jews, and their families, provides some fundamental information necessary for those considering mixed marriage or intermarriage. For the author "intermarriage" is a union in which the non-Jewish partner has converted to Judaism before the wedding ceremony. It will also be helpful to rabbis in their counseling of couples contemplating interfaith marriages.

—————. Jews and Non-Jews: Getting Married. New York: Union of American Hebrew Congregations, 1984.

A manual developed with the purpose of explaining interfaith marriages from the perspective of a Reform Jew committed to the perpetuation of Judaism. The author reflects upon the Jewish wedding, children, and the chances of success of interfaith marriages.

Sklare, Marshall, ed. The Jew in American Society. New York: Behrman House, 1974.

Arnold Schwartz's chapter, "Intermarriage in the United States," is a lucid and scholarly look at how Jews feel about intermarriage. He provides several examples of rabbis who view intermarriage as a problem for, and thus a threat to, the Jewish community. He also examines Jewish demography, intermarriage rates, several studies on intermarriage, and the effects of intermarriage on the Jewish community and its future.

O. Liturgy, Spirituality, Prayer, Holidays

This section is composed of liturgical works, prayer guides, and books on festivals and spirituality.

Bacchiocchi, Samuele. From Sabbath to Sunday: A Historical Investigation of the Rise of Sunday Observance in Early Christianity. Rome: Pontifical Gregorian University Press, 1977.

If the liturgist's task is to bring people to a new understanding of worship, then this will prove to be a useful book. Bacchiocchi, a Seventh-day Adventist and the first non-Catholic to graduate from the Pontifical Gregorian University in Rome, argues that the adoption of Sunday instead of the Sabbath occurred in the Church of Rome a century later than originally thought. He contends that the change did not take place in the primitive Church of Jerusalem by reason of apostolic authority. He also looks at other factors pertinent to Jewish-Christian relations that may have influenced the change, i.e., anti-Jewish feelings, repressive Roman laws enacted against the Jews, etc.

Brickner, Balfour. An Interreligious Guide to Passover and Easter. New York: Commission on Interfaith Activities, 1969.

The goal of this booklet is for Christians and Jews to come to a better understanding of their differences. These two holidays offer a unique opportunity for understanding. Sections include the history and meaning of Passover, a comparison of Passover and Easter, and an explanation of the rites and symbols of the festivals organized so that a rabbi and a minister can share in the teaching.

Carson, D. A., ed. From Sabbath to Lord's Day: A Biblical, Historical, and Theological Investigation. Grand Rapids: Zondervan, 1982.

This work is in part a response to Bacchiocchi's argument that Sunday became a substitute for the Sabbath. The authors, who represent a conservative evangelical Protestant perspective, have tackled a question that frequently comes up in Jewish-Christian dialogue. They conclude that Sunday was the new day of worship for the earliest Christians. Technical in places, it will still be useful for seminaries, where this question frequently arises.

Feeley-Harnik, Gillian. The Lord's Table: Eucharist and Passover in Early Christianity. Philadelphia: University of Pennsylvania Press, 1981.

A new approach to understanding the table traditions in the New Testament and Judaism in Jesus' time. The author analyzes the relationship of the Passover tradition in Judaism and the Last Supper tradition found in the Gospels.

Finkel, Asher, and Lawrence Frizzell, eds. Standing before God: Studies on Prayer in Scripture and Tradition in Honor of John M. Oesterreicher. New York: Ktav, 1981.

Twenty-four essays have been contributed to this volume in honor of John M. Oesterreicher, founder and director of the Institute of Judaeo-Christian Studies, on the occasion of his seventy-fifth birthday. Scholars from all over the world have written on worship in Scriptures, prayer in tradition, and reflections on biblical and religious themes.

Gavin, F. The Jewish Antecedents of the Christian Sacraments. New
    York: Ktav, 1969.

    Lectures on "Judaism and Sacramentalism," "Jewish Proselyte and
    Christian Convert," and "B'racha [prayer] and Eucharist." Recent
    scholarship makes this work dated and one-dimensional.

Guilding, Aileen. The Fourth Gospel and Jewish Worship: A Study of
    the Relation of St. John's Gospel to the Ancient Jewish Lectionary
    System. Oxford, England: Oxford University Press, 1960.

    The author reviews the ancient systematic readings and then
    demonstrates how the fourth evangelist has utilized Jesus' sermons
    against the background of the Jewish liturgical year.

Idlesohn, Abraham Z. Jewish Liturgy and Its Development. New York:
    Schocken, 1967.

    A thorough history of Jewish liturgy. Jewish elements in the early
    Christian liturgy are treated in an appendix.

Klenicki, Leon, and Gabe Huck, eds. Spirituality and Prayer: Jewish
    and Christian Understandings. New York: Paulist, 1983.

    A set of essays that explore the spiritual traditions found in Judaism
    and Christianity. A contribution to the ongoing dialogue between
    Jews and Christians that examines, in depth, the topics of prayer
    and spirituality.

Lapide, Pinchas E. Hebrew in the Church: The Foundations of Jewish-
    Christian Dialogue. Trans. Erroll F. Rhodes. Grand Rapids: Eerdmans,
    1984.

    A scholarly survey of, and commentary on, Christian and Jewish efforts
    to translate the New Testament and the Christian liturgy into Hebrew.

Le Deaut, Roger. The Message of the New Testament and the Aramaic
    Bible. Trans. Stephen F. Miletic. Rome: Biblical Institute Press,
    1982.

    The author's goal in this work was to "demonstrate how ancient Jewish
    liturgy and the Aramaic translations connected with it constitute
    a capital source for illustrating the message of the New Testament."

Le Deaut, Roger, Annie Jaubert, and Kurt Hruby. The Spirituality of
    Judaism. Trans. Paul Barrett. St. Meinrad, Ind.: Abbey, 1977.

    The richness of Jewish spirituality is explored in this work by three
    Catholic scholars. Written for Catholics to enrich their understanding
    of Jewish worship.

Littell, Marcia Sachs, ed. <u>Liturgies on the Holocaust</u>. New York: E. Mellen/ Anne Frank Institute, 1986.

Sabbath services, sermons, and liturgical expressions with songs, readings, and prayers are made available in this work that is excellent for use on the Days of Remembrance. These essays offer Jewish and Christian clergy a mode through which to help the laity "seek reconciliation and to renew faith in humanity and commitment to life."

Oesterley, W.O.E. <u>The Jewish Background of the Christian Liturgy</u>. Gloucester, Mass.: P. Smith, 1965.

This study of the Jewish liturgy and pre-Christian elements in the Jewish liturgy demonstrated the influence early Jewish worship had on Christian worship. A comprehensive work with indexes of subjects, biblical references, references to ancient authors and ancient writings, rabbinical references, and modern authors.

Petuchowski, Jakob J., and Michael Brocke, eds. <u>The Lord's Prayer and Jewish Liturgy</u>. New York: Seabury, 1978.

The book as a whole is uneven, but one can glean useful information. Divided into four parts: 1) "The Hebrew Bible," 2) "The Prayers of the Synagogue," 3) "The New Testament," and 4) "Practical Applications." Concludes with a helpful bibliographical chapter.

Polish, Daniel F., and Eugene J. Fisher, eds. <u>Liturgical Foundations of Social Policy in the Catholic and Jewish Traditions</u>. Notre Dame, Ind.: University of Notre Dame Press, 1983.

Essays in this commendable volume examine the way the two faith communities utilize their liturgical traditions to approach problems in the areas of environment, health care, peace, and social commitment. Contributors include Lawrence A. Hoffman, John A. Gurrieri, Walter S. Wurzburger, Dennis Krouse, John T. Pawlikowski, Jules Harlow, Edward J. Rilmartin, and Jonathan I. Helfand. Hoffman and Gerard S. Sloyan offer, respectively, Jewish- and Catholic assessments on the liturgical basis for social policy.

Saldarini, Anthony J. <u>Jesus and Passover</u>. New York: Paulist, 1984.

The images, rituals, and symbols of the Jewish feast of Passover are investigated in the light of its origins, Jesus' lifetime, the Gospels, and Easter. Easy reading about the holiday of hope and remembrance.

Schlesinger, Hugh, and Humberto Porto. <u>Prayers of Blessing and Praise for All Occasions</u>. Mystic, Conn.: Twenty-Third Publications, 1987.

These prayers can help meet the spiritual needs of Jews and Christians who come to pray together in joint religious ritual. There are one hundred different prayers for people, their professions and community, significant events and occasions, social issues and values, and much more.

Simpson, W. W. <u>Light and Rejoicing</u>: <u>A Christian's Understanding of</u>
<u>Jewish Worship</u>. Belfast, Ireland: Christian Journals, 1976.

Meant for non-Jewish readers, Simpson's work is a practical guide
to the vitality of living Jewish worship and the need for Christians
to gain an appreciation of Judaism.

Werner, Eric. <u>The Sacred Bridge</u>: <u>The Interdependence of Liturgy and</u>
<u>Music in Synagogue and Church during the First Millennium</u>. New
York: Columbia University Press, 1959.

A very thorough and scholarly exploration of the early use of organized
forms of common worship in Judaism and Christianity. The title
indicates the author's belief that there is a bridge between the two
religions that has enabled exchange of liturgy and music.

P. Mission

A selection of works that consider evangelization, proselytism, mission,
and witness.

Anderson, Gerald H., and Thomas F. Stransky, eds. <u>Mission Trends No.</u>
<u>5</u>: <u>Faith Meets Faith</u>. New York: Paulist/Eerdmans, 1981.

Christian church leaders, educators, lay persons, and missionaries
reflect on the meeting of Christianity and other faiths. Essays from
the Orthodox, Protestant, and Roman Catholic traditions consider
religious pluralism, interfaith dialogue, mission and witness,
confrontation, universalism, values, and the like.

Bamberger, Bernard J. <u>Proselytism in the Talmudic Period</u>. New York:
Ktav, 1968. Originally published in 1939.

Considered to be a definitive treatment, Bamberger's research led
him to the conclusion that there was generally a favorable view of
Jewish proselytism in this period. This book will be helpful for a
better understanding of Jewish attitudes towards converts.

Blumstock, Robert Edward. <u>The Evangelization of Jews</u>: <u>A Study of</u>
<u>Interfaith Relations</u>. Eugene: University of Oregon Press, 1964.

Doctoral dissertation that concentrates on two aspects of the mission
to the Jews. It examines factors of interfaith relations in the U.S.
and then investigates the anti-Jewish foundations of the American
Board of Mission to the Jews.

Cohen, Martin A., and Helga Croner, eds. <u>Christian Mission-Jewish Mission</u>.
New York: Paulist, 1982.

The Stimulus Foundation has produced a very useful, critical discussion
of the significance of mission for Christianity and Judaism. Eight
essays by ministers, rabbis, and scholars address the historical context
of Christian mission, contemporary Christian perspectives, and Jewish
attitudes towards these perspectives.

Croner, Helga and Leon Klenicki, eds. Issues in the Jewish-Christian Dialogue: Jewish Perspectives on Covenant and Mission. New York: Paulist, 1979.

Jewish scholars direct their reflective skills toward issues raised by Christian statements and religious pluralism. This contribution, another in the "Studies in Judaism and Christianity" series, adds constructively to interreligious dialogue and contemporary Jewish thought.

Eichhorn, David Max. Evangelizing the American Jew. Middle Village, N.Y.: Jonathan David, 1978.

Arranged historically, from the colonial period to the present, this book chronicles the efforts of Christians to convert Jews, specifically Christians who are making a concerted effort to attract Jews. This is a convincingly documented portrayal of a disputed practice in the dialogue.

Fleischner, Eva. Judaism in German Christian Theology since 1945: Christianity and Israel Considered in Terms of Mission. Metuchen, N.J.: Scarecrow, 1975.

This work (Fleischner's Ph.D. dissertation) provides useful support for the need for dialogue. She states that "mission to the Jews must give way to true 'dialogue'." This approach will be welcomed by many Jews and Christians, while other Christians will feel that it abandons the essence of Christianity, which requires conversion mission.

Hart, Lewis A. A Jewish Reply to Christian Evangelists. New York: Bloch, 1906.

Thirty-one articles written as communications to The Jewish Times of Montreal. The articles, a response to active Christian evangelism of the Jews, are divided into three sections: 1) "On Christian Attempts to Convert Jews," 2) "Some Questions Answered," and 3) "An Answer to Christian Evangelists."

Jocz, Jakob. Christians and Jews: Encounter and Mission. London: SPCK, 1966.

A series of lectures delivered at Princeton Theological Seminary by Jocz, a well-known Hebrew Christian. Although the author suggests confrontation rather than conversion in Christian encounters with Jews, his arguments indicate that missionizing should be a primary motivation.

Levine, Samuel. You Take Jesus, I'll Take God: How to Refute Christian Missionaries. Los Angeles: Hamorah, 1980.

Piercing questions are presented in this polemical work against Christian missionaries and Messianic Jews.

Sigal, Gerald. The Jew and the Christian Missionary: A Jewish Response to Missionary Christianity. New York: Ktav, 1981.

> Over seventy-five biblical passages used by Christian missionaries when attempting to convert Jews are examined in detail. An assessment is made on the relation of the passage to the religious beliefs of both Christianity and Judaism.

Troki, Isaac ben Abraham. Faith Strengthened: 1200 Biblical Refutations to Christian Missionaries. Trans. Moses Mocatta. New York: Ktav, 1970.

> Although this work is specifically for Jews, it has found an audience among many Christians, despite its polemical nature. Over four hundred years old, this powerful refutation of Christian polemics is still pertinent to the question of missionizing among the Jews.

Q. Issues in the Dialogue

This section is comprised of books that discuss certain specific issues in the dialogue, or that define encounter, conversation, and dialogue for Jewish-Christian relations.

Agus, Jacob Bernard. Dialogue and Tradition: The Challenges of Contemporary Judaeo-Christian Thought. New York: Abelard-Schuman, 1971.

> The author, a prolific Jewish scholar, analyzes Judaism's dialogue with itself and with Christians, historians, the "New Atheists," and secular ideologists. The key concern throughout the book "is the tension between tradition and dialogue." Included in the section on Jewish-Christian dialogue is Agus's response to Augustine Bea's The Church and the Jewish People and Jean Danielou's Dialogue with Israel.

Althouse, LaVonne. When Jew & Christian Meet. New York: Friend Press, 1966.

> The material is quite dated, but for one studying advancements in the dialogue in the last twenty-five years, this book would prove useful. For beginning a dialogue to help combat prejudice, other books published recently are more useful.

Barth, Markus. Israel and the Church: Contribution to a Dialogue Vital for Peace. Richmond, Va.: John Knox, 1969.

> In the light of the 1967 Arab-Israeli war, Barth believes it is time for a renewal of the dialogue between Christians and Jews. These theological essays are divided into three sections: 1) "What Can a Jew Believe about Jesus--and Still Remain a Jew?" 2) "Was Paul an Anti-Semite?" and 3) "Israel and the Church in Paul's Epistle to the Ephesians."

Bird, Thomas E., ed. Modern Theologians: Christians and Jews. Notre
Dame, Ind.: University of Notre Dame Press, 1967.

Concise essays on ten of the more important theologians who have
had (and are still having) a major effect on Catholic, Jewish, and
Protestant theology. The ten theologians include Martin Buber, John
Courtney Murray, Josef Hromadka, Bernard Haring, Edward
Schillebeeckx, John A. T. Robinson, Bernard Lonergan, John Hick,
Abraham Joshua Heschel, and Henri de Lubac.

Bitton-Jackson, Livia. Madonna or Courtesan? The Jewish Woman in
Christian Literature. New York: Seabury, 1982.

This interesting work "is an attempt to shed light on the deceptive
nature of the myth-making process which has so often led one human
being to become the perpetrator of injustice and another its victim."

Brandon, S. G. F. The Judgment of the Dead: An Historical and Comparative
Study of the Idea of a Post-Mortem Judgment in the Major Religions.
London: Weidenfeld and Nicolson, 1967.

The subtitle accurately reflects the content of the book. Brandon
provides a provocative analysis of the history of the major religions'
belief in some kind of judgment after death. He traces its history
in Ancient Egypt and Mesopotamia, the Hebrew religion, Graeco-Roman
culture, Christianity, Islam, and the Eastern religions.

Braybrooke, Marcus. Interfaith Organizations 1893-1979: An Historical
Directory. New York: E. Mellen, 1980.

Concerned mostly with interreligious conferences of the last hundred
years. Although the directory has limited use (it is only seven pages
in length and many entries are without addresses), the rest of the book
does serve the purpose of recording the historical dimensions of the
interfaith movement.

Buber, Martin. Between Man and Man. New York: Macmillan, 1948.

An amplification of Buber's I and Thou, this book of five short works
contains essays on the nature of dialogue, education, and philosophical
anthropology.

————. I and Thou. Trans. and prologue by Walter Kaufmann. New
York: Scribner, 1970.

Although proclaimed as "insightful" and "classic," the thought is obtuse.
Thus it will probably prove useful to a limited audience, e.g., upper-level
graduates and above. It offers an intense religious dimension that
serious scholars will find worth exploring.

Cohen, Arthur A. The Myth of the Judaeo-Christian Tradition and Other
Dissenting Essays. New York: Harper and Row, 1970.

Cohen examines the Judaeo-Christian tradition and determines that
it is inaccurate to refer to a "Judaeo-Christian" tradition at all. In

fact, serious Jews and Christians are actually theological enemies. The myth serves to blur distinctions between the two faiths. He attempts to overcome these problems with his suggested Judaeo-Christian humanism that will "hear in each other the sounds of truth."

Croner, Helga, compiler. More Stepping Stones to Jewish-Christian Relations: An Unabridged Collection of Christian Documents 1975-1983. New York: Paulist, 1985.

A continuation of the first work on Christian documents, this book also contains commentaries by Jorge Mejia, Alice L. Eckardt, and Mordecai Waxman.

————. Stepping Stones to Further Jewish-Christian Relations. Foreword by Edward A. Synan. New York: Stimulus, 1977.

A compilation of official documents dealing with Jewish-Christian relations. The Roman Catholic documents include statements by authorities in the Vatican and in the United States, Europe, and Latin America (joint Jewish-Christian). Protestant documents include statements by the World Council of Churches and various church groups.

Cournos, John. An Open Letter to Jews and Christians. New York: Oxford University Press, 1938.

An effectively argued plea for Jews and Christians to unite in common causes, i.e., the struggle for freedom, social justice, etc. The author sees Jesus as the meeting point and believes there should be a Jewish reclamation of Jesus.

Coward, Harold. Pluralism: Challenge to World Religions. Maryknoll, N.Y.: Orbis, 1985.

The attitudes of Buddhism, Christianity, Hinduism, Islam, and Judaism toward each other are examined. Coward uses these reactions to the challenge of pluralism to develop new guidelines for interreligious dialogue. A well-written presentation.

Danielou, Jean. Dialogue with Israel. Baltimore: Helicon, 1968.

A short collection of essays on topics of importance (early Judaism and Christianity, later mysticism and metaphysics, some Jewish views of Jesus, anti-Judaism) in the Jewish-Christian dialogue. Danielou investigates these various issues with an understanding that might serve as a model to all who wish to re-examine their own positions. Jacob Agus replies succinctly to Danielou's questions and problems.

Daum, Annette and Eugene J. Fisher. The Challenge of Shalom for Catholics and Jews: A Dialogical Discussion Guide to the Catholic Bishops' Pastoral on Peace and War. New York: Union of American Hebrew Congregations, 1985.

This discussion guide will be valuable for Jews and Christians who wish to unite to promote peace. Those dialogue groups that have gone beyond the introductory stage and have begun to deliberate on specific issues will find this book helpful.

Davis, Lenwood G., compiler. Black-Jewish Relations in the United States, 1752-1984: A Selected Bibliography. Westport, Conn.: Greenwood, 1984.

Although much of Black-Jewish relations does not deal specifically with the Jewish-Christian encounter, there are many aspects that are pertinent.

Eckardt, A. Roy. Christianity and the Children of Israel. New York: King's Crown, 1948.

The earliest of Eckardt's books on the dialogue, this is an examination of the theological rationale that, historically, has led to problems in Jewish-Christian relations. He surveys the attitudes of neo-Reformation writers, chiefly the Niebuhrs, and looks at the "Jewish question."

_____. Elder and Younger Brothers: The Encounter of Jews and Christians. New York: Scribner, 1967.

In what was a ground-breaking work, Eckardt's moral and theological exposition challenges Christians to rethink the question of the legitimacy of Judaism and Israel's right to exist. This work of reconciliation reflects upon anti-Judaism, the covenant of the Jews, the tragedy of the Holocaust, and the lack of reaction by the Christian community to the 1967 Israeli-Arab war.

_____. Jews and Christians: The Contemporary Meeting. Bloomington: Indiana University Press, 1986.

Eckardt, one of the premier thinkers in today's Jewish-Christian encounter, asks some complex questions and tackles controversial issues in a well-written and insightful volume on the developments of the dialogue. This work admirably utilizes recent and current literature from Jewish and Christian theologians and philosophers.

_____. Your People, My People: The Meeting of Jews and Christians. New York: Quadrangle, 1974.

Eckardt's writings are bold and pointed and these essays are no exception. He brings to the dialogue timely statements on anti-Judaism and the Christian's predicament, the silence and "neutralism" of Christians after the Six Day War, and the future of the Jewish-Christian relationship.

Edelman, Lily, ed. Face to Face: A Primer in Dialogue. New York: Anti-Defamation League of B'nai B'rith, 1967.

Seventeen short essays with material that will be helpful as preparation for Jews beginning rapprochement with Christians. There is a variety of topics presented in Jewish-Christian differences and Catholic, Jewish, Protestant, and historic views of Vatican Council II.

Fisher, Eugene J., and Leon Klenicki, eds. Pope John Paul II on Jews and Judaism 1979-1986. Washington, D.C.: United States Catholic Conference, 1987.

This short work chronicles the Pope's addresses on Jews and on the need for dialogue. His statements are preceded by commentary.

Fisher, Eugene J., and Daniel F. Polish, eds. The Formation of Social Policy in the Catholic and Jewish Traditions. Notre Dame, Ind.: University of Notre Dame Press, 1980.

These papers, from a dialogue held at the University of Notre Dame, represent Jewish and Christian perspectives on social policy questions. Topics include "Social Policy-Making Structures of Our Religious Communities," "Religion and Family Policy," "Religion and National Economic Policy," "Religion and International Human Rights," and "Methodological Conclusions." A useful introduction precedes each set of papers.

Fisher, Eugene J., A. James Rudin, and Marc H. Tanenbaum, eds. Twenty Years of Jewish-Catholic Relations. New York: Paulist, 1986.

The most up-to-date anthology on Jewish-Catholic relations available, this book has essays by distinguished Jewish and Christian theologians, including Lawrence Boadt, Michael J. Cook, John T. Pawlikowski, Irving Greenberg, the editors, and several others. Topics include Nostra Aetate, Israel, the Bible, and philosophical and religious thought.

Gordon, Haim. Dance, Dialogue, and Despair: Existentialist Philosophy and Education for Peace in Israel. Birmingham: University of Alabama Press, 1986.

This book chronicles the Education for Peace project undertaken during the years 1979 to 1982 at Ben-Gurion University of the Negev. The endeavor was intended to encourage dialogue between Jews and Arabs by utilizing Buberian existentialist philosophy. Gordon, who directed the project, employs the principles that Martin Buber developed for dialogue and then records the resulting discussions. The outcome is engaging action research.

Greenspahn, Frederick E., ed. Contemporary Ethical Issues in the Jewish and Christian Traditions. New York: Ktav, 1986.

The orientation of Jews and Christians can often be in opposition on ethical questions. This volume of essays by distinguished scholars analyzes the differences of the two traditions in the area of science and technology, sexuality, and social justice.

—————. The Human Condition in the Jewish and Christian Traditions. New York: Ktav, 1986.

A look at the classical positions on human nature, sin and atonement, and eschatological hopes. The authors attempt "to make contemporary sense" of their tradition's conceptions of these issues. Scholars contributing to this volume include Richard Rubenstein, Steven Schwarzschild, Michael Wyschogrod, Monika Hellwig, Robert Kress, Carl Peters, Langdon Gilkey, Clark Pinnock, and David Wells.

Greenstone, Julius H. The Messiah Idea in Jewish History. Philadelphia: Jewish Publication Society, 1906.

An important aspect in Judaism is the belief in a messiah. This work examines this concept in biblical times, the second commonwealth, the talmudic period, the rise of rationalism, the development in the Kabbalah, the effects of Kabbalistic speculations, religious reform and Zionism, and the liturgy. Christians and Jews alike would profit from a better understanding of the history of this concept.

Hargrove, Katharine T., ed. The Star and the Cross: Essays on Jewish Christian Relations. Milwaukee: Bruce, 1966.

Dialogic essays that show the beginning of the fruitful discussions of the early sixties. Hargrove has collected these writings (generally coupling one by a Jewish writer with one on a corresponding topic by a Catholic scholar) from a variety of sources and has skillfully arranged them in three parts, "Unity in Diversity," "Tension," and "Toward Deeper Unity."

Herberg, Will. Protestant, Catholic, Jew: An Essay in American Religious Sociology. Garden City, N.Y.: Doubleday, 1955.

The author describes this book as "a study of one aspect of the religious situation in this country from a sociological standpoint." The aspect he speaks of is the interrelationship of Catholic, Jew, and Protestant in American religious life.

Howe, Reuel L. The Miracle of Dialogue. Greenwich, Conn.: Seabury, 1963.

In the same vein as Buber's work on dialogue, to heighten communication "between man and man." This short work will suggest to any reader the fundamentals of dialogue.

Jacquet, Constan H., Jr., ed. Yearbook of American & Canadian Churches 1987. Nashville: Abingdon, 1987.

Containing information for many different faiths, this volume is a useful resource with directories for cooperative organizations, religious bodies, international agencies, ecumenical agencies, theological seminaries and Bible colleges, religious periodicals, and service agencies. It also includes statistical and historical data.

Jocz, Jakob. A Theology of Election: Israel and the Church. New York: Macmillan, 1958.

From the perspective of a Hebrew Christian, the author examines the theological issue of "election." The central question he explores is: Can the Church and the Jewish people both be Israel?

Klenicki, Leon, and Geoffrey Wigoder, eds. <u>A Dictionary of the Jewish-</u>
<u>Christian Dialogue.</u> New York: Paulist, 1984.

An important book for those interested in knowing the terminology
of the Jewish-Christian dialogue. Each topic is explained in two
essays, one by a Jewish and one by a Christian scholar. The essays
on these thirty-four topics will help all who are involved in the dialogue
to become better informed.

Knight, George A.F., ed. <u>Jews and Christians:</u> <u>Preparation for Dialogue.</u>
Philadelphia: Westminster, 1965.

The book aims "to encourage Jewish-Christian dialogue, to help prepare
the Church for such dialogue, to furnish resource materials for
discussion, and to raise the questions significant for such a dialogue."
The editor prefaces each chapter with explanatory remarks. Developed
at the encouragement of the Department of Evangelism of the National
Council of Churches.

Lapide, Pinchas E., and Jurgen Moltmann. <u>Jewish Monotheism and Christian</u>
<u>Trinitarian Doctrine.</u> Trans. Leonard Swidler. Philadelphia: Fortress,
1981.

Each author has written an essay, followed by a dialogue between
the two on the conflict between the trinity and monotheism. Their
positions are not representative of their traditions. Both the translator
and Jacob B. Agus have written forewords for the book. Lapide and
Moltmann have issued a common declaration that proclaims a challenge
for the two faiths.

Lapide, Pinchas E., and Karl Rahner. <u>Encountering Jesus--Encountering</u>
<u>Judaism: A Dialogue.</u> New York: Crossroad/Continuum, 1987.

Lay, Thomas, ed. <u>Jewish-Christian Relations.</u> St. Marys, Kans.: St. Mary's
College Press, 1966.

The proceedings of an institute held at St. Mary's College, St. Marys,
Kansas (February 21-22, 1965), a Catholic community college which
decided it needed to improve its knowledge of the Jewish community.
Jewish speakers, addressing topics relevant to Jewish-Christian
relations, include Jakob J. Petuchowski, Marc H. Tanenbaum, Morris
Margolies, Elbert L. Sapinsley, and David Rabinovitz.

Martin, Malachi. <u>The Encounter.</u> New York: Farrar, Straus, and Giroux,
1969.

Martin looks at the truth claims of each of the three major Western
religions--Judaism, Christianity, Islam--and assesses them in light
of contemporary scholarship. A fascinating set of scenarios
("ecumenical," "dominance," "underground," "externalization,"
"re-internalization," and "human consensus"), entitled "Historical
Prognoses," makes up the fourth section of this volume.

McInnes, Val Ambrose, ed. Renewing the Judeo-Christian Wellsprings. New York: Crossroad/Continuum, 1987.

Mollenkott, Virginia Ramey, ed. Women of Faith in Dialogue. New York: Crossroad, 1987.

Catholic, Jewish, Muslim, and Protestant women discuss their identity, community struggles, justice in the world, and the future agenda. Contains eighteen outstanding essays, a model interreligious service, and guidelines for founding local chapters of Women of Faith.

Neuhaus, Richard John, ed. Jews in Unsecular America. Grand Rapids: Eerdmans/Center for the Study of the American Jewish Experience, 1987.

An exploration of Jewish and Christian desire to nurture a democratic and pluralistic society. Interreligious dialogue has paved the way for trust between the two faiths that will help make this possible. Essays by Milton Himmelfarb, Jonathan D. Sarna, Marvin R. Wilson, David Novak, and Paul T. Stallsworth.

Oesterreicher, John M. Ecumenism and the Jews. West Hartford, Conn.: Saint Joseph College, 1969.

Examines the question: "Are the Jews partners in the ecumenical movement, or not?" Although it seems clear that the author believes the ecumenical movement is for those who profess Jesus as their Savior, Oesterreicher also believes Jews are partners in a movement of greater scope, "the kingdom of God."

————, ed. The Bridge. Five vols. New York: Pantheon, 1956-70.

A yearbook of Jewish-Christian relations by the Institute for Judaeo-Christian Studies, at Seton Hall University. It contains studies perspectives, surveys, documents, book reviews, and illustrations. Although this work does not constitute a dialogue since only Roman Catholics have contributed, it is generally designed for Christians to gain "a deeper understanding of their treasures."

Ophals, Paul D., and Marc H. Tannenbaum, eds. Speaking of God Today: Jews and Lutherans in Conversation. Philadelphia: Fortress, 1986.

Records the first national-level conversation between Jewish and Lutheran scholars. Controversial theological issues were frankly discussed in the areas of law, grace, and election. The other sections of the book chronicle subsequent dialogue on the topics of land, people, state, and how we speak of God today.

Osten-Sacken, Peter von der. Christian-Jewish Dialogue: Theological Foundations. Philadelphia: Fortress, 1986.

A critical look at how the Jewish-Christian dialogue has advanced in Germany, "the country where the Holocaust occurred." The author seeks to develop a Christology with an openness to Judaism.

Parkes, James. Prelude to Dialogue: Jewish-Christian Relationships.
New York: Schocken, 1969.

Lectures and articles by one of Christianity's foremost authorities
on Judaism and Jewish-Christian relations. These papers are a
distinguished contribution to the furthering of good relations between
Jews and Christians. Parkes presents an historical analysis of four
areas in the dialogue: "The Nature of Judaism," "Judaism among
the World's Religions," "Israel," and "Theological Foundations."

Pawlikowski, John T. What Are They Saying about Jewish-Christian
Dialogue? New York: Paulist, 1980.

The state of Jewish-Christian relations is surveyed in this marvelous
volume. Pawlikowski reviews the positions of prominent Christian
and Jewish theologians in the areas of New Testament, anti-Judaism,
covenant theology, Jesus, Israel, and the Holocaust. Will serve as
an excellent introduction to the status of the field, although it is
amazing to reflect on how much has happened since this work was
published.

Peck, Abraham J., ed. Jews and Christians after the Holocaust.
Philadelphia: Fortress, 1982.

These sensitively written papers, presented at a major symposium
on "Religion in a Post-Holocaust World," are impressive. Particularly
noteworthy is Rosemary Radford Ruether's "Christology and
Jewish-Christian Relations" (also included in her book To Change
the World: Christology and Cultural Criticism).

Rivkin, Ellis. The Shaping of Jewish History: A Radical New Interpretation.
New York: Scribner, 1971.

This work, admired by many Christians involved in the dialogue,
attempts to look at the process by which Judaism has defined itself
throughout history. This process, says the author, has led to the Jews'
unique status in many societies.

Rousseau, Richard W., ed. Christianity and Judaism: The Deepening
Dialogue. Scranton, Pa.: Ridge Row, 1983.

An excellent anthology with important essays bearing on the progress
being made in the reconstruction of a Christology sensitive to Jewish-
Christian relations. Those essays helpful to this topic include: A.
Roy Eckardt's "Christians and Jews: Along a Theological Frontier,"
Isaac C. Rottenberg's "Fulfillment Theology and the Future of
Jewish-Christian Relations," Eugene B. Borowitz's "Anti-Semitism
and the Christologies of Barth, Berkouwer and Pannenberg," and Clark
Williamson's "Christ against the Jews: A Review of Jon Sobrino's
Christology." Other essays reflect the subtitle and the openness
the members of each faith feel towards the other.

Rudavsky, Tamar, ed. Divine Omniscience and Omnipotence in Medieval Philosophy: Islamic, Jewish, and Christian Perspectives. Boston: D. Reidel, 1985.

A collection of essays on Islamic, Jewish, and Christian formulations of theories of divine predicates, particularly omnipotence, omniscience, and the challenge of human freedom. The medieval (and contemporary, when pertinent) discussions in these three traditions, along with their texts, are analyzed by scholars from all three perspectives.

Rudin, A. James, and Marvin R. Wilson, eds. A Time to Speak: The Evangelical Jewish Encounter. Grand Rapids: Eerdmans/Center for Judaic-Christian Studies, 1987.

This volume is based on a conference, "Evangelicals and Jews: Coming of Age," held at Gordon College in Wenham, Massachusetts (February 28-March 1, 1984). It contains several essays by distinguished evangelical and Jewish scholars. In discussing the need for dialogue the editors state that it is because "it is a time for evangelicals and Jews alike to speak out boldly and honestly to each other, to come to know and understand each other as people and not as spiritual abstractions."

Ruether, Rosemary Radford, ed. Religion and Sexism: Images of Woman in the Jewish and Christian Traditions. New York: Simon and Schuster, 1974.

Ruether has selected essays that consider Judaism's and Christianity's contributions to misogynism and "in shaping the traditional cultural images that have degraded and suppressed women." This theme is examined in the Scriptures, the Talmud, medieval and Reformation theology, and the theology of Barth and Tillich.

Ruether, Rosemary Radford, and Eleanor McLaughlin, eds. Women of Spirit: Female Leadership in the Jewish and Christian Traditions. New York: Simon and Schuster, 1979.

Lucid, concise, and readable study of women's leadership in Judaism and Christianity.

Scharper, Philip, ed. Torah and Gospel: Jewish and Catholic Theology in Dialogue. New York: Sheed and Ward, 1966.

An excellent book documenting the claim that the mid-sixties were the beginning of a trend that has continued to this day: a move from goodwill on the social level to the more significant and worthy encounter of theological confrontation. The theologians (including notables such as Solomon Grayzel, John B. Sheerin, Samuel Sandmel, Gerard S. Sloyan, Roland E. Murphy, and Jacob Agus) who participated in this symposium, held at St. Vincent's Archabbey in January of 1965, discussed biblical scholarship, freedom of conscience, Israel, past and future relations, and worship.

Schneider, Peter. The Dialogue of Christians and Jews. New York: Seabury, 1967.

The author seeks to clarify past misunderstandings in the Jewish-Christian relationship and thus enable each to learn in a dialogue beneficial to both traditions.

Seltzer, Sanford, and Max L. Stackhouse. The Death of Dialogue and Beyond. New York: Friendship, 1969.

Compiled after the 1967 Arab-Israeli conflict, these articles and papers have been assembled to present views on the lull in the dialogue in reaction to this crisis. Important essays by Malcolm L. Diamond, Balfour Brickner, Philip Scharper, Frank M. Cross, Jr., Rosemary Radford Ruether, Krister Stendahl, W. D. Davies, David Flusser, and Manfred H. Vogel.

Spong, John Shelby, and Jack Daniel Spiro. Dialogue: In Search of Jewish-Christian Understandings. Prologue by Frank Edwin Eakin, Jr. New York: Seabury, 1975.

A short, captivating dialogue between a rabbi and an Episcopal clergyman in Richmond, Virginia. They touch upon theological issues with sensitivity and warmth.

Swidler, Leonard J., ed. Scripture and Ecumenism: Protestant, Catholic, Orthodox, and Jewish. Pittsburgh: Duquesne University Press, 1965.

Primarily a Christian enterprise, except for a well-written essay by Stephen Schwarzchild, the concern here is not Jewish-Christian dialogue. However, Schwarzchild helps clarify confusion on what the ecumenical movement means in regards to the Jews.

Talmage, Frank E., ed. Disputation and Dialogue: Readings in the Jewish-Christian Encounter. New York: Ktav/Anti-Defamation League of B'nai B'rith, 1975.

An extremely important set of essays (thirty-seven) by well-known Jewish and Christian scholars. There are five sections, entitled "Verus Israel," "Messiah and Christ," "Law and Gospel—Letter and Spirit," "The Scepter of Judah," and "Impasse, Coexistence, Dialogue." Worth special note is the classic Jewish anti-dialogue statement "Judaism in the Post-Christian Era" by Eliezer Berkovits.

Tanenbaum, Marc, Marvin Wilson, and A. James Rudin, eds. Evangelicals and Jews in an Age of Pluralism. Grand Rapids: Baker, 1984.

This book continues the spirited conversation of evangelicals and Jews recorded in the editors' first collection of essays. Jews and evangelicals who believe they have little to talk about will find much more than they expected here.

————. Evangelicals and Jews in Conversation. Grand Rapids: Baker, 1978.

Evangelicals and Jews work together to overcome stereotypes and nurture spiritual bonds. There are essays by Jewish and evangelical scholars on their shared perspectives, the messiah, the meaning of Israel, interpretation of Scripture, responses to moral crises and social ferment, religious pluralism, and the future.

Thompson, Norma, and Bruce Cole, eds. The Future of Jewish-Christian Relations. Schenectady, N.Y.: Character Research, 1982.

These essays, most of which were presented at a conference on behalf of Lee A. Belford's noble efforts for the dialogue, are helpful to the Jewish reader who wishes to understand how Christian theologians grapple with their faith in a pluralistic world.

van Buren, Paul M. The Burden of Freedom: Americans and the God of Israel. New York: Seabury, 1976.

By examining the mystery of freedom, a short and partial reconstruction of Christian theology is offered by one of the better-known American theologians. Van Buren, who is on a "continuing quest for the concrete," expects Christian theologians to take advantage of economic, historical, political, and social facts that will enable them better to grasp the relationship of Christianity and Judaism.

Von Hammerstein, Franz, ed. Christian-Jewish Relations in Ecumenical Perspective with Special Emphasis on Africa: A Report on the Conference of the WCC Consultation on the Church and the Jewish People. Jerusalem, 16-26 June, 1977. Geneva: World Council of Churches, 1978.

The World Council of Churches has put the dialogue into a wider context by including African and Asian Christians. These conference proceedings provide Christian perspectives from the nations of Kenya, Tanzania, Rhodesia, Nigeria, Ethiopia, Ghana, and Thailand.

Werblowsky, Zwi. Jewish-Christian Relations. London: Council of Christians and Jews, 1973.

A short lecture delivered by Zwi Werblowsky, Professor of Comparative Religion at the Hebrew University, Jerusalem, for the thirtieth annual general meeting of the Council of Christians and Jews. Werblowsky illustrates the impact of several events in recent history on the Jewish-Christian relationship.

Wood, James E., Jr., ed. Jewish-Christian Relations in Today's World. Waco, Tex.: Baylor University Press, 1971.

Most of these essays were originally presented at a symposium on Jewish-Christian relations at Baylor University between January 24-26, 1971. The symposium was called to make available scholarly interpretations of Jews' and Christians' common concerns and to further Jewish-Christian understanding through academic channels of teaching and research.

Yates, George A., ed. In Spirit and in Truth: Aspects of Judaism and Christianity. London: Hodder Stoughton, 1934.

Historically this book is significant since it constitutes the first Jewish-Christian symposium to be published in England. Some of the topics include: approaches to God, the reality of God, the defeat of pain, the problem of evil, views of atonement, social teaching, ideals for human society, devotional life, the nature of revelation, and the nature of religious experience.

Zeik, Michael, and Martin Siegel, eds. <u>Root and Branch</u>: The <u>Jewish/Christian Dialogue</u>. Williston Park, N.Y.: Roth, 1973.

Semi-popular study of several important issues in the dialogue. Includes essays by Asher Finkel on the relationship of the Passover story and the Last Supper, Ellis Rivkin on the Pharisaic background of Christianity, Joseph A. Grassi on anti-Judaism in the Gospels, John T. Pawlikowski on Pauline baptismal theology, Thomas P. Anderson on nationalism, James Finn and Michael Zeik on Israel, Gregory Baum on the doctrinal basis for Jewish-Christian dialogue, and Martin Siegel on Jewish-Christianity.

R. Bibliographies

Blewett, Robert P. "Annotated Bibliographies Regarding Christian-Jewish Relations." 1987. Available through Interfaith Resources, Inc., 1328 Oakwood Drive, Anoka, Minnesota 55303.

These bibliographies cover four areas: history, theology, disputation and dialogue, and antisemitism. Each series of resources is divided into early Church and medieval and modern time period.

Cargas, Harry James. <u>The Holocaust</u>: <u>An Annotated Bibliography</u>. Second ed. Chicago: American Library Association, 1986.

Quality annotations make this an extremely useful resource for anyone wishing to study the history and implications of the Holocaust. Cargas's evaluations of over five hundred books cover a wide range of topics in a very thorough fashion.

Celnik, Isaac, and Max Celnik. <u>A Bibliography on Judaism and Jewish-Christian Relations</u>. New York: Anti-Defamation League of B'nai B'rith, 1965.

A selected bibliography of Judaism with brief annotations on its history, literature, beliefs, practices, institutions, and the Jewish-Christian encounter from its origins until 1964. Although this book was written when Jewish-Christian relations were just beginning to blossom (and as a result this section is very short), it is still useful for its annotations on the classics of history and literature in Judaism.

Cohen, Iva. <u>Israel</u>: <u>A Bibliography</u>. New York: Anti-Defamation League of B'nai B'rith, 1970.

Extensive and thorough annotations on the history of Israel and its culture. This bibliography contains sections on history, geography, archaeology, Zionism, politics, social structure, economy, education, the Kibbutz, the Arab-Israeli conflict, literature, and books for young people.

Cracknell, Kenneth. "Bibliography: Christian-Jewish Dialogue." Modern Churchman 26 (1984): 40-48.

Most of the books included are available only in England. However, there are a few American editions in print and it is useful to know what is happening in the dialogue on the international scene.

Eckardt, A. Roy. "Recent Literature on Christian-Jewish Relations." Journal of the American Academy of Religion 49 (1981): 99-114.

A scholarly review of the literature with an extensive listing of titles relating to the Holocaust and Christian anti-Judaism. There is also an excellent compilation of research in the areas of "Political Theology," "Jewish Influences on Christian Thought," "The Integrity of Judaism," and "Witness and Mission."

Fisher, Eugene J. "A New Maturity in Christian-Jewish Dialogue: An Annotated Bibliography 1979-83." Face to Face: An Interreligious Bulletin 11 (1984): 29-43.

The explosion of material in recent years has made this well-organized bibliography extremely helpful for students and scholars alike. Fisher has divided the article into thirteen different sections: "Documenting the Dialogue," "The New Testament and Judaism," "The Trial of Jesus," "The Relationship between the Scriptures," "The Patristic Period," "The Medieval Period," "The Modern Period: Jews and Christians in America," "Mission and Witness Reconsidered," "Toward a Christian Theology of Judaism," "Jewish Responses to Christianity," "Liturgy, Spirituality, Catechetics," "The Holocaust and Christian-Jewish Relations," and "Muslim-Jewish-Christian Relations."

Jackson, Herbert C., ed. Judaism, Jewish-Christian Relations, and the Christian Mission to the Jews: A Select Bibliography. New York: Missionary Research Library, 1966.

This bibliography, done by the Missionary Research Library at the request of the World Council of Churches' Committee on the Church and the Jewish People, lists over one thousand books, pamphlets, and articles.

Library, Union Theological Seminary in Virginia. Christian Faith Amidst Religious Pluralism: An Introductory Bibliography. Richmond, Va.: Union Theological Seminary in Virginia, 1980.

A teaching bibliography that lists print and non-print media in the areas of: Christianity and other religions (including African religions, Buddhism, Hinduism, Islam, Judaism, Sikhism, and Zoroastrianism); history and phenomenology of religion; philosophy and theology of religion; theology and practice of mission; and Third World theology. The media sections are particularly useful. Would be of great value to teachers and professors in Christian education who wish to explore further the use of pluralism for their classes. Available from the Union Theological Seminary in Virginia for $5.00.

Muffs, Judith Hershlag. The Holocaust in Books and Films. New York: Center for Studies on the Holocaust, Anti-Defamation League of B'nai B'rith, 1982.

Well-organized resource guide intended for librarians, students, and teachers in search of a greater understanding of the Holocaust. The annotated list of books and films provides useful descriptions of a wide range of material on and about the Holocaust. Headings include "European Jewry before the Holocaust," "The Third Reich," "Holocaust Overview," "Camps, Ghettos, in Hiding," "Collaboration and Indifference," "Resistance and Rescue," "War Criminals," "Survivors and the Generation After," "After the Holocaust: Reflection and Literary Analyses," "Nature of Human Behavior," "Analogies," "The Jews," "Prejudice and Anti-Semitism," and "The Controlled Society." Also includes a list of Holocaust centers and curriculum material.

Pawlikowski, John T. "The Bi-Polar Experience." New Catholic World 21 (1974): 43-47.

An introduction, for the Christian reader, to topics of central concern for those involved in the Jewish-Christian dialogue. These books, which touch upon issues that are important to, and significant for, contemporary Judaism, represent a good selection of the literature published in the early seventies.

Szonyi, David M. The Holocaust: An Annotated Bibliography and Resource Guide. New York: Ktav, 1985.

An extensive listing of resource materials on the Holocaust. This reference guide includes not only annotations of non-fiction works, but also of fiction, books for younger readers, and imaginative literature. Included within this research tool is a filmography, list of Holocaust education centers, research institutes, sample curricula for public school courses on the Holocaust, and a good deal more. This reference is an excellent starting point for anyone who wishes to begin a study of the subject.

Talmage, Frank. "Judaism on Christianity: Christianity on Judaism." In The Study of Judaism: Bibliographical Essays. New York: Anti-Defamation League of B'nai B'rith/Ktav, 1972.

Over seventy books and articles are included in this first-rate bibliographical article. It is composed of two sections, "The Image of Christianity in Judaism," and "The Christian View of Judaism." The organization of the material (late antiquity, middle ages, modern times), the list of publications cited in the text, and the supplementary list of titles make this a useful resource.

Wood, James E. "Selected and Annotated Bibliography on Jewish-Christian Relations." <u>Journal of Church and State</u> 13 (1971): 317-40.

More than 150 books dealing expressly with the relationship between Judaism and Christianity. Wood, who has also edited a book about Jewish-Christian relations, alphabetically organizes a list of books with short, descriptive annotations. This article lists most of the books written before 1972, but, because of the explosion of published research in the field, lacks many works that have already become classics.

S. Pamphlets

Since there is a myriad of issues, and books have not been written about all of them, a section on pamphlets available on Jewish-Christian relations is included here. The titles are generally descriptive of the content of the pamphlet. Prices have been included when available. Please write the organizations and publishers to obtain a copy of the pamphlets.

<u>Analysis of Notes on the Correct Way to Present the Jews and Judaism in Preaching and Catechesis of the Roman Catholic Church.</u> By Annette Daum. $2.00. Union of American Hebrew Congregations, Department of Interreligious Affairs, 838 Fifth Avenue, New York, New York 10021.

<u>Approaching Early Christian Writings: Some Jewish Perspectives.</u> By Michael J. Cook. Hebrew Union College-Jewish Institute of Religion, 3101 Clifton Avenue, Cincinnati, Ohio 45220.

<u>Building a Marriage on Two Altars.</u> By Elizabeth and William Genne. <u>Public Affairs Pamphlet 466 (1971).</u>

<u>Caring for the Dying Person.</u> By Los Angeles Roman Catholic/Jewish Respect Life Committee. Free. American Jewish Committee, Interreligious Affairs Committee, 6505 Wilshire Boulevard, Suite 315, Los Angeles, California 90048.

<u>The Challenge of Shalom for Catholics and Jews.</u> $4.00. Union of American Hebrew Congregations, Department of Interreligious Affairs, 838 Fifth Avenue, New York, New York 10021.

<u>The Challenge of the Holocaust for Christian Thinking.</u> By John T. Pawlikowski. $2.50. Anti-Defamation League of B'nai B'rith, 823 United Nations Plaza, New York, New York 10022.

<u>Children of Abraham.</u> By Edward W. Bauman. American Jewish Committee, 165 East 56 Street, New York, New York 10022.

<u>Christians and Jews: Suggestions for Dialogue.</u> By James A. Carpenter. Foreword Movement Publications, 412 Sycamore Street, Cincinnati, Ohio 45202.

106 Bibliography

Christianity and Jewish-Christian Relations in American Rabbinical School Programs. By Samuel Weintraub. $3.00. American Jewish Committee, 165 East 56 Street, New York, New York 10022.

Commemorations for Yom Hashoah: Holocaust Remembrance Day. National Conference of Christians and Jews, 71 Fifth Avenue, New York, New York 10003.

A Covenant of Care: A Jewish-Catholic Reflection on the Religious Contribution to Health Care and Medical Ethics. By Los Angeles Roman Catholic/Jewish Respect Life Committee. Free. American Jewish Committee, Interreligious Affairs Committee, 6505 Wilshire Boulevard, Suite 315, Los Angeles, California 90048.

Covenant or Covenants? A Historical Reflection on the Notion of Covenant. By Los Angeles Priest/Rabbi Committee. Free. American Jewish Committee, Interreligious Affairs Committee, 6505 Wilshire Boulevard, Suite 315, Los Angeles, California 90048.

Dimensions of the Holocaust. A Series of Lectures Presented at Northwestern University and Coordinated by the Department of History. By Elie Wiesel et al. $3.50. Anti-Defamation League of B'nai B'rith, 823 United Nations Plaza, New York, New York 10017.

Ecumenical Considerations on Jewish-Christian Dialogue: Dialogue with People of Living Faiths. World Council of Churches, 150 route de Ferney, 1211 Geneva 20, Switzerland.

An Experimental Haggadah. Union of American Hebrew Congregations, Department of Interreligious Affairs, 838 Fifth Avenue, New York, New York 10021.

Explaining Christmas to the Jewish Child. By Lois Miller Weinstein. Minute-Print, Inc., P.O. Box 989, Williamsville, New York 14221.

From Death to Hope: Liturgical Reflections on the Holocaust. By Eugene J. Fisher and Leon Klenicki. $1.50. Anti-Defamation League of B'nai B'rith, 823 United Nations Plaza, New York, New York 10017.

Good Friday Worship: Jewish Concerns—Christian Response. $3.00. National Institute for Catholic-Jewish Education, 1307 South Wabash Avenue, Room 224, Chicago, Illinois 60605. Ecumenical Institute for Jewish-Christian Studies, 26275 Northwestern Highway, Southfield, Michigan 48076.

A Guide to Interreligious Dialogue. By Judith Hershcopf and Morris Fine. $0.50. American Jewish Committee, 165 East 56 Street, New York, New York 10022.

Guidelines for Dialogue with Black Churches. Union of American Hebrew Congregations, Department of Interreligious Affairs, 838 Fifth Avenue, New York, New York 10021.

Guidelines on Dialogue with People of Living Faiths and Ideologies. $1.75.
World Council of Churches, 150 route de Ferney, 1211 Geneva 20,
Switzerland.

A Holocaust Memorial Service for Christians--Yom HaShoah. National
Conference of Christians and Jews, 71 Fifth Avenue, New York, New
York 10003.

If I Marry outside My Religion. By Algernon D. Black. Public Affairs
Pamphlet 204 (1954).

The Image of Jews in Christian Teaching. Judith H. Banki. $1.00. American
Jewish Committee, 165 East 56 Street, New York, New York 10022.

Interfaith Teacher Training Program on Festivals, Life Cycle Events, Prayer,
and Houses of Worship in the Christian and Jewish Faiths. $1.50.
National Conference of Christians and Jews, 360 Delaware Avenue,
Suite 106, Buffalo, New York 14202.

The International Council of Christians and Jews: A Brief History. By
William W. Simpson. International Conference of Christians and Jews,
Werlestrasse 2, 6148 Heppenheim, P.O. Box 305, Federal Republic
of Germany.

An Interreligious Guide to Passover and Easter. $1.00. Union of American
Hebrew Congregations, Department of Interreligious Affairs, 838 Fifth
Avenue, New York, New York 10021.

Interreligious Interaction: A Program Guide. Union of American Hebrew
Congregations, Department of Interreligious Affairs, 838 Fifth Avenue,
New York, New York 10021.

Introduction and Planning Principles and Guidelines for Joint Worship. Union
of American Hebrew Congregations, Department of Interreligious
Affairs, 838 Fifth Avenue, New York, New York 10021.

Jerusalem. By Teddy Kollek. $1.50. Anti-Defamation League of B'nai
B'rith, 823 United Nations Plaza, New York, New York 10017.

Jesus Christ between Jews and Christians. By Paul M. van Buren. $0.35.
Forward Movement Publications, 412 Sycamore Street, Cincinnati,
Ohio 45202.

Jewish and Roman Catholic Reflections on Abortion and Related Issues.
By Los Angeles Roman Catholic/Jewish Respect Life Committee. Free.
American Jewish Committee, Interreligious Affairs Committee, 6505
Wilshire Boulevard, Suite 315, Los Angeles, California 90048.

Jewishness and Jesus. By Daniel C. Juster. InterVarsity Press, Downers
Grove, Illinois 60515.

Jews and Catholics: Taking Stock. By Judith Banki and Alan L. Mittleman.
$0.35. American Jewish Committee, 165 East 56 Street, New York,
New York 10022.

Jews and Christians in Joint Worship. Union of American Hebrew
Congregations, Department of Interreligious Affairs, 838 Fifth Avenue,
New York, New York 10021.

Jews and Christians: Teaching about Each Other. $6.00. Union of
American Hebrew Congregations, Department of Interreligious Affairs,
838 Fifth Avenue, New York, New York 10021.

Jews and Judaism in Catholic Education. By Rose Thering. $5.00.
American Jewish Committee, 165 East 56 Street, New York, New
York 10022. Anti-Defamation League of B'nai B'rith, 823 United
Nations Plaza, New York 10017.

Kinship Recalled: Members and Friends of the Institute Celebrate the
Bond between Jews and Christians. Ed. John M. Oesterreicher, Institute
for Judaeo-Christian Studies, Seton Hall University, South Orange,
New Jersey 07079.

Lenten Pastoral Reflection: Homiletic and Pastoral Aids for
Catholic-Jewish Interaction in Lenten and Holy Week Liturgies. By
Los Angeles Priest/Rabbi Committee. Free. American Jewish
Committee, Interreligious Affairs Committee, 6505 Wilshire Boulevard,
Suite 315, Los Angeles, California 90048.

A Liturgical Interpretation in Narrative Form of the Passion of Jesus
Christ with a Dramatic Arrangement for Congregational Use. By
John T. Townsend. National Conference of Christians and Jews,
71 Fifth Avenue, New York, New York 10003.

Martyrs of the Decalogue: Reflections on Pope John Paul's Pilgrimage
to Auschwitz. By John M. Oesterreicher. Institute of Judaeo-Christian
Studies, Seton Hall University, South Orange, New Jersey 07079.

The Meaning and Conduct of Dialogue. By Dean M. Kelley and Bernhard
E. Olson. $0.35. National Conference of Christians and Jews, 71
Fifth Avenue, New York, New York 10003.

Messianic Hope: A Jewish Perspective/A Christian Perspective. By Judith
Banki and Eva Fleischner. $1.00. American Jewish Committee, 165
East 56 Street, New York, New York 10022.

Nes Ammim. American Friends of Nes Ammim, Grange and Chadwick
Roads, Teaneck, New Jersey 07666.

A New Look at Prejudice: Program Implications for Educational
Organizations. By Helen Foss. National Conference of Christians
and Jews, 71 Fifth Avenue, New York, New York 10003.

A Notion of the Kingdom: Catholic-Jewish Reflections. By Los Angeles Priest/Rabbi Committee. Free. American Jewish Committee, Interreligious Affairs Committee, 6505 Wilshire Boulevard, Suite 315, Los Angeles, California 90048.

The Nuclear Reality. By Los Angeles Roman Catholic/Jewish Respect Life Committee. Free. American Jewish Committee, Interreligious Affairs Committee, 6505 Wilshire Boulevard, Suite 315, Los Angeles, California 90048.

Official Guidelines for Episcopal-Jewish Relations in the Areas of Interfaith Worship, Christian Education, Evangelism and the Jewish People, and Marriage between Christians and Jews. $1.50. The Episcopal Diocese of Newark, 24 Rector Street, Newark, New Jersey 07201.

Out of Many: A Study Guide to Cultural Pluralism in the United States. By Oscar Handlin. $1.50. Anti-Defamation League of B'nai B'rith, 823 United Nations Plaza, New York, New York 10017.

The Passover Celebration: A Haggadah for the Seder. By Leon Klenicki. $1.90. Anti-Defamation League of B'nai B'rith, 823 United Nations Plaza, New York, New York 10017.

Principles, Guidelines & Suggestions: I. Jews and Christians in Joint Worship. II. Christian Usage of Jewish Prayers & Customs. III. Celebration of Judaic Roots: Projects. Office on Christian-Jewish Relations, National Council of the Churches of Christ in the U.S.A., 475 Riverside Drive, New York, New York 10115.

The Proceedings of the Center for Jewish-Christian Learning: Inaugural Lecture Series. By Marc H. Tanenbaum, Paul M. van Buren, and Michael McGarry. College of St. Thomas, 2115 Summit Avenue, St. Paul, Minnesota 55105.

The Proceedings of the Center for Jewish-Christian Learning: 1987 Lecture Series. By Abba Ebban, Eugene B. Borowitz, John T. Pawlikowski, and Michael Shermis. College of St. Thomas, 2115 Summit Avenue, St. Paul, Minnesota 55105.

The Process of Dialogue: Purpose and Scope, Leadership and Planning Bibliography. National Conference of Christians and Jews, 71 Fifth Avenue, New York, New York 10003.

A Reappraisal of the Christian Attitude to Judaism. By James Parkes. Parkes Library, Royston, England.

The Rediscovery of Judaism. Ed. John M. Oesterreicher. Institute of Judaeo-Christian Studies, Seton Hall University, South Orange, New Jersey 07079.

Root and Branches: Biblical Judaism, Rabbinic Judaism, and Early Christianity. By Leon Klenicki and Eugene J. Fisher. A Pace Monograph. $3.00. Saint Mary's Press, Terrace Heights, Winona, Minnesota 55987.

A Seminary Exchange: The First Decade. Reflective Comments on the
Educational Exchange between Hebrew Union College, Los Angeles,
and St. John's Roman Catholic Seminary, Camarillo, 1973-83. Free.
American Jewish Committee, Interreligious Affairs Committee, 6505
Wilshire Boulevard, Suite 315, Los Angeles, California 90048.

The Single Parent Family. By Los Angeles Roman Catholic/Jewish Respect
Life Committee. Free. American Jewish Committee, Interreligious
Affairs Committee, 6505 Wilshire Boulevard, Suite 315, Los Angeles,
California 90048.

The Teaching of Contempt. By Jules Isaac. $1.00. Anti-Defamation
League of B'nai B'rith, 823 United Nations Plaza, New York, New
York 10017.

Theological Education for the Church's Relation to the Jewish People.
By Paul M. van Buren. $0.75. American Jewish Committee, 165
East 56 Street, New York, New York 10022.

Vatican-Jewish Meeting Commemorates Twenty Years Progress in
Catholic-Jewish Relations since "Nostra Aetate." By Marc H.
Tanenbaum. $0.25. American Jewish Committee, 165 East 56 Street,
New York, New York 10022.

What Viewers Should Know about . . . the Oberammergau Passion Play,
1980. By Judith Banki. $1.50. American Jewish Committee, 165
East 56 Street, New York, New York 10022.

Within Context: Guidelines for the Catechetical Presentation of Jews
and Judaism in the New Testament. Ed. Eugene J. Fisher. Silver
Burdett and Ginn, Morristown, New Jersey.

The Worship of Good Friday: Jewish Concerns. By A. James Rudin./Jews
and Christians: The Road Ahead. By John T. Pawlikowski. American
Jewish Committee, 165 East 56 Street, New York, New York 10022.

III.
Articles

The purpose of this chapter is to alert readers to relatively current and important articles in the field. It consists of annotations for twenty-five of some of the most substantial articles concerning Jewish-Christian relations. The articles were selected with the help of a survey which included most of the members of the speakers bureau and some of the leading scholars in the field.

The following have been included: 1) articles that would help those unfamiliar with the field to gain an understanding of the meaning and significance of Jewish-Christian relations; 2) articles considered among the most important in the field, which break new ground for Jewish-Christian understanding; 3) articles that have helped in one's development as a religious scholar/lecturer/teacher/author; 4) articles that have been recommended to colleagues. Not all articles belong in every category.

In the section following the twenty-five articles, there is a listing of other articles that, although they were not annotated, are nevertheless significant to the understanding of specific issues within this burgeoning field.

Banki, Judith Hershkopf. "The Image of Jews in Christian Teaching." Journal of Ecumenical Studies 21 (1984): 437-51.

Banki reviews the Protestant, Roman Catholic, and German studies, sponsored by the American Jewish Committee, on the representation of Jews in Christian teaching. Follow-up studies have shown that there have been gains made in the presentation of Jews and Judaism in Christian textbooks but that these textbooks still promote inaccurate generalizations and negative stereotypes. Improved teacher training, sensitive textbook preparation, and a higher priority for the elimination of a negative portrayal and inclusion of positive information about Jews and Judaism are all part of the solution.

Baum, Gregory. "The Doctrinal Basis for Jewish-Christian Dialogue." The Month 224 (1967): 232-46.

The central considerations of this essay are the appropriateness of the Church's attempt to convert the Jews in the name of Jesus Christ and the place of Judaism in human salvation for Christian belief. Baum responds to these problems by proposing that Judaism is a living religion with much to offer to Christianity, viz., common patrimony and brother/sisterhood. He also believes that the Church should not engage in proselytization of Jews but, instead, Christians should become involved in dialogue with open intentions and without a hidden agenda.

Berger, David. "Jewish-Christian Relations. A Jewish Perspective." Journal of Ecumenical Studies 20 (1983): 5-32.

Berger states, "No area of Jewish-Christian relations has been left untouched by the fundamental transformations of the last two decades." This article reviews the gains and the problems they raise in the Jewish-Christian encounter since Vatican II. He presents a perceptive assessment of the problems of dialogue, mission and covenant, anti-Judaism, the State of Israel, and ethics and public policy.

Cook, Michael J. "Anti-Judaism in the New Testament." Union Seminary Quarterly Review 38 (1983): 125-38.

A well-written, incisive look at the arguments for and against the presence of anti-Judaism in the New Testament. Cook acknowledges that there is anti-Jewish polemic in the New Testament and asks Christians not that they share Jewish interpretations but that they "understand how Jews can see the matter that way."

————. "Jesus and the Pharisees: The Problem As It Stands Today." Journal of Ecumenical Studies 15 (1978): 441-60.

Cook provides a scholarly examination of the literature that considers Jesus' relationship with the Pharisees. In a thorough analysis he reviews the deficiencies of many previous studies, defines their methodological problems, and suggests that scholars who wish to undertake a proper study of the subject first achieve expertise in both the New Testament and rabbinic literature.

Culbertson, Philip. "Doing Our Own Homework: Fifteen Steps Toward Christian-Jewish Dialogue in Local Congregations." Journal of Ecumenical Studies 20 (1983): 118-23.

Fifteen helpful suggestions that Christians should consider before coming to dialogue. They include viewing Judaism as a living religion; giving up positions of exclusiveness and superiority; identifying the commonalities of the two traditions; repudiating anti-Judaism; challenging Christian self-righteousness; clarifying what Christians have to offer Judaism; considering the negative image of the Jews portrayed in liturgy; acknowledging the lessons of the Holocaust; and rethinking mission strategy.

————. "The Pharisaic Jesus and His Parables." Christian Century 102 (1985): 74-77.

Culbertson calls for Christians to interpret the meaning of the parables in the context of the Jewish milieu in which they were told. By doing this, he believes, a more accurate portrayal of the Pharisees will appear, one that likely identifies Jesus as a first-century Jew who was a member of the Pharisaic movement.

Eckardt, A. Roy. "Anti-Semitism Is the Heart." Theology Today 41 (1984): 301-8.

> Eckardt, unfailing in his support for Jews, Judaism, and the State of Israel, forcefully writes about the evil of Christian anti-Judaism and how it lies at the heart of Jewish-Christian relations. He presents critical arguments against those Christians who would define and evaluate the Jews.

Everett, Robert H. "The Impact of the Holocaust on Christian Theology." Christian Jewish Relations 15 (1982): 3-11.

> Questions posed by the Holocaust event for the Christian are considered in this articulate and forceful article. Everett considers lies that Christians tell about Jews, a re-examination of traditional theological doctrines and teachings about Jesus, and the necessity of Christian repentance for a post-Holocaust future.

Fisher, Eugene J. "The Evolution of a Tradition: From Nostra Aetate to the Notes." Christian-Jewish Relations 18 (1985): 32-47.

> Fisher provides a sensitive appraisal of the controversy surrounding the 1985 "Notes on the Correct Way to Present Jews and Judaism in Preaching and Catechesis." He has traced the development of the Church's official attitude towards the Jewish people by utilizing a chart that shows the clarification that has occurred since Nostra Aetate in 1965, and the "Guidelines and Suggestions for Implementing Nostra Aetate" issued in 1975. His appraisal includes a look at Jewish concerns for the shortcomings of the "Notes."

_____. "Research in Christian Teaching Concerning Jews and Judaism: Past Research and Present Needs." Journal of Ecumenical Studies 21 (1984): 421-36.

> In this thorough review of the literature, Fisher analyzes studies and statements that have attempted to eliminate negative stereotypes of Jews and Judaism. Such detrimental themes include "a latent Marcionite approach to the Hebrew Scriptures," "the crucifixion and the deicide charge," and "legalism and the Pharisees." Fisher advances several helpful suggestions that Christians can use to cope with these negative stereotypes. He also supplies the reader with the many positive elements Judaism has to offer the Christian, i.e., "permanent validity of the Jewish covenant," "a dialogical Catechesis," and "Jesus' Jewishness."

_____. "Typical Jewish Misunderstandings of Christianity." Judaism 22 (1973): 21-32.

> Fisher presents a position paper with examples of Jewish misunderstandings regarding the nature of Christianity. He explores some of the possible historical origins for these misunderstandings, some of which include: 1) "Christianity is polytheistic because of the trinity," 2) "Christianity has dogma, Judaism has ethics as means of salvation," 3) "Christianity as ascetic; Judaism as the golden mean," 4) "Paul as bad guy; Christianity as hellenistic Judaism," and 5) "Christians believe that only Christians can be saved."

Greenberg, Irving. "Judaism and Christianity after the Holocaust." Journal of Ecumenical Studies 12 (1975): 521-51.

This article is the classic call for Christianity and Judaism to "confront the Holocaust event and seek its meaning." Greenberg believes that traditional responses to the Holocaust are inadequate, that it is necessary to live in dialogical tension, and that although the credibility of faith is called into question, secular options are now impossible. Mandatory reading for all those who wish to engage in post-Holocaust reflection.

————. "The Relationship of Judaism and Christianity: Toward a New Organic Model." Quarterly Review 4 (1984): 4-22.

Greenberg proposes a model that "would allow both sides to respect the full nature of the other in all its faith-claims." It does this and much more in a remarkably lucid portrayal of how the two traditions can both accept each other and become relevant religions of redemption for the modern world.

Harrelson, Walter. "Christian Misreadings of Basic Themes in the Hebrew Bible." Quarterly Review 2 (1982): 58-66.

The misreading of certain topics in the Hebrew Scriptures has led to their misuse, i.e., polemical purposes. Harrelson analyzes these misinterpretations and lays the framework for better relations between Christians and Jews. These misreadings include: God's judgment on Israel in which Jews are seen as betraying the covenant; the return to Judah from Babylon, seen as a time of moral decay; and the promises of the prophets, whose images are seen as operating only historically and not eschatologically.

Kung, Hans, and Pinchas Lapide. "Is Jesus a Bond or Barrier? A Jewish-Christian Dialogue." Journal of Ecumenical Studies 14 (1977): 466-83.

These two scholars find much upon which to agree, especially regarding the historicity of Jesus. There are, however, areas in which they disagree; for example, Kung believes that Jesus' execution took place because of primarily religious rather than political factors, whereas Lapide feels that Jesus' death was the political responsibility of the Romans. The article is presented in the form of a dialogue with Walter Strolz posing questions to the two scholars.

Pawlikowski, John T. "Jews and Christians: The Contemporary Debate." Quarterly Review 4 (1984): 23-36.

In this "state of the dialogue" piece, Pawlikowski ably explores the relevant issues in the current Jewish-Christian encounter. He looks at the crucifixion story, the relevance of Judaism to the Christian message, an appreciation of the Hebrew Scriptures, the role of the Pharisees, the place of Israel in the world, the necessity of reflection on the Holocaust, and a Christology sensitive to the Jewish covenant. He believes that the most promising route to further theological development is in understanding that "Christianity and Judaism are distinctive religions, each with a unique faith perspective despite their historic links."

Ruether, Rosemary Radford. "An Invitation to Jewish-Christian Dialogue: In What Sense Can We Say That Jesus Was the 'Christ'?" The Ecumenist 10 (1972): 1-10.

A discerning look at the problems that are created when Christians proclaim Jesus as the Messiah. Ruether suggests that Jesus is a Christ-in-process rather than the Messiah of Israel who ushers in the messianic age.

Rylaarsdam, J. Coert. "The Two Covenants and the Dilemma of Christology." Journal of Ecumenical Studies 9 (1972): 249-70.

The author proposes that a paradox exists in the way Christians interpret Jesus. It exists because present-day Christianity frequently utilizes an historical interpretation in preference to the eschatological understanding of early Christianity.

Stendahl, Krister. "The Apostle Paul and the Introspective Conscience of the West." Harvard Theological Review 56 (1963): 199-215.

This article is considered one of the groundbreaking works in Pauline theology. Stendahl suggests that "the West for centuries has wrongly surmised that the biblical writers were grappling with problems which no doubt are ours, but which never entered their consciousness." This has helped lead the way to reinterpreting Paul and arriving at the conclusion, like that of other Pauline scholars, that Paul was an advocate of Jewish-Christian solidarity.

Swidler, Leonard. "The Jewishness of Jesus: Some Religious Implications for Christians." Journal of Ecumenical Studies 18 (1981): 104-13.

This is a delightfully well-written article that makes three points. The first is that traditional Christian dichotomies, such as faith and works, law and grace, justice and love, are false; the second is that Jesus (Swidler employs the title Rabbi Jeshua) is Christ for the Gentiles but not the messiah promised to the Jews; and third, that Christians will be able to understand the Gospel only if they interpret it Jewishly. He also makes a plea to Christians on the necessity of studying "the history and present reality of their relations with Jesus' co-religionists, the Jews."

van Buren, Paul M. "Judaism in Christian Theology." Journal of Ecumenical Studies 18 (1981): 114-27.

Van Buren develops in this article what a systematic theology "might be like if there were to be a genuine recognition and affirmation of Judaism within Christian theology." As he attempts to reach this goal, he explores the consequences of ecclesiology, the Trinity, Christology, and revelation that are sensitive to the Jewish people.

————. "Probing the Jewish-Christian Reality: How My Mind Has Changed." Christian Century 98 (1981): 665-68.

The author, who has become an important figure in the Jewish-Christian dialogue, chronicles his move from work in the philosophy of religion to the task of systematic theology. This move began in the 1970s when he gained an appreciation of Judaism. It has since led him to develop one of the more thoughtful approaches of a Christian theologian to the understanding of living Judaism, what he calls a "theology of the Jewish-Christian reality."

Williamson, Clark M. "The New Testament Reconsidered: Recent Post-Holocaust Scholarship." Quarterly Review 4 (1984): 37-51.

Williamson sums up recent scholarship done in the areas of Paul and the Pharisees. He looks at models of New Testament interpretation that place Jesus and Paul against the Jews and concludes that a fairer interpretation of the Apostolic Writings will take into consideration the context of first-century Judaism. It will also depict the Pharisees in a better light, especially as Jesus and Paul related to them.

Wilson, Marvin R. "An Evangelical View of the Current State of Evangelical-Jewish Relations." Journal of the Evangelical Theological Society 25 (1983): 139-60.

Wilson, considered the leading evangelical scholar in evangelical-Jewish relations, presents a well-written paper on different aspects of the Jewish-evangelical dialogue. He covers recent interactions, such as jointly-sponsored area conferences, and factors motivating Jews and evangelicals to meet. He also suggests several promising possibilities for future projects between Jews and evangelicals.

OTHER SIGNIFICANT ARTICLES

These articles all merit greater attention than can be given here. They are listed at the request of scholars, rabbis, ministers, priests, and important members of the laity, who feel that the content of the articles will be useful to those with an interest in exploring further some of the results of the Jewish-Christian encounter.

Axel, Larry E. "Christian Theology and the Murder of the Jews." Encounter 40 (1979): 129-41.

Ben 'Chorin, Shalom. "The Image of Jesus in Modern Judaism." Journal of Ecumenical Studies 11 (1974): 401-30.

Berkhof, Hendrikus. "Israel As a Theological Problem in the Christian Church." Journal of Ecumenical Studies 6 (1969): 329-47.

Berkovits, Eliezer. "Judaism in the Post-Christian Era." Judaism 15 (1966): 74-84.

Bleich, J. David. "Survey of Recent Halakhic Periodical Literature: Teaching Torah to Non-Jews." Tradition 18 (1980): 192-211.

Borowitz, Eugene. "A Call for Ecumenical Polemics." Religious Education 62 (1967): 107-12.

Boys, Mary. "Questions 'Which Touch the Heart of Our Faith.'" Religious Education 76 (1981): 636-56.

Cook, Michael J. "Interpreting 'Pro-Jewish' Passages in Matthew." Hebrew Union College Annual 54 (1983): 135-47.

Culbertson, Philip. "Changing Christian Images of the Pharisees." Anglican Theological Review 64 (1982): 539-61.

————. "New Christian Theologies of Covenant." Reconstructionist 51 (1985): 15-19, 32.

————. "Re-thinking the Christ in Jewish-Christian Dialogue." Ecumenical Trends 13 (1984): 1-5.

Davies, W.D. "Paul and the People of Israel." New Testament Studies 24 (1977): 4-39.

Eckardt, A. Roy. "Christians and Jews: Along a Theological Frontier." Encounter 15 (1979): 89-127.

————. "Is There a Way Out of the Christian Crime? The Philosophic Question of the Holocaust." Holocaust and Genocide Studies 1 (1986): 121-26.

————. "Jurgen Moltmann, the Jewish People and the Holocaust." Journal of American Academy of Religion 44 (1976): 675-91.

Eckardt, Alice L. "The Holocaust: Christian and Jewish Responses." Journal of the American Academy of Religion 42 (1974): 453-69.

————. "Post-Holocaust Theology: A Journey out of the Kingdom of Night." Holocaust and Genocide Studies 1 (1986): 229-40.

Evans, Carl D. "The Church's False Witness against Jews." Christian Century 99 (1982): 530-33.

Everett, Robert H. "Judaism in Nineteenth-Century American Transcendentalist and Likural Protestant Thought." Journal of Ecumenical Studies 20 (1983): 396-414.

Fisher, Eugene J. "Ani Ma'amin: Directions in Holocaust Theology." Interface 5 (1980): 1-5.

————. "The Holocaust and Christian Responsibility." America 144 (1981): 118-21.

—————. "Twenty Years After Vatican II: The Church Is Still Struggling to Define Its Relationship with the Jewish People." Jewish Monthly (1985): 20-25.

Fleck, G. P. "Jesus in the Post-Holocaust Jewish-Christian Dialogue." Christian Century 100 (1983): 904-906.

—————. "On Jewish-Christian Dialogue." Christian Century 100 (1983): 1086-87.

Flusser, David. "A New Sensitivity in Judaism and the Christian Message." Harvard Theological Review 61 (1968): 107-27.

Fournier, Marie H. "The Evolution of Relations between Christians and Jews: From 1973-1983." Pro Mundi Vita Bulletin 95-96 (1983-84): 1-68.

Gaston, Lloyd. "Israel's Enemies in Pauline Theology." New Testament Studies 28 (1982): 400-423.

—————. "The Messiah of Israel as Teacher of the Gentiles: The Setting of Matthew's Christology." Interpretation 29 (1975): 24-40.

Greenberg, Blu. "Report of a Jewish Teacher." The Ecumenist 12 (1974): 84-86.

Greenberg, Irving. "The New Encounter of Judaism and Christianity." Barat Review 3 (1967): 113-25.

—————. "New Revelations and New Patterns in the Relationship of Judaism and Christianity." Journal of Ecumenical Studies 16 (1979): 249-67.

Harrington, Daniel J. "The Jewishness of Jesus: Facing Some Problems." Catholic Biblical Quarterly 49 (1987): 1-13.

Inch, Morris A. "Jews and Evangelicals." Christianity Today 23 (1979): 24-26.

Kantzer, Kenneth. "Concerning Evangelicals and Jews." Christianity Today 26 (1981): 12-15.

Kelley, John J. "Christian Strategy on the Passion Play." The Ecumenist 24 (1986): 38-44.

Kelly, Joseph G. "Lucan Christology and the Jewish/Christian Dialogue." Journal of Ecumenical Studies 21 (1984): 688-708.

LaSor, William Sanford. "Protestants and Jews." Judaism: A Quarterly Journal of Jewish Life and Thought 35 (1986): 10-15.

McCauley, Deborah, and Annette Daum. "Jewish-Christian Feminist Dialogue: A Wholistic Vision." Union Seminary Quarterly Review 38 (1983): 147-90.

Modras, Ronald. "Jews and Poles: A Relationship Reconsidered." *America* 146 (1982): 5-8.

Moore, George Foot. "Christian Writers on Judaism." *Harvard Theological Review* 14 (1921): 197-254.

Pawlikowski, John T. "The Road Ahead for Jews and Christians." *The Priest* 43 (1987): 31-40.

Pierand, Richard V. "Evangelicals and Jews STrive for Mutual Understanding." *Christianity Today* 28 (1984): 29.

Pogrebin, Letty Cottin. "Anti-Semitism in the Women's Movement." *Ms* 10 (1982): 45-46, 48, 62, 65, 66, 69-72.

Rottenberg, Isaac C. "Fulfillment Theology and the Future of Christian-Jewish Relations." *Christian Century* 97 (1980): 66-69.

_____. "Should There Be a Christian Witness to the Jews?" *Christian Century* 94 (1977): 352-56.

Sanders, James. "Torah and Christ." *Interpretation* 29 (1975): 372-90.

Sandmel, Samuel. "Parallelomania." *Journal of Biblical Literature* 81 (1962): 1-13.

Siegman, Henry. "A Decade of Catholic-Jewish Relations—A Reassessment." *Journal of Ecumenical Studies* 15 (1978): 243-60.

Soloveitchik, Joseph B. "Confrontation." *Tradition* 6 (1964): 5-29.

Stendahl, Krister. "Jesus and the Kingdom." *The Alumni Bulletin* (Bangor Theological Seminary) 42 (1967): 6-14.

Stransky, Thomas F. "Focusing on Jewish-Catholic Relations." *Origins* 15 (1985): 65-70.

Stravinskas, Peter. "The Mass: Catholic Ritual, Jewish Pedigree." *National Catholic REgister* (1986): 1-7.

Swidler, Leonard. "The Dialogue Decalogue: Ground Rules for Interreligious, Interideological Dialogue." *Journal of Ecumenical Studies* 20 (1983): 1-4.

van Buren, Paul M. "Theological Education for the Church's Relationship to the Jewish People." *Journal of Ecumenical STudies* 21 (1984): 489-505.

Williamson, Clark M. "Anti-Judaism in Process Christologies?" *Process Studies* 10 (1980): 73-92.

Wilson, Marvin R. "Christians and Jews: Competing for Converts." *Christianity Today* 24 (1980): 28-30.

————. "The Jewish Concept of Learning: A Christian Appreciation." Christian Scholar's Review 5 (1976): 350-63.

————. "Zionism as Theology: An Evangelical Approach." Journal of the Evangelical Theological Society 22 (1979): 27-44.

Wyschogrod, Michael. "A New Stage in Jewish-Christian Dialogue." Judaism 31 (1982): 355-65.

Zucker, Wolfgang. "Thirty Years after Holocaust: A Midrash for the Church." Lutheran Forum (1975): 6-10.

IV.
Journals

This chapter is composed of four sections:

1. the most important journals and newsletters in the field of Jewish-Christian relations,
2. journals that have published special issues on aspects of Jewish-Christian relations, with a list of the articles they contain,
3. journals that occasionally publish important articles in the field, with titles of the articles they contain, and
4. other journals and newsletters significant to the field of interreligious dialogue.

Those who are interested in the field will find this chapter most useful in comparing journals, their particular emphases, size, frequency of publication, etc., and may use the data to make a more informed choice about subscription. In the subscription information "-P" means "to present" and the eight-digit number following the date is the ISSN number.

1. The most important journals and newsletters in the field of Jewish-Christian relations which frequently publish special issues on aspects of Jewish-Christian relations.

Christian Jewish Relations

Institute of Jewish Affairs Ltd., 11 Hertford Street, London W1Y 7DX, England; 1968-P, 0144-2902, quarterly, $20.00 a year.

This journal advances "education in the field of human relationships, with particular reference to the history and social conditions of the Jewish people both past and present, and of the communities of which they have formed or form part and to the causes of racial and religious stress."

Dialogue & Alliance

International Religious Foundation, Inc., JAF Box 2347, New York, New York 10116; 1987-P, 0891-5881, quarterly, $20.00 a year.

This journal aims to facilitate dialogue and alliance among the religions of the world as a means of promoting world peace and harmony.

Dispatch from Jerusalem

Bridges for Peace, P.O. Box 33145, Tulsa, Oklahoma 74153; six times a year, $15.00 a year.

"Our endeavor is to present positive news and perspectives from Israel in order to encourage understanding, support and intercessory prayer for the people and land of Israel. This is accomplished through the Dispatch, lectures, seminars, our study mission program, Operation Ezra, and other bridge-building projects."

Explorations

American Institute for the Study of Religious Cooperation, 401 North Broad Street, Philadelphia, Pennsylvania 19108; 1987-P, six times a year, free.

The purpose of the newsletter is to "focus the attention of Jews and Christians on two mutual concerns: their common origins, and the present relations of Jews and Christians in the world. It seeks to celebrate not only similarities but also differences."

Face to Face: An Interreligious Bulletin

Anti-Defamation League of B'nai B'rith, 823 United Nations Plaza, New York, New York 10017; 1975-P, quarterly, $12.00 a year.

This periodical contains important articles on various aspects of the Jewish-Christian dialogue. Each issue deals with one facet of this dialogue in depth. Prominent spokesmen from the Christian and Jewish communiteis present their perspective on topics of mutual concern.

Immanuel: A Bulletin of Religious Thought and Research in Israel

Anti-Defamation League of B'nai B'rith, 823 United Nations Plaza, New York, New York 10017; 0302-8127, bi-annually, $10.00 a year.

"Aims to meet the considerable academic interest in recent developments in Israel in the religious and theological areas and helps foster a better understanding between Christians and Jews. It also publishes relevant translations of material written in Hebrew which would otherwise be inaccessible to interested readers abroad. Also included, for its international audiences, are original contributions, summaries of articles, book reviews and descriptions of current biblical scholarship and Judaic studies."

Interreligious Currents

Union of American Hebrew Congregations, 838 Fifth Avenue, New York, New York 10021; 1982-P, quarterly.

This short newsletter, put out by UAHC's Department of Interreligious Affairs, contains articles on issues such as Nostra Aetate, the "Notes," and anti-Judaism. It also contains information about congregations across the U.S. and their involvement in the Jewish-Christian dialogue.

Interreligious Newsletter

American Jewish Committee, 165 East 56th Street, New York, New York 10022, 1977-P, quarterly, $27.50 a year.

This newsletter is published by the Interreligious Affairs Department of the AJC. It is a "review of trends and developments in interreligious affairs." It keeps its readers up-to-date on local AJC chapters involved in the interfaith movement.

Journal of Ecumenical Studies

Temple University, Room 511 Humanities Building, Temple University, Philadelphia, Pennsylvania 19122; 1964-P, 0022-0558, quarterly, $17.50 a year.

This journal is the standard in the field for ecumenical work in religion. It contains articles by many preeminent theologians. It also includes reviews of current literature, abstracts of important articles, and events in the ecumenical world. It is essential reading for those interested in interreligious dialogue.

National Conference of Christians and Jews Newsletter

National Conference of Christians and Jews, 71 Fifth Avenue, New York, New York 10003; 1928-P, quarterly, free.

"News to keep its national constituencies abreast of program developments and other interesting activities of NCCJ."

National Dialogue Newsletter

National Dialogue Newsletter, P.O. Box 849, Stamford, Connecticut 06904; 1985-P, quarterly, $5.00 a year.

"This newsletter is committed to the improvement of communication in the field of Jewish-Christian dialogue. Most of its articles will be addressed to this area."

NICM: Journal for Jews and Christians in Higher Education

National Institute for Campus Ministries, Anabel Taylor Hall, Cornell University, Ithaca, New York 14853; 1976-P, 0362-0794, quarterly, $20.00 a year.

SIDIC (Service International de Documentation Judeo-Chretienne)

SIDIC, Via del Plebescito 112, Rome 00186, Italy; 1968-P, three times a year, $14.00 a year.

The aim of SIDIC is "to promote understanding and respect between Jews and Christians; to make known the heritage which Christianity and Western culture have received from the Jewish people; to encourage the study of Jewish tradition and emphasize its importance for Christianity and for all mankind."

2. Journals that have published <u>special issues</u> on Jewish-Christian relations, the dialogue, or the Holocaust, with a list of the articles they contain. Between the information for each journal and the article(s) it contains is the volume, number, year, and theme, if one was given, of the issue. Example: 76: 1 (1987), "Jewish-Christian Dialogue."

American Journal of Theology & Philosophy

American Journal of Theology & Philosophy, Augusta College, Augusta, Georgia 30910; 1980-P, 0194-3448, three times a year, $9.00 a year, $17.00 for two years, and $24.00 for three years.

2: 3 (1981), "American Theology after Auschwitz" includes

The Uniqueness and Universality of the Holocaust . . . . . Michael Berenbaum
How Shall We Now Exegete the Apostolic Writings . . . . . Paul M. van Buren
New Images of Sinai in a Post-Holocaust World . . . . . . S. Daniel Breslauer
Evaneglical Christians and Holocaust Theology . . . . Stephen T. Davis

Anglican Theological Review

Anglican Theological Review, Inc., 600 Haven Street, Evanston, Illinois 60201; 1919-P, 0003-3286, quarterly, $15.00 a year.

64: 4 (1982), includes

On Christians and Jews in Dialogue: An Introductory Essay . . . . . James A.
    Carpenter
Love and Law in Judaism and Christianity . . . . Alan T. Davies
Law and Love in Jewish Theology . . . . Byron L. Sherwin
The Covenant: How Jews Understand Themselves and Others . . . . Elliot N.
    Dorff
The Covenant Concept: Judaism and Christianity. . . . . Norma H. Thompson
Two Pictures of the Pharisees: Philosophical Circle or
    Eating Club . . . . Jacob Neusner
Changing Christian Images of the Pharisees . . . . Philip Culbertson
Occasions of Grace in Paul, Luke, and First-Century Judaism . . John Koenig

The Annals of the American Academy of Political and Social Sciences

Sage Publications, Inc., 275 South Beverly Drive, Beverly Hills, California 90212; 1891-P, 0002-7162, bi-monthly, $26.00 a year.

450 (1980), "Reflections on the Holocaust" includes

Historical Antecedents: Why the Holocaust? . . . . Claude R. Foster, Jr.
Racism and German Protestant Theology: A Prelude to the
    Holocaust . . . . Alan T. Davies
Genocide: Was It the Nazis' Original Plan? . . . . Yehuda Baue
Punitive Threat to National Security as Nuremberg Defense for
    Genocide . . . . Robert Wolf
Holocaust Business: Some Reflections on Arbeit Macht Frei . . John K. Rot
Children of Hippocrates: Doctors in Nazi Germany . . . . Jack S. Boozer

Chicago Theological Seminary Register

Chicago Theological Seminary, 5757 University Avenue, Chicago, Illinois 60637; 1910-P, three times a year, $2.00 a year.

76: 1 (1986), "Jewish-Christian Dialogue" includes

Christian Life Magazine

Christian Life Missions, 396 East Street and Charles Road, Carol Stream, Illinois 60188; 1939-P, 0009-5427, monthly, $15.95 a year.

46: 7 (1984), "The Land" includes

Conservative Judaism

Rabbinical Assembly, 3080 Broadway, New York, New York 10027; 1951-P, 0010-6542, quarterly, $15.00 a year.

38: 1 (1985), includes

Reflections on the 20th Anniversary of <u>Nostra Aetate</u> .... Yocheved Muffs
Interpreting <u>Nostra Aetate</u> .... Eugene J. Fisher
<u>Nostra Aetate</u>, the Jews and the Future of Dialogue ..... Byron D. Cytron
Jewish-Christian Relations: A New Development ...... Dan Cohn-Sherbok
Liberation Theology--A Response .... Paul M. van Buren

Dialog

Dialog, Inc., 2375 Como Avenue, St. Paul, Minnesota 55108; 1962-P, 2012-2033, quarterly, $14.00 a year.

16 (1977), "Judaism" includes

Report from Jerusalem .... Franklin Sherman
Judaism and Christianity: A Theology of
    Co-Existence .... Harold H. Ditmanson
Biblical Faith and Political Life .... Milton Kotler
The "Jews" in the Fourth Gospel .... Regina Fuller
Anti-Semitism and the Christologies of Barth, Berkouwer,
    Pannenberg .... Eugene B. Borowitz
The Jews and Christian Ingratitude .... Jeffery G. Sobosan

Ecumenical Bulletin

Executive Council of the Episcopal Church, Ecumenical Office, 815 Second Avenue, New York, New York 10017; 1973-P, six times a year, $6.00 a year.

8: 44 (1980), includes

The Continuing Christian Need for Judaism .... John S. Spong
A Jewish Perspective: This Moment in Jewish-Christian
    Relations .... Daniel F. Polish
A Roman Catholic Perspective: The Interfaith Agenda ... Eugene J. Fisher
How One Diocesan Committee on Jewish Relations
    Functions .... Lee A. Belford
Three That Worked: A Report on Episcopal-Jewish Projects
    in Long Island .... Lawrence McCoombe and Annette Daum
Jews and Christians in Joint Worship:
    A Symposium .... Robert L. Turnipseed and Balfour Brickner
Project Yachad: A Model of Continuing Jewish-Christian
    Dialogue in Ohio .... Philip Culbertson

Ecumenical Trends

Graymoor Ecumenical Institute, 475 Riverside Drive, Room 528, New York, New York 10115; 1971-P, 0360-9073, monthly (except August), $7.00 a year.

16: 3 (1987), "What Do Jews Want to Say to Christians?" includes

Are We Both God's People? .... Leon Klenicki
Auschwitz, Israel, the Contemporary Jewish Experience and
  the Future of the Dialogue .... Daniel Polish
Jewish-Christian Encounter in Israel .... David Rosen
Recent Jewish Perspectives on Christianity .... Barry D. Cytron
Catholic-Jewish Relations in Latin America .. Luis Eduardo Castano Cardona
SIDIC--An International Service for Jewish-Christian
  Documentation .... Shirley Sedawie

Ecumenism

Canadian Centre for Ecumenism, 2065 Sherbrook Street, West, Montreal,
Quebec H3H 1G6, Canada; 1965-P, 0383-4301x, quarterly, $10.00 a year.

76 (1984), "The Christian-Jewish Dialogue" includes

Jewish-Christian Dialogue in Montreal: Personal Reflections .. E. D. Fleming
Glimpses of the Past, Present and Future: Christian-Jewish
  Dialogue of Toronto .... Edith Land
Christian-Jewish Relations in the U.S.A.--A Catholic View.. Eugene J. Fisher
From Fellowship, Tea and Sympathy, to a Change of Heart: The
  Interreligious Dialogue in the United States .... Leon Klenicki
A Glimpse of Jewish-Christian Dialogue around the
  World .... Victor C. Goldbloom
The SIDIC Centre - Rome .... Margaret McGrath
Commemorating the Holocaust as Christians .... Stephane Valiquette
Marriage between Jews and Roman Catholics .... Stephane Valiquette

Encounter

Christian Theological Seminary, Box 88267, Indianapolis, Indiana 46208;
1956-P, 0013-7081, quarterly, $12.00 a year.

40: 2 (1979), "Christians and Jews" includes

Christians and Jews: Along a Theological Frontier .... A. Roy Eckardt
Christian Theology and the Murder of Jews .... Larry E. Axel

39: 3 (1978), "Judaic-Christian Relations" includes

Dialogue: Interpersonal and Interfaith .... Harold E. Hatt
Comprehending Religious Diversity .... Samuel C. Pearson, Jr.
A New Paradigm for Reading Romans.............. Calvin L. Williamson
Brother Isaac, Sister Ruth .... David Owen

42: 2 (1981), "Post-Holocaust Theology" includes

Travail of a Presidential Commission........... A. Roy and Alice Eckardt
Theological Aspects of the Holocaust .... Yechiel Ilsar
Martyrdom and Chrisma .... S. Daniel Breslauer
The Holocaust: Its Implications for Church and Society
  Problematic .... John T. Pawlikowski
Christians and Jerusalem .... Thomas A. Idinopulos
The Holocaust God .... Frederick Sontag

Genesis 2: An Independent Voice for Jewish Renewal

Rebirth 2, Inc., 99 Bishop Allen Drive, Cambridge, Massachusetts 02139; 1969-P, 0016-6669, eight times a year, $10.00 a year.

16: 6 (1985), "Focus on Jewish-Christian Relations" includes

The Politics of God . . . . Balfour Brickner
The Popes and Zionism . . . . Irving Greenberg
The Seder—A Ritual for Christians? . . . . Herman J. Blumberg
A Mixed Marriage . . . . Ruth Geller
When a Rabbi Studies the New Testament . . . . Michael R. Greenwald
Forty Years Later, the Rescuers Gather . . . . Alan Rosen

Greek Orthodox Theological Review

Holy Cross Orthodox Press, 50 Goddard Avenue, Brookline, Massachusetts 02146; 1954-P, 0017-3894, quarterly, $13.00 a year.

22: 1 (1977), includes

Greek Orthodox-Jewish Relations in Historical
 Perspective . . . . Demetrios J. Constantelos
Greek Orthodox-Jewish Relations in Historical Perspective . . . . . Zvi Ankori
Ethics in the Greek Orthodox Tradition . . . . Stanley Harakas
Judaism and Eastern Orthodoxy: Theological
 Reflections . . . . Theodore Stylianopoulous
Judaism and the New Testament . . . . Jacob B. Agus
Religion and Nationalism in the Byzantine Empire and After:
 Conformity or Pluralism? . . . . Deno J. Geanakoplos
Nationalism and Religion in the Contemporary World . . . . . . Salo W. Baron
The Influences of Jewish Worship on Orthodox Christian
 Worship . . . . George S. Bebis
Tribal Agathas . . . . Eric Werner

Interpretation: A Journal of Bible and Theology

Union Theological Seminary in Virginia, 3041 Brook Road, Richmond, Virginia 23227; 1947-P, 0020-9643, quarterly, $11.00 a year, $27.00 for three years.

39: 4 (1985), includes

The Law and the Coexistence of Jews and Gentiles
 in Romans . . . . Jacob Nuesner
The Book That Reads Us . . . . John B. Rogers, Jr.
Some Theological Implications of the Holocaust . . . . Gerard S. Sloyan

New Catholic World

Paulist Fathers, Paulist Press, 997 Macarthur Boulevard, Mahwah, New Jersey 07430; 1865-P, six times a year, $10.00 a year, $19.00 for two years, $27.00 for three years.

228: 1367 (1985), "Christian/Jewish Relations Twenty Years after Vatican II" includes

Jewish Views of Christianity . . . . David Novak
The Two Covenants . . . . Joseph Kelly
The Role of Scripture in Catholic-Jewish Relations . . . . Lawrence Boadt
The Faith of the Jewish People . . . . Walter S. Wurzburger
Catholic-Jewish Reconciliation: Three Major Contributions to
    the Dialogue . . . . Eugene J. Fisher
Publishing in the Service of Christian-Jewish Relations . . . . . . Helga Croner
Nostra Aetate Twenty Years Later . . . . Leon Klenicki
Education for Catholic-Jewish Relations . . . . Carol Rittner

Philosophical Forum

Philosophical Forum, Inc., c/o City University of New York, Box 239, 17 Lexington Avenue, New York, New York 10010; 1942-P, 0031-806X, quarterly, $12.00 a year.

16: 1-2 (1985), "Philosophy and the Holocaust" includes

The Concept of Genocide . . . . Bereel Lang
The Origin of Extermination in the Imagination . . . . William Gass
Skepticism, Narrative, and Holocaust Ethics . . . . Philip Hallie
Can Evil Be Banal? . . . . Nathan Rotenstreich
Hannah Arendt's View of Totalitarianism and
    the Holocaust . . . . Gertrude Ezorsky
How to Make Hitler's Ideas Clear? . . . . John K. Roth
Measuring Responsibility . . . . A. Zvie Bar-On
The Theological Implications of the Holocaust . . . . George Schlesinger
Forgiveness and Regret . . . . Martin P. Golding
Christianity and the Final Solution . . . . William L. Reese

Quarterly Review

United Board of Higher Education and Ministry and United Methodist Publishing House, 1007 19th Avenue, Box 871, Nashville, Tennessee 37202; 1980-P, 0270-9287, quarterly, $15.00 a year.

4: 4 (1984), "Focus on Jewish-Christian Relations" includes

The Relationship of Judaism and Christianity: Toward a New
    Organic Model . . . . Irving Greenberg
Jews and Christians: The Contemporary Dialogue . . . . . John T. Pawlikowski
The New Testament Reconsidered: Recent Post-Holocaust
    Scholarship . . . . Clark M. Williamson
The Jewish "No" to Jesus and the Christian "Yes"
    to Jews . . . . J. (Coos) Schoneveld
Heschel's Significance for Jewish-Christian Relations . . . . Eva Fleischner
Homiletical Resources from the Hebrew Bible
    for Lent . . . . Michael Chernick

Reconstructionist

Federation of Reconstructionist Congregations and Hauvarot, 270 West 89th Street, New York, New York 10024; 1935-P, 0034-1495, eight times a year, $20.00 a year.

51: 3 (1986), includes

New Christian Theologies of Covenant . . . . Philip Culbertson
Jews and Fundamentalists . . . . Nathan Perlmutter
Steps and Missteps in a Jewish-Christian Dialogue:
    A Review Essay . . . . Peter Manchester

Religion and Intellectual Life

Associates for Religion and Intellectual Life, College of New Rochelle, New Rochelle, New York 10801; 1983-P, 0741-0549, quarterly, $25.00 a year.

3: 4 (1986), includes

The Story Is Not Yet Over . . . . David B. Burrell
Paul M. van Buren's Re-Understanding of Judaism
    and Christianity . . . . Shamai Kanter
The Context of Jesus Christ: Israel . . . . Paul M. van Buren
Not a Reversal but a Recovery . . . . Maureena Fritz
Jesus the Jew in the Apostolic Writings . . . . Lloyd Gaston
On the Value of Religious Boundaries . . . . Neil Gillman
Truth as Revealed in Scripture . . . . Arthur F. Glasser
A New Context for Christology . . . . Clark M. Williamson
Christology: The Immovable Object . . . . Michael Wyschogrod

Religious Education

Religious Education Association, 409 Prospect Street, New Haven, Connecticut 06510; 1906-P, quarterly, $35.00 a year for membership, $17.50 a year for students.

76: 6 (1981), "Jewish-Christian Dialogue" includes

Dialogue and Conflict: Jewish-Christian Relations Today . . . . Walter Jacob
The Torah: A Bridge? . . . . Katherine T. Hargrove
Judaism and Christianity: Sources of Convergence . . . . Jack D. Spiro
The Continuing Christian Need for Judaism . . . . John S. Spong
Questions "Which Touch on the Heart of Our Faith" . . . . Mary C. Boys
Samuel Sandmel's Philosophy of Religious Education:
    "To Speak the Truth in Love" . . . . Jay A. Holstein
A Bibliography on Judaism for Christian Education: Part II . . Joel Rembaum

18: 1 (1986), "Issues in Jewish and Christian Religious Education" includes

The Impact of John Dewey on Jewish Education . . . . Kerry Olitzky
Pluralism and Jewish Education . . . . Simon Greenberg

Jewish Studies and Religious Studies .... David Blumenthal
Hebrew Bible in Colleges and Universities .... Jon Levenson
Elliot Eisner's Artist's Model of Education .... H. A. Alexander
To See the World through Jewish Eyes .... Howard Bogot
Nostra Aetate: A Turning Point in History .... Maureena Fritz
Preparation for Teaching about Religion in Public Schools .. Thayer Warshaw
Oral Tradition: Legacy of Faith for the Black Church .... Ella Mitchell
The Future of the Past: History and Policy Making
    in Religious Education......................... Jack L. Seymour

Review and Expositor

Southern Baptist Theological Seminary, 2825 Lexington Road, Louisville, Kentucky 40280; 1903-P, 0034-6373, quarterly, $9.00 a year, $23.00 for three years.

84: 2 (1987), "The New Testament and Judaism" includes

The New Testament and Judaism: An Historical
    Perspective on the Theme .... Michael J. Cook
Rabbinic Judaism and Early Christianity: From
    the Pharisees to the Rabbis .... Michael J. Cook
A Gospel Portrait of the Pharisees .... Donald E. Cook
The Concept of the Messiah in Second Temple
    and Rabbinic Literature .... Lawrence H. Schiffman
The Concept of the Messiah: A Baptist Perspective .... Frank Stagg
The Gospel of John and the Jews .... Michael J. Cook
The Gospel of John and the Jews .... R. Alan Culpepper
The Rabbinic Understanding of Covenant .... Lawrence H. Schiffman
Paul on the Covenant .... Charles H. Talbert
A Survey of Some Introductions to the Old Testament ...... Marvin E. Tate

Shofar

Jewish Studies Program, Purdue University, Recitation 222, Purdue University, West Lafayette, Indiana 47907; 1981-P, 0882-8539, quarterly, $10.00 a year.

3: 2 (1985), includes

A New Maturity in Christian-Jewish Dialogue: An
    Annotated Bibliography 1975-1983 .... Eugene J. Fisher
The Evolution of Christian-Jewish Dialogue .... John T. Pawlikowski
The Oberammergau Passion Play and Modern
    Anti-Semitism................................. Gordon M. Mork

Theology Today

Science Press, P.O. Box 29, Princeton, New Jersey 08542; 1943-P, 0040-57 36, quarterly, $14.00 a year.

41: 3 (1984), includes

Acting Redemptively .... Diogenes Allen
The Jewish-Christian Agenda .... Solomon S. Bernards

Whence Anti-Semitism? .... W. Eugene March
Buber: Biography as Dialogue .... Elena Malits
Contemporary Encounter .... William A. Hartfelder
A Jewish Feminist View .... Annette Daum
Anti-Semitism Is the Heart ....A. Roy Eckardt

Union Seminary Quarterly Review

Union Theological Seminary, 3041 Broadway, New York, New York 10027; 1945-P, 0362-1545, quarterly, $10.00 a year, $18.00 for two years, $25.00 for three years.

30: 2 (1983), "Christianity and Anti-Judaism," includes

Anti-Judaism in the New Testament .... Michael J. Cook
Contemporary Christian Theology and a Protestant
    Witness for the Shoah .... A. Roy Eckardt
Jewish-Christian Feminist Dialogue: A Wholistic
    Vision .... Deborah McCauley and Annette Daum
The Holy Land in Jewish-Christian Dialogue .... David Klatzker
Corner-Stone, Stumbling Stone: Christian Problems
    in Viewing Israel .... Robert L. Brashear

3. Journals that occasionally publish important articles in the field of Jewish-Christian relations, with titles of the articles they contain.

America

Jesuits of the United States and Canada, 106 West 56th Street, New York, New York 10019; 1909-P, 0002-7049, weekly, bi-weekly during the summer, $25.00 a year.

144: 6 (1981), includes

The Holocaust and Christian Responsibility .... Eugene J. Fisher

152: 14 (1985), includes

Catholics and Jewish Prayer .... Daniel J. Harrington

154: 3 (1986), includes

Surprises and Fears of Ecumenism: Twenty Years
    after Vatican II .... Thomas F. Stransky

154: 5 (1986), includes

Nostra Aetate in Cultural Perspective .... David M. Bossman
The Jewish-Catholic Dialogue: Twenty Years
    after Nostra Aetate .... Thomas F. Stransky

Center Journal

Center for Christian Studies, 237 North Michigan Street, South Bend, Indiana 46601; 1981-P, quarterly, $25.00 a year.

4: 1 (1984), includes

After the Holocaust: What Then Are We to Do? . . . . John X. Evans

Christian Century

Christian Century Foundation, 407 South Dearborn Street, Chicago, Illinois 60605; 184-P, 0009-5281, weekly, $24.00 a year.

102: 3 (1985), includes

The Pharisaic Jesus and His Gospel Parables . . . . Philip Culbertson

100: 29 (1983), includes

Jesus in the Post-Holocaust Jewish-Christian Dialogue . . . . . Peter G. Fleck

Christianity and Crisis

Christianity and Crisis, Inc., 537 West 121st Street, New York, New York 10027; 1941-P, 0009-5745, nineteen times a year, $21.00 a year.

41: 9 (1981), includes

What Do We Really Think of Judaism . . . . Philip Culbertson

42: 9 (1982), includes

What Did Jesus Ask?. . . . . Pinchas E. Lapide

43: 3 (1983), includes

How Shall the Jews of America Be Jewish? . . . . Arthur Hertzberg

Christianity Today

Christianity Today, Inc., 465 Gundersen Drive, Carol Street, Illinois 60188; 1956-P, 0009-5753, eighteen times a year, $21.00 a year.

25 (1981), includes

Evangelical and Jewish Leaders Probe the Realities
   behind the Labels . . . . Tom Minnery

Commonweal

Commonweal Publishing Co., Inc., 232 Madison Avenue, New York, New York 10016; 1924-P, 0010-3330, bi-weekly, $20.00 a year.

112: 463 (1985), includes

Jews & Catholics: Taking Stock, Why the Vatican's
    Notes Were Disappointing . . . . Judith Banki and Alan L. Mittleman

Currents in Theology and Mission

Christ Seminary, 539 North Grand Street, St. Louis, Missouri 63103; 1974-P, 0098-2113, bi-monthly, $8.50 a year.

11 (1984), includes

Anti-Semitism as Christian Legacy . . . . Ralph W. Klein

Hebrew Union College Annual

Ktav Publishing House, Inc., 900 Jefferson Street, Hoboken, New Jersey 07030; 1927-P, 0360-9049, annually.

54 (1983), includes

Interpreting "Pro-Jewish" Passages in Matthew. . . . . Michael J. Cook

Horizons Biblical Theology

Pittsburgh Theological Seminary, 616 North Highland Avenue, Pittsburgh, Pennsylvania 15206; 1979-P, 0195-9085, semi-annually, $10.00 a year, $7.00 for students.

5: 2 (1983), includes

Aspects of Dual Covenant Theology: Salvation . . . . Phillip Sigal

International Bulletin of Missionary Research

Overseas Ministry Study Center, Box 2057, Ventor, New Jersey 08406; 1950-P, 0272-6122, quarterly, $14.00 a year.

8: 2 (1984), includes

Christianity and Judaism: Continuity and Discontinuity . . . . W.S. Campbell

7: 1 (1983), includes

Ecumenical Considerations on Jewish-Christian
    Dialogue . . . . World Council of Churches, Executive Committee

Journal of the American Academy of Religion

Scholars Press, P.O. Box 1608, Decatur, Georgia 30031; 1933-P, 0002-7189, quarterly, $50.00 a year.

49: 1 (1981), includes

Recent Literature on Christian-Jewish Relations . . . . A. Roy Eckardt

53: 3 (1985), includes

The Christian Blasphemy . . . . Robert T. Osborn

Journal of the Evangelical Theological Society

Evangelical Theological Society, 4747 College Avenue, San Diego, California 92115; 1958-P, 0360-8808, quarterly, $15.00 a year.

25: 2 (1982), includes

An Evangelical View of the Current State of
    Evangelical-Jewish Relations . . . . Marvin R. Wilson
The Jewish Leaders in MAtthew's Gospel: A Reappraisal . . . . D. A. Carson

King's Theological Review

University of London, King's College, Strand, London WC2R 2LS, England; 1978-P, 0143-5922, bi-annually, $11.00 a year.

6: 2 (1983), includes

Jewish-Christian Dialogue: A New Proposal . . . . Dan Cohn-Sherbok

Missiology

American Society of Missiology, 600 Walnut Avenue, Scottsdale, Pennsylvania 15603; 1973-P, 0091-8296, quarterly, $15.00 a year.

7: 4 (1979), includes

Towards Redefining Our Mission--With Respect to the Jewish
    People . . . . David-Maria Jaeger

Modern Churchman

Modern Churchman's Union, School House, Leysters, Leominster, Herefordshire HR6 OHB, United Kingdom; 1911-P, quarterly, 0026-7597, $9.00 a year.

26: 2 (1984), includes

Bibliography: Christian-Jewish Dialogue . . . . Kenneth Cracknell

Modern Judaism

Johns Hopkins University Press, 701 West 40th Street, Suite 275, Baltimore, Maryland 21211; 1981-P, 0276-1114, three times a year, $20.00 a year.

2: 3 (1982), includes

Recent Publications in the Jewish-Christian Dialogue:
    A Review Essay .... Marc Saperstein

PACE: Professional Approaches for Christian Educators

Saint Mary's Press, Terrace Heights, Winoma, Minnesota 55987; 1970-P, yearly volume consisting of eight monthly sections, $56.00 a year.

Several volumes have issues that have special concern for those interested in Jewish-Christian relations.

Process Studies

School of Theology at Claremont, Center for Process Studies, 1325 North College Avenue, Claremont, California 91711; 1971-P, 0360-6503, quarterly, $12.00 a year.

10: 3-4 (1980), includes

Anti-Judaism in Process Christologies? .... Clark Williamson

Sh'ma

Sh'ma, Inc., Box 567, Port Washington, New York 11050; 1970-P, bi-weekly except June, July, and August, $22.00 a year.

13: 260 (1983), includes

Jewish-Christian Relations in America .... Solomon S. Bernards
The Futility of Interfaith Relations .... Ethel C. Fenig
Interfaith: An Israeli Perspective .... Geoffrey Wigoder

16: 302 (1985), includes

Nostra Aetate--After 20 Years .... Alfred Wolf
On Not Speaking to Christians--Ever! .... Barry Cytron

Witness

Episcopal Church Publishing, Co., Box 359, Ambler, Pennsylvania 19002; 1917-P, 0197-8896, monthly except August, $15.00 a year.

65: 1 (1982), includes

Christians and Jews in Context .... Barbara Krasner

4. Other journals and newsletters significant to the field of interreligious dialogue.

Ateismo e dialogo

Segretariato per i non credenti, 00120 Vatican City; 1966-P, quarterly.

Bulletin of Christian Institutes of Islamic Studies

Formerly Al-Basheer. Henry Martyn Institute, P.O. Box 153, Hyderabad 500001, A. P., India; 1978-P, quarterly.

Center for Holocaust Studies Newsletter

Center for Holocaust Studies, 1609 Avenue J, Brooklyn, New York 11230; 1984-P, quarterly.

Centerpoint: A Journal of Interdisciplinary Studies

City University of New York, 33 West 42nd Street, Room 208, New York, New York 10036; 1974-84.

Ching Feng

Christian Study Centre on Chinese Religion and Culture, Tao Fong Shan, P.O. Box 153, Shatin, N.T., Hong Kong; 1957-P, 0009-4668, quarterly, $10.00 a year.

Christian Institute of Sikh Studies Bulletin

Barin Union Christian College, Batala, Punjab, India; occasional.

Christian News from Israel

Ministry of Religious Affairs, Box 1167, 30 Jaffa Street, Jerusalem, Israel; 1949-P, 0009-5532, semi-annually, $5.00 a year.

Christian Peace Conference Bulletin

International Secretariat of the Christian Peace Conference, Jungmannova 9, Prague 1, Czechoslovakia; 1962-P, 0009-5567, quarterly, $9.70 a year.

Commentary

American Jewish Committee, 165 East 56th Street, New York, New York 10022; 1945-P, 0010-2601, monthly, $33.00 a year.

Communio Viatorum

Ecumenical Institute, comenius Faculty of Theology, Knokovna, Jungmanova 9, 110-00 Prague, Czechoslovakia; 1958-P, 0010-3713, quarterly, free.

138 Journals

Current Dialogue

Formerly The Church and the Jewish People Newsletter. World Council of Churches, 150 route de Ferney, Box 66, 1211 Geneva 20, Switzerland, 1978-P, quarterly, free.

Dansalan REsearch Center Papers

P.O. Box 5430, Iligan City 8801, Philippines, occasional.

Dialogue

Ecumenical Institute for Study and Dialogue, 490/5 Havelock Road, Colombo 6, Sri Lanka; 1963-P, 0012-2181, tri-annually, $3.00 a year.

Dimensions: A Journal of Holocaust Studies

Anti-Defamation League of B'nai B'rith, 823 United Nations Plaza, New York, New York 10017; 1985-P, 0882-1240, tri-annually, $12.00 a year, $20.00 for two years.

Ecumenical Review

World Council of Churches, 475 Riverside Drive, Room 1062, New York, New York 10115; 1948-P, 0013-0796, $15.00 a year.

The Ecumenist

Paulist Press, 997 Macarthur Boulevard, Mahwah, New Jersey 07430; 1962-P, 0013-080X, bi-monthly, free.

Exchange: Bulletin of Third World Christian Literature

Department of Missiology, Interuniversity Institute for Missiological and Ecumenical Research, Boehaavelaan 43, Leiden, The Netherlands; 1972-P, tri-annually.

Flambeau

Association of Theological Schools in Central and West Africa, Editions CLE, B.P. 4048, Yaounde, Cameroun; 1964-P, quarterly.

Harvard Theological Review

Harvard Divinity School, 45 Francis Avenue, Cambridge, Massachusetts 02138; 1908-P, 0017-8160, quarterly, $12.00 a year.

Holocaust and Genocide Studies: An International Journal

Pergamon Press, Fairview Park, Elmsford, New York 10523, 1986-P, 8756-6583, bi-annually, $25.00 a year.

International Bulletin of Missionary Research

Formed by the merger of Gospel in Context and Occasional Bulletin of Missionary Research. Overseas Ministries Study Center, P.O. Box 2057, Ventor, New Jersey 08406; 1977-P, 0272-6122, quarterly.

International Review of Mission

Commission on World Mission and Evangelism of the World Council of Churches, 150 route de Ferney, 1211 Geneva 20, Switzerland, 1912-P, quarterly, $15.00 a year.

Japanese Religions

NCC Center for the Study of Japanese Religions, c/o Kyoto Diocese of the Japan Episcopal Church, 602 Karasuma-Shimotachiuri, Kamikyo-Ku, Kyoto, Japan; 1959-P, 0448-8954, irregular, $10.00 a year.

Jewish Quarterly Review

Dropsie University, Broad and York Streets, Philadelphia, Pennsylvania 19132; 1909-P, 0021-6682, quarterly, $35.00 a year.

Journal of Biblical Literature

Scholars Press, P.O. Box 1608, Decatur, Georgia 30031; 1982-P, 0021-9231, quarterly, $50.00 a year.

Journal of Dharma

Center for Study of World Religions, Dharmaram College, Bangalore, India 0253-7222; 1975-P, quarterly, $15.00 a year.

Journal of Jewish Studies

Oxford Centre for Postgraduate Hebrew Studies, Oriental Institute, Pusey Lane, Oxford OX1 2LE, England; 1948-P, 0022-2097, semi-annually, $30.00 a year.

Journal of Reform Judaism

Central Conferences of American Rabbis, 21 East 40th Street, 14th Floor, New York, New York 10016; 1953-P, 0149-7124, quarterly, $15.00 a year.

Journal of Religion

University of Chicago Press, 5757 University Avenue, Chicago, Illinois 60037; 1927-P, 0022-4189, quarterly, $22.00 a year.

Journal of Religion in Africa

E.J. Brill, Leiden, The Netherlands, 1967-P, 0022-4200, tri-annually.

Journal of Religious Studies

Cleveland State University, Department of Religion, Cleveland, Ohio 44115; 1972-P, 0193-3064, semi-annually, $4.00 a year.

Journal of Religious Thought

Howard University Press, Howard University, 2900 Van Ness Street, NW, Washington, D.C. 20008; 1943-P, 0022-4235, semi-annually, $12.00 a year.

Judaica

Judaica Verlag, Etzelstr 19, CH-8038, Zurich, Switzerland; 1945-P, 0022-5724, quarterly, $13.00 a year.

Judaism

American Jewish Congress, 15 East 84th Street, New York, New York 10028; 1952-P, 0022-5762, quarterly, $12.00 a year.

Junge Kirche

Verlag Junge Kirche, Mathildenstrasse 86, 2800 Bremen 1, West Germany; 1933-P, 0022-0139, monthly, $27.50 a year.

Lest We Forget

Newsletter of the Anne Frank Institute of Philadelphia, P.O. Box 2147, Philadelphia, Pennsylvania 19103; 1975-P, quarterly, $25.00 a year.

LWF Report

Lutheran World Federation, 150 route de Ferney, 1211 Geneva 20, Switzerland; 1953-P, 0024-760X, quarterly, $7.50 a year.

Masses Ouvrieres

23, rue Jean-de-Beauvais, 75005 Paris, France; 1945-P, monthly.

Midstream

Theodor Herzl Foundation, Inc., 515 Park Avenue, New York, New York 10022, 1955-P, 0026-332X, ten times a year, $15.00 a year.

The Month

Society of Jesus, English Providence, 114 Mount Street, London W14 6AH, England; 1864-P, 0026-7597, monthly, $18.00 a year.

Moody Monthly

Moody Bible Institute, 820 North LaSalle Drive, Chicago, Illinois 60610; 1900-P, 0027—806, monthly, $16.95 a year.

Al-Mushir

Christian Study Centre, 126-B Murree Road, Rawalpindi, Pakistan; 1959-P, quarterly, $10.00 a year.

The Muslim World

Duncan Black Macdonald Center at Hartford Seminary Foundation, 55 Elizabeth Street, Hartford, Connecticut 06105; 1911-P, 0027-4909, quarterly, $15.00 a year.

Neues Forum: Zeitschrift fur den Dialog

Museumstrasse 5, A-1070 Vienna, Austria; 1967-P, monthly.

Parole et Societe: Revue bimestrielle du christianisme social

Librairie Protestante, 140 Bd. Saint-Germain, Paris 6e, France; 1972-P, bi-monthly.

Polish Review

Polish Institute of Arts and Science of America, 59 East 66th Street, New York 10021; 1956-P, quarterly, 0032-2970, $20.00 a year.

Pro Mundi Vita

Rue de la Limite 6, B-1030 Brussels, Belgium; 1963-P, quarterly.

Reform Judaism

Union of American Hebrew Congregations, 838 Fifth Avenue, New York, New York 10021; 1972-P, 0482-0819, quarterly, $10.00 a year, $5.00 a year for students.

Reformed Journal

William B. Eerdmans Publishing Co., 225 Jefferson Street, Grand Rapids, Michigan 49503; 1951-P, 0486-252X, monthly, $12.00 a year.

Religion and Society

Bulletin of the Christian Institute for the Study of Religion and Society, P.O. Box 4600, 17 Miller's Road, Bangalore 560 046, India; 1953-P, 0034-3951, quarterly, $15.00 a year.

Saint Luke's Journal of Theology

School of Theology, University of the South, Sewanee, Tennessee 37375; 1957-P, 0036-309X, quarterly, $10.00 a year, $19.00 for two years, $27.00 for three years.

Secretariatus pro non Christianis Bulletin

Palazzo S. Calisto, Vatican City; 1966-P, tri-annually.

Shoah: A Review of Holocaust Studies

Zachor, The Holocaust Resource Center of the National Jewish Resource
Center, 250 West 57th Street, New York, New York 10107; 1978-P,
0197-2960, quarterly, $10.00 a year.

Tradition: A Journal of Orthodox Jewish Thought

Rabbinical Council of America, 275 Seventh Avenue, New York, New
York 10001; 1958-P, 0041-0608, quarterly, $18.00 a year, $32.00 for two
years, $45.00 for three years.

V.
Congresses

Congresses, conferences, symposia, forums, seminars, encounters, meetings, dialogues, colloquia, consultations, and workshops on or about Jewish-Christian relations held since 1965 have been listed.

Organization of the entry consists of the theme and/or congress title if available, sponsor(s), place, and date.

1989

Eleventh National Workshop on Christian-Jewish Relations. Tentatively titled "Jews and Christians within the American Experience." Multiple national and local sponsors. Charleston, South Carolina. March 27-30, 1989.

1988

"Remembering for the Future: The Impact of the Holocaust and Genocide on Jews and Christians." Council of Christians and Jews, Pergamon Press, and Holocaust and Genocide Studies. Oxford, England. July 10-14, 1988.

1987

"Jesus before Christianity." Jewish Community Relations Council, Christian Theological Seminary, and Indiana Interreligious Commission on Human Equality. Indianapolis, Indiana. March 23, 1987.

"Jewish, Christian and Humanistic Contributions toward Peace and Conflict Resolution." Institute of Judaeo-Christian Studies, Seton Hall University, South Orange, New Jersey. March 3-4, 1987.

"The Jewish/Christian Reality." Fourth Annual Consultation of the Associates for Religion and Intellectual Life. Religion and Intellectual Life. Duke University, Durham, North Carolina. June 15-18, 1987.

"Jewish History, Philosophy, and Theology int he Curriculum of a Catholic University." Institute of Judaeo-Christian Studies, Seton Hall University, South Orange, New Jersey, June 8-26, 1987.

"Jews and Christians: Listening to Each Other." Tenth National Workshop on Christian-Jewish Relations. Multiple national and local sponsors. Minneapolis, Minnesota. November 8-12, 1987.

"New Testament and Judaica/Judaism." Center for Jewish-Christian Studies, Chicago Theological Seminary. Chicago, Illinois. January 21, 1987.

"Overcoming Prejudice—An Educational Challenge." International Colloquium. International Council of Christians and Jews. Fribourg, Switzerland. July 12-17, 1987.

"The Parting of the Ways: A Study Conference on the Self-definition of Christianity and Rabbinic Judaism in the First to Fifth Centuries C.E." Centre for the Study of Judaism and Jewish/Christian Relations and Council of Christians and Jews. Westhill College, Selly Oak, Birmingham, England. September 2-9, 1987.

"Power and Powerlessness in Light of the Holocaust: A Dialogue between Christians and Jews." Syracuse Area Interreligious Council, Jewish-Christian Dialogue Project in the United Church of Christ, Le Moyne College, and Syracuse University. Syracuse, New York. March 30-31, 1987.

"A Precious Legacy—The Contribution of the Jews to the Culture of Central and Eastern Europe in the Nineteenth and Twentieth Century." Second Seminar of Jews and Christians from the East and the West. International Council of Christians and Jews. "Wilhelmshohe" Buckow, East Germany. September 13-17, 1987.

1986

"Acts of Courage/Stories of Faith." Jewish Community Relations Council, Christian Theological Seminary, and Indiana Interreligious Commission on Human Equality. Indianapolis, Indiana. March 10, 1986.

An African Christian-Jewish Consultation. International Jewish Committee on Interreligious Consultations and World Council of Churches. Nairobi, Kenya. November 10-14, 1986.

"Christians and Jews and the Covenant." National Conference of Christians and Jews and Shalom Hartman Institute for Advanced Judaic Studies. Jerusalem, Israel. December 28, 1986-January 28, 1987.

"Coming to Grips with Our Past: Forging Our Future." Ninth National Workshop on Christian Jewish Relations. Multiple national and local sponsors. Baltimore, Maryland. May 13-16, 1986.

"Consultation on the Church and the Jewish People." World Council of Churches. Arnoldshain, West Germany. February 10-14, 1986.

"Cultural and Religious Encounter between Jews, Christians and Muslims—Lessons from the Past." International Council of Christians and Jews. Madrid, Toledo, and Salamanca, Spain. July 6-11, 1986.

"God and Exodus: The Meaning of Liberation." Seventh Jewish-Lutheran-Catholic Graymoor Conversation. Interfaith Affairs Department of the Anti-Defamation League of B'nai B'rith, Division of Theological Studies of the Lutheran Council (U.S.A.), and Graymoor Ecumenical Institute. Garrison, New York. Nov. 12-13, 1986.

"How Jews and Christians Look at Jesus." Center for Jewish-Christian Learning, College of St. Thomas. St. Paul, Minnesota. November 19-20, 1986.

"Identity and Commitment in the Interreligious Encounter." International Council of Christians and Jews. Jerusalem, Israel. December 21, 1986-January 1, 1987.

International Symposium on Jewish-Christian Dialogue since the Eighteenth Century. Duisburg University. Evangelische Akademie Mulheim, Duisburg, West Germany. March 2-6, 1986.

"Jewish-Christian Relations in the Classical Period: Implications for the Present." Center for Jewish-Christian Studies, General Theological Seminary. New York, New York. November 9, 1986.

"Jewish-Christian Relations in the Medieval Period: Implications for the Present." Center for Jewish-Christian Studies, General Theological Seminary. New York, New York. November 9, 1986.

"Jewish Life at the Time of Jesus." Catholic Jewish Relations Council of Northeast Queens. Forest Hills, New York. September 23, 1986, November 26, 1986, and March 10, 1987.

"Judaism and Christianity: The View from the University Classroom." Indiana University. Bloomington, Indiana. May 28, 1986.

"The New Anti-Semitic Disease: Terminable or Interminable?" The Divinity School Committee on Jewish-Christian Relations. Yale University, New Haven, Connecticut. April 9, 1986.

"1986 Symposium—The State of Our Relations." Christian Conference of Connecticut. Woodbridge, Connecticut. October 29, 1986.

"One God, Three Religions: Hope for Reconciliation." Hope Interfaith Center, Bethlehem. Rome, Italy. January 24, 1986.

"Salvation and Redemption in Judaism and Catholicism." Second International Catholic-Jewish Theological Colloquium. School of Theology of the St. Thomas Pontifical University, Centro Pro Unione-Friars of the Atonement, and SIDIC. Rome, Italy. November 4-6, 1986.

"Symbols of Faith." Archdiocese of Los Angeles Commission on Ecumenical and Interreligious Affairs, Wilshire Boulevard Temple, and the Islamic Center of Southern California. Los Angeles, California. January 29, 1986.

"Symposium on the New Testament and Judaism." Interreligious Affairs Department of Anti-Defamation League of B'nai B'rith, Interfaith Witness Department of the Southern Baptist Home Mission Board, and Southern Baptist Theological Seminary. Louisville, Kentucky. March 31-April 3, 1986.

1985

First Pan-American Conference on Catholic-Jewish Relations. American Jewish Committee and the National Conference of Brazilian Bishops. Hebraica Center, Sao Paulo, Brazil. November 3-5, 1985.

"How to Preach and Teach about the Jews." Institute of Judaeo-Christian Studies. Seton Hall University. South Orange, New Jersey. October 11, 1985.

"Jewish-Christian Dialogue and Its Contribution to Peace." International Council of Christians and Jews and Interchurch Peace Council in Hungary. Budapest, Hungary. November 17-20, 1985.

"Jewish-Christian Relations: Where Have We Been? Where Are We Going?" Atlantic School of Theology. Halifax, Nova Scotia, Canada. November 17, 1985.

"Jewish History in Non-Jewish Historiography and History Teaching." International Council of Christians and Jews. Arnoldshain, West Germany. May, 1985.

"Jews and Christians in Dialogue—Twentieth Anniversary of Vatican II Statement Nostra Aetate." Center for Jewish-Christian Learning, College of St. Thomas. St. Paul, Minnesota. November 18-19, 1985.

"Paul and the Torah." Jewish Community Relations Council, Christian Theological Seminary and Indiana Interreligious Commission on Human Equality. Indianapolis, Indiana. March 4, 1985.

"Reconciliation: Mutual Tolerance or Shared Responsibility?" International Council of Christians and Jews. Dublin, Ireland. July 21-24, 1985.

"Religion, Politics and Ideology: American Perspectives." Anti-Defamation League of B'nai B'rith. Indiana University, Bloomington, Indiana. January 14-16, 1985.

"Third Observance of Nostra Aetate." Ecumenical and Interreligious Affairs Commission of the Los Angeles Archdiocese. Los Angeles, California. October 17, 1985.

Twelfth Meeting of the International Catholic-Jewish Liaison Committee. Holy See's Commission for Religious Relations with the Jews and International Jewish Committee on Interreligious Consultations. Rome, Italy. October 28-30, 1985.

1984

"The Authority and Interpretation of Scripture in Judaism and Christianity." American Jewish Congress and the Vatican. Institute of Jewish-Christian Research of the Theological Faculty of Luzern, Lucerne, Switzerland. January, 1984.

"The Catholic Church and Hitler's War against the Jews." Institute of Judaeo-Christian Studies, Seton Hall University. South Orange, New Jersey. October 7, 1984.

"Evangelicals and Jews: Coming of Age." Third National Conference of Evangelical Christians and Jews. Gordon College and Department of Interreligious Affairs, American Jewish Committee. February 28-March 1, 1984.

"Faith in Humankind: Rescuers of Jews during the Holocaust." U.S. Holocaust Memorial Council. State Department in Washington, D.C. September 17-19, 1984.

First Jewish-Christian-Muslim Trialogue in the Western United States. Multiple Sponsors. Pitzer College, Claremont, California. February 8-9, 1984.

"Gateways to New Understandings." Eighth National Workshop on Christian-Jewish Relations. Multiple national and local sponsors. St. Louis, Missouri. October 29-November 1, 1984.

"Jewish-Christian Relations: A Look Ahead." Anti-Defamation League of B'nai B'rith. Indiana University, Bloomington, Indiana. December 10-13, 1984.

"Judaism in Christian Theological Education: Why? How? What?" Weston School of Theology, Harvard Divinity School, and Boston Theological Institute. Cambridge, Massachusetts. March 8, 1984.

"Liberation: Impulses from Jewish Passover and Christian Easter." International Council of Christians and Jews. Unteerjoch/Allgau, West Germany. April 26-May 1, 1984.

"Life after Auschwitz." Fifth Lutheran-Jewish-Roman Catholic Colloquium. Division of Theological Studies, Lutheran Council in the U.S.A., Anti-Defamation League of B'nai B'rith, and Graymoor Ecumenical Institute. Graymoor in Garrison, New York. November 13-14, 1984.

"Purpose and Strategy in Jewish-Christian Relations." International Council of Christians and Jews. Vallombrosa/Saltino, Italy. 1984.

"Seminary Education and Christian-Jewish Relations." Sierra Madre, California. March, 1984; Chicago, Illinois. April, 1984.

"To See Ourselves As Others See Us: The Theory of the Other in the Formative Age of Christianity and Judaism." Brown University Judaic Studies Program. Brown University, New York, New York. August 6-10, 1984.

"Toward a Theology of the Jewish-Christian Reality." Jewish Community Relations Council, Christian Theological Seminary, and Indiana Interreligious Commission on Human Equality. Indianapolis, Indiana. March 5, 1984.

"Toward a Universal Theology of Religion." Journal of Ecumenical Studies and Religion Department at Temple University. Philadelphia, Pennsylvania. October 17-19, 1984.

1983

"Israel for Christians." Jewish Community Relations Council, Christian Theological Seminary, and Indiana Interreligious Commission on Human Equality. Indianapolis, Indiana. March 4, 1983.

"Liberation in the Jewish and Christian Traditions." Third Seminar in Ireland on Jewish-Christian Relations. Irish School of Ecumenics. Dublin, Ireland. April 13-14, 1983.

"Luther, Lutheranism, and the Jews." Lutheran World Federation and the International Jewish Committee on Interreligious Consultations. Stockholm, Sweden. July 11-13, 1983.

"The Next Generation of Christian-Jewish Relations." Seventh National Workshop on Christian-Jewish Relations. Multiple national and local sponsors. Boston, Massachusetts. April 24-28, 1983.

"Poles and Jews: Myth and Reality in the Historical Context." Institute of East and Central Europe of Columbia University and Center for Israeli and Jewish Studies of Columbia University. New York, New York. March 6-10, 1983.

"The Search for Peace--Our Responsibility As Jews and Christians." International Council of Christians and Jews. Amsterdam, Holland. 1983.

1982

"The Family in Jewish and Christian Tradition." Second Seminar in Ireland on Jewish-Christian Relations. Irish School of Ecumenics. Dublin, Ireland. May 20-21, 1982.

"Has God Rejected His People?" Jewish Community Relations Council, Christian Theological Seminary, and the Indiana Interreligious Commission on Human Equality. Indianapolis, Indiana. May 2, 1982.

"Human Responsibility for the Creation--A Challenge for Jews and Christians in the World of Today." International Council of Christians and Jews. Hallig Hooge, West Germany. 1982.

"Jews and Christians between the Past and the Future." International Council of Christians and Jews. Berlin, West Germany. 1982.

"Liberation Theology and Judaism." Irish School of Ecumenics. Dublin, Ireland. March 13-14, 1982.

"Revelation: Torah, Christ, Muhammad." Department of Theology at Birmingham University, Edward Cadbury Trust, and United Reformed Church. Birmingham, England. September, 1982.

"The Sanctity of Life in an Age of Violence." Synagogue Council of America and National Conference of Catholic Bishops. Notre Dame University, Notre Dame, Indiana. November, 1982.

"In Search of Peace: Interfaith Perspectives." Sixth Annual Workshop of Two Traditions in Dialogue. Los Angeles, California. November, 1982.

1981

Consultation on the Church and the Jewish People. World Council of Churches. London-Colney, England. June 22-26, 1981.

First Seminar in Ireland on Jewish-Christian Relations. Irish School of Ecumenics. Dublin, Ireland. June 25-26, 1981.

"Image of the Other: The Presentation of Judaism in Christian Education and Christianity in Jewish Education." International Council of Christians and Jews. Heppenheim, West Germany. 1981.

"In the Image of God: The Challenge of Diversity." Sixth National Workshop on Christian-Jewish Relations. Multiple national and local sponsors. Milwaukee, Wisconsin. October 26-29, 1981.

"Lutherans and Jews: The Concept of the Human Being in the Lutheran and Jewish Traditions." First International Consultation. Copenhagen, Denmark. July 6-8, 1981.

"Religious Education in Germany." International Council of Christians and Jews. Heppenheim, West Germany. June 28, 1981.

"The Root and the Wild Olive." Faith and Order Conference. Indiana Council of Churches. Fort Wayne, Indiana. November 4-6, 1981.

"Seasons of Joy: Teaching about Each Other." Second Annual Catholic-Jewish Colloquium. Anti-Defamation League of B'nai B'rith, Union of American Hebrew Congregations, Hebrew Union College, the Archdiocese of New York, and Dioceses of Brooklyn and Rockville Center. Hebrew Union College-Jewish Institute of Religion, New York, New York. March, 1981.

1980

"Anglicans and Jews: Law and Religion in Contemporary Society." Consultants to the Archbishops of Canterbury and York on Interfaith Relations and the International Jewish Committee on Interreligious Consultations. Amport House, Andover, England. November 26-28, 1980.

"Christian Scholars Ask What Jesus' Jewishness Means Today." Graymoor Ecumenical Institute. Garrison, New York. December, 1980.

"Faith after Auschwitz." International Council of Christians and Jews. Sigtuna, Switzerland. 1980.

"Israel in Jewish-Christian Relations." International Council of Christians and Jews. Neve Ilan, Israel. 1980.

"Jews and Christians: Do We Live in the Same World?" Fifth National Workshop on Christian-Jewish Relations. Multiple national and local sponsors. Dallas, Texas. April 28-May 1, 1980.

"Religion and the Crisis of Modernity." World Council of Churches and the International Jewish Committee on Interreligious Consultations. Toronto, Canada. August 31-September 3, 1980.

1979

"Judaism in Christian Theology and Preaching: New Horizons or Old Dilemmas?" Hendricks Chapel and B. G. Rudolph Lectures, Syracuse University. Temple Society of Concord, Syracuse, New York. October, 1979.

"Religious Responsibility and Human Rights." International Council of Christians and Jews. New York, New York. June, 1979.

"Seminar on Judaism and Christianity in Dialogue." Princeton Theological Seminary. Princeton, New Jersey. February 12-15, 1979.

"Seminar on the Muslim-Jewish-Christian Faith Communities As Transnational Actors for Justice and Peace." Center for International Affairs, the Divinity School of Harvard University, and Interreligious Peace Colloquium of Washington, D.C. Cambridge, Massachusetts. March, 1979.

1978

"Sacred Values in a Dehumanized World." Fourth National Workshop on Christian-Jewish Relations. Multiple national and local sponsors. Los Angeles, California. November 6-9, 1978.

1977

A Christian Orthodox/Jewish Encounter. Lucerne, Switzerland. 1977.

"Living Together in an Age of Pluralism." Third National Workshop on Christian-Jewish Relations. Multiple national and local sponsors. Southfield, Michigan. April 19-21, 1977.

Third Annual Conference Workshop on Christian-Jewish Relations. Christian-Jewish Dialogue of Toronto and Holy Blossom Temple. Wycliffe College in the University of Toronto, Toronto, Canada. 1977.

1976

"Israel: Its Significance and Realities." International Council of Christians and Jews. Jerusalem, Israel. June, 1976.

Second Annual Conference Workshop on Christian–Jewish Relations. Christian-Jewish Dialogue of Toronto and Holy Blossom Temple. Wycliffe College in the University of Toronto, Toronto, Canada. February, 1976.

1975

"Life to the Seed: The Year for Opening Communications." First Episcopal-Jewish Colloquium in the United States. Diocese of Southern Ohio with the Episcopal Council of Greater Cincinnati, Hebrew Union College, and American Jewish Committee. Cincinnati, Ohio. March 16-17, 1975.

"New Dimensions in Christian-Jewish Relations." Second National Workshop on Christian-Jewish Relations. Multiple national and local sponsors. Memphis, Tennessee. October 28-30, 1975.

"The Worshiping Community—Jews and Christians." World Council of Churches Consultation of the Church and the Jewish People. Sigtuna, Sweden. June 6-11, 1975.

1974

First Annual Conference Workshop on Christian-Jewish Relations. Christian-Jewish Dialogue of Toronto and the Holy Blossom Temple. Wycliffe College in the University of Toronto, Toronto, Canada. Fall, 1974.

1973

First National Workshop on Catholic-Jewish Relations. Secretariat for Catholic-Jewish Relations of the National Conference of Catholic Bishops. Bergamo Center, Dayton, Ohio. November 27-29, 1973.

"Jewish-Christian Dialogue: Sorting Out the Issues—Symposium on Auschwitz." New York, New York. June 3-6, 1973.

"Jewish-Christian Relations and the Curriculum." North American Academy of Ecumenists and the National Conference of Christians and Jews. Villanova University, Villanova, Pennsylvania. March 23-25, 1973.

1972

First National Greek Orthodox-Jewish Colloquium. Greek Orthodox Archdiocese of North and South America and Department of Interreligious Affairs, American Jewish Committee. January 25-26, 1972.

1971

"The State and the Religious Community: Lutheran and Jewish Perspectives." Third U.S. Lutheran-Jewish Colloquium. American Jewish Committee and Lutheran Council in the U.S.A. Brandeis University, Waltham, Massachusetts. November 17-18, 1971.

1970

"Promise, Land, Peoplehood—Jewish and Christian Perspectives." Lutheran Council in the U.S.A. and American Jewish Committee. Concordia Seminary, St. Louis, Missouri. May 26-27, 1970.

1969

"About Jews and Judaism: An Interreligious Colloquy." American Jewish Committee and New York Theological Seminary. New York, New York. September 23–October 21, 1969.

1968

"Overcoming the Barriers to Communication." International Conference of Christians and Jews. York University, Toronto, Canada. 1968.

1965

"Torah and Gospel: Jewish and Catholic Theology in Dialogue." St. Vincent's Archabbey. Latrobe, Pennsylvania. January, 1965.

VI.
Media

This chapter lists 16mm film, filmstrips, video cassettes, records, and audio-cassettes. Categories include:

A. Jewish-Christian Relations
B. Holocaust
C. Israel
D. Anti-Judaism
E. Immigrant Contributions

The symbols below each entry represent distributors, producers, or film libraries where each type of media is located. The symbol code and addresses are listed on pages 170-75. Please write to the institution or organization for rental details.

Production dates of the media were provided when available; "n.d." indicates no date. Prices listed with commercial distributors are purchase prices; prices listed with seminary and university film libraries are rental fees. In many cases it was not possible to provide an annotation.

A. Jewish-Christian Relations

The Book and the Idol. 1955. $14\frac{1}{2}$ minutes/color/video cassette. $15.00.

> Using both Jewish and Christian archaeological artifacts, the film traces the emergence of monotheism and its conflict with paganism in the early civilization of Israel. The film displays many ancient and revered holy objects.

ADL

Changes in Roman Catholic Attitudes toward the Jews. n.d. By Francis
L. Filas. 55 minutes/cassette, mono.

UTSV

The Christian Dialogue with Judaism. 1961. Christian Faith and Other
Faiths, No. 1. By Stephen Charles Neill. Cassette, mono.

UTSV

Christian Theology in Israel. 1983. 30 minutes/color/video cassette. $40.00.

A discussion of the special problems facing Christian theologians in the Holy Land. With Dr. Paul M. van Buren, Professor of Religion, Temple University, Philadelphia, Pennsylvania, and Dr. Alvin Rosenfeld, Director of the Jewish Studies Program, Indiana University, Bloomington, Indiana (Indiana University Discussion Series).

ADL IU

Christians and Jews—A Troubled Brotherhood. n.d. 95 frames/color/2 filmstrips/LP record or cassette plus discussion guide. $31.95.

To help Jews and Christians work on improving relationships, and for use in high school classes working on prejudice and bigotry.

AHC

Hope against Hope. 1983. 30 minutes/color/video cassette. $40.00.

A discussion of the Italian-Jewish community during the Renaissance. With Dr. David Ruderman, Teacher of Jewish History and Thought, History Department, University of Maryland and Dr. Todd Endelman, Associate Professor of History, University of Michigan, Ann Arbor, Michigan (Indiana University Discussion Series).

ADL IU

Jesus in Jewish and Christian Literature. 1983. 30 minutes/color/video cassette. $40.00.

Christian and Jewish scholars discuss the changing portrayal of Jesus in Jewish and Christian literature. With Dr. Pinchas Lapide, Gottingen University and Kirchilsche Hochschule, West Germany; Dr. Gerard S. Sloyan, Professor of Religion and New Testament Studies, Temple University, Philadelphia, Pennsylvania, and Dr. Alvin Rosenfeld, Director of the Jewish Studies Program, Indiana University, Bloomington, Indiana (Indiana University Discussion Series).

ADL IU

Jewish and Christian Elements in the Western Philosophical Tradition. 1967. 70 minutes/2 cassettes, mono.

UTSV

The Jewishness of Jesus. Thesis Theological Cassettes 8: 1 (1977). By Samuel Sandmel. 23 minutes/cassette, mono.

UTSV

Jews and the Ecumenical Council. n.d. By Eric Goldman. 57 minutes/cassette, mono.

UTSV

Jews, Muslims, and Christians. 1983. 30 minutes/color/video cassette. $40.00.

An exploration of the religious and cultural differences and similarities among Jews, Muslims, and Christians. With Daniel Pipes, History Department, University of Chicago, and Dr. Alvin Rosenfeld, Director of the Jewish Studies Program, Indiana University, Bloomington, Indiana (Indiana University Discussion Series).

ADL IU

The Judaeo-Christian Dialogue. 1964. By Jakob Jocz. Missions Lectureship, No. III. Cassette, mono.

UTSV

Judaism and the New Testament. 1974. 30 minutes /b & w/16 mm film.

NCCC UTSV

Judaism in the Age of Jesus. 1968. By Samuel Sandmel. 27 minutes/cassette, mono.

UTSV

The Messianic Idea in Jewish History. 1983. 30 minutes/color/video cassette. $40.00.

A discussion of the personalities and theologies of messiahs throughout Jewish history. With Dr. Gerson Cohen, Chancellor of the Jewish Theological Seminary, New York, New York, and Dr. Alvin Rosenfeld, Director of the Jewish Studies Program, Indiana University, Bloomington, Indiana (Indiana University Discussion Series).

ADL IU

Ninth National Workshop on Christian-Jewish Relations. "Coming to Grips with Our Past: Forging Our Future." 1986. Cassettes of varying lengths. $4.50 for individual tapes, full set $99.00 Add $1.00/tape, maximum $7.00 for shipping.

Opening Session:
Eugene J. Fisher, Arie Brouwer, David Gordis.

Plenaries:
Christianity in the Context of Second Temple Judaism
"The Teaching of Jesus in His Context," Daniel Harrington.
"Approaching Early Christian Writings: Some Jewish Perspectives," Michael Cook.
The Parting of the Ways: Issues, Problems, Consequences
"A Jewish Perspective," Martha Himmelfarb.
"A Christian Perspective," John S. Gager.

Medieval Development: Institutionalizing the Tensions and Conflicts
  "Scholastics, Scholars and Saints," Jaroslav Pelikan.
  "The Jewish Situation: Rabbis and Philosophers," Jeremy Cohen.
Dialogue after the Holocaust and the Situation Today
  "Jewish Concerns after the Holocaust," Irving Greenberg.
  "Christian Concerns after the Holocaust," John T. Pawlikowski.
Workshops:
  "Jewish/Christian Relations in the Classroom: A Workshop for
    Educators," (two cassettes) Eugene J. Fisher, Judith H. Banki.
  "A Workshop on the Holocaust," Franklin Littell, Judith Muffs,
    Alan Udoff.
  "How to Conduct Local Interfaith Dialogue," Alfred Wolf,
    Royal M. Vadikan.
  "Faith As a Source of Daily Living," Delores Leckey, Mark G.
    Loeb.
  "Feminist Concerns in Judaism and Christianity," Gloria
    Albrecht, Shiela Russian, Jacqueline G. Wexler.
  "Passion Plays and Holy Week Liturgies," Jack Kelley, Alan
    Mittleman.
  "Religion and Public Schools," Roger A. Emmert, Stephen Fuchs,
    Elliott Wright.
  "The Rise of Evangelicals: Implications for Jewish-Christian
    Relations," A. James Rudin, George J. Sheridan.
  "The U.S. Economy: Religious Perspectives," Ronald
    Kreitemeyer, David Saperstein.
  "Jewish-Christian-Muslim Relations in U.S. Society," Clark
    Lobenstine, Robert D. Crane, Elaine K. Hollander.
  "Jewish and Christian Liturgies: Developments Reflecting the
    Interfaith Encounter," Asher Finkel, Lawrence Frizzell.
  "Jewish and Christian Understandings of the State of Israel,"
    Robert O. Freedman, J. Bryan Hehir, Robert L. Brashear.
  "Apartheid: Jews and Christians Confront Racism," John
    Richard, A. James Rudin.
  "How Communities Confront Violence and Extremism," Edward
    Leavy, Stanley Sollins.
  "Looking at the Biblical Text," Leon Klenicki, Edward Dobson.
  "Religious Freedom in Eastern Europe and the Soviet Union,"
    Ann Gillen, Isaac C. Rottenberg, Stephen D. Solender.
  "War and Peace in a Nuclear Age," Annette Daum, Walter
    Sullivan.
Walters Art Gallery:
  "Judaism and the Genesis of Christian Art," Robert P. Bergman.
Panel Discussion:
  Panel Discussion by Plenary Speakers. Alan Udoff, Moderator.
Closing Ceremony

CPU

Our Common Bonds. Thesis Theological Cassettes 5: 9 (1974), by Marc
  H. Tanenbaum. 21 minutes/cassette, mono.

  UTSV

The Relationship between Christianity and Judaism. 1972. By W. D. Davies.
50 minutes/6 cassettes, mono.

UTSV

What Conversation Can There Be between Christianity and Judaism? 1961.
Faith in Action Series. No. 10. By Will Herberg. 14 minutes/7 in.
reel tape, 3-3/4 ips., mono.

UTSV

B. Holocaust

About the Holocaust. n.d. 26 minutes/color/video cassette. Purchase
$40.00.

A young American woman, daughter of a survivor of the Nazi death
camps, tells about her personal search for knowledge of the Holocaust
years and explains why the study of the Holocaust is important now,
though it is many years after the events. Produced by the Holocaust
Survivors Film Project, Inc., the videotape, which includes first-hand
accounts from a number of survivors, as well as documentary footage,
reveals the fate of European Jewry in the decade between 1935 and
the end of the Second World War.

ADL

Act of Faith. 1961. 28 minutes/b & w/16 mm film/video cassette. 16
mm film rental $40.00, purchase $350.00, 3/4" video $350.00, 1/2" video
$260.00.

This is the dramatic story of the heroic Danish resistance movement
against Hitler, originally presented on CBS-TV. Filmed in Denmark,
it is a first-hand account of the role played by the Danish people in
saving their Jewish compatriots from Nazi extermination.

ADL AF CBS CF SUCB

Ages of Anguish: The Holocaust. 1978. 124 frames/color/filmstrip with
15 minute cassette, mono., and guide.

UTSV

The Anatomy of Nazism. n.d. 55 frames/color/filmstrip and kits available.
Purchase $15.00.

An historic presentation of the social, cultural, economic, and political
workings of fascism in Hitler's Germany. Although focused on Germany,
this filmstrip succeeds in reflecting the general threat to democracy
of all forms of totalitarianism.

ADL

Anne Frank in Maine. 1979. 28 minutes/color/16 mm film/video cassette/
     discussion guide. 16 mm rental $40.00, purchase $375.00, video cassette
     $40.00.

     The Junior High School class in Kennebunk, Maine learns about the
     Holocaust. Students question adults who lived through those years.
     Gradually, the whole community becomes involved. When the class
     decides to perform The Diary of Anne Frank, the local church provides
     the stage. The minister, townspeople, students and their parents
     comment on the Holocaust study program and its effect on the children
     involved. Helpful for those developing programs for teaching about
     the Holocaust in their communities.

     ADL SUCB

Anne Frank: Legacy for Our Time. n.d. 19 minutes and 65 frames each/
     b & w/2 filmstrips with audio/discussion guide. Purchase set $81.00.

     The story of Anne Frank unfolds as portions of her diary reveal how
     the different periods of her life were shaped by world events: her
     early years in Germany, her childhood in Amsterdam, the two years
     spent in hiding in the "secret annex," and her tragic end in the Bergen-
     Belsen concentration camp. Using the Anne Frank story as a catalyst,
     the filmstrip examines the relationship between prejudice and
     discrimination, identifies the elements of fascism, and describes
     the roles played by propaganda and scapegoating when Jews are
     exploited by fascists. Showing how Jews and other groups were treated
     by the Nazis, the filmstrip examines neo-fascist groups that exist
     today.

     ADL

Avenue of the Just. 1978. 55 minutes/color/16mm film/video cassette.
     16mm film rental $50.00, purchase $450.00, video cassette $70.00.

     In Jerusalem, at the Yad Vashem memorial to the six million Jews
     who perished during the Holocaust, there is a garden surrounded by
     a tree-lined walk which commemorates heroism and life. Each tree
     on the Avenue of the Just bears the names of a Christian who saved
     Jewish lives during the terrible Hitler years. Ten of these valiant
     people—and some of the people they rescued—recount their personal
     experiences in this extraordinary film. The film explores the
     motivations of the rescuers whose deeds imperiled their friends, their
     families, and themselves. Filmed in the United States, Western Europe,
     and Israel, "The Avenue of the Just" includes interviews with Anne
     Frank's father, with the people who hid the Frank family in an
     Amsterdam warehouse, and sequences showing the house today.

     ADL AF

The Camera of My Family: Four Generations in Germany: 1845-1945.
     1979. 18 minutes/color/filmstrip 123 frames/video cassette/discussion
     guide. Video cassette $40.00, purchase filmstrip $40.00.

     An award-winning production which tells the story of one upper-middle
     class German Jewish family, set against a search for personal identity.

When Catherine Hanf Noren, photographer and author, finds a collection of family photographs which reveals her "secret past," she begins her quest for knowledge about her relatives and herself. Her discovery of their lives in Germany until the Second World War and their fate during the years of Nazi rule symbolize the fate of all European Jewry during the Holocaust years.

ADL

Confronting the Moral Implications of the Holocaust. n.d. 58 minutes/ cassette. $7.50.

Raul Hilberg, one of the leading scholars on the Holocaust, approaches it as a twentieth-century phenomenon in its bureaucratic and technological character. Using the German railroad system as a case in point, Hilberg draws a chilling picture of the people who played a part in the slaughter.

ADL

The Courage to Care. n.d. 16mm film/color/video cassette. 16mm film rental $35.00, purchase $350.00, video purchase 1/2" $60.00, 3/4" $40.00.

A film about non-Jews who rescued Jews during the Holocaust; exceptional both as an educational resource and for personal enlightenment. A variety of materials has been developed for use in conjunction with this film.

ADL

Forever Yesterday. 1980. 55 minutes/color/video cassette. Rental only, $50.00.

Produced by WNEW-TV in cooperation with the Holocaust Survivors Film Project, this Emmy Award-winning documentary consists of unforgettable interviews with Jewish survivors who tell about the past: their lives in pre-Nazi Europe, the round-ups, the transports, the camps, and liberation. They present a wealth of details about what life was like amidst death during the years of the Holocaust.

ADL MM

Genocide. 1975. 52 minutes/color/16mm film/discussion guide. Rental only, $75.00.

A documentary film that tells the inhuman story of Hitler's "final solution." Set within an historic frame--from the 1920s, when waves of anti-Semitism swept through Germany, to 1945, when the remnants of European Jewry were released from the death camps--the film exposes the methodical insanity of the Nazi era. Extraordinary film footage, much of it never presented elsewhere, and interviews with death camp survivors, as well as with Germans who were directly involved in implementing the "final solution," combine to make this the definitive documentary on the Holocaust. Produced by Thames Television as part of "The World at War" series, narrated by Sir Laurence Olivier.

ADL AF PU

Joseph Schultz. 1973. 14 minutes/color/16mm film/video cassette, 16 mm film rental $30.00, purchase $240.00, purchase video $120.00.

Vital questions concerning personal moral choice vs. obedience to authority are raised in this film based on an actual incident which occurred during the Second World War. Joseph Schultz is a soldier in the Nazi army fighting in Yugoslavia. He has been a "good soldier," following orders which resulted in death and destruction. Yet, one day when Schultz is ordered to take his place as a member of a firing squad and execute a group of villagers, he refuses to raise his rifle. Forced to choose between killing or being killed, Schultz is executed with them.

ADL AF BYU IU KSU PU PSU SU SUNB WP UCB UI UM UN UP UW WP

Let My People Go. 1969. 54 minutes/b & w/16mm film. $37.00.

The Jews in dispersion are seen through the lens of the Holocaust and the establishment of a homeland as a haven for Jewish refugees.

FI FSU NIU ULI UM UNE

Light and Shadow. n.d. 19 minutes/color/16mm film. Rental $30.00, purchase $235.00.

Among the 6,000,000 people who perished in the Holocaust, there were some who shared a unique kinship. They were artists who came to Paris in the 1920s and 1930s to live in the midst of an intellectual and artistic ferment. This film focuses on the lives and works of fifteen artists. With their paints and brushes, each captured a personal vision of the world. Their canvases reveal the enormous talent of these artists who would soon share a common fate: they were all to perish in the death camps.

ADL

Memorial. n.d. 17 minutes/color/16mm film. Rental $15.00.

Although no major underground movement arose in Nazi Germany, a few brave people sought vainly to resist the madness of the Third Reich. For their efforts, they perished. The heroic attempts of these clergymen, labor leaders and students—all non-Jews—are recounted, through World War II documentary films, still photographs, and contemporary sequences filmed in West Berlin at a church built as a memorial to their valor. Produced under the auspices of the government of the city of West Berlin.

ADL AF SUCB

Memory of a Moment. n.d. 10 minutes/color/video cassette. Purchase
3/4" $50.00, 1/2" $40.00.

In this MacNeil-Lehrer News Hour segment with Canadian Broadcasting
Corporation's reporter Jerry Thompson, two men whose lives touched
forty years ago are reunited on the anniversary of the liberation of
Buchenwald. Robert Waisman, who had been imprisoned in the German
concentration camp, and Leon Bass, a black American who participated
in their liberation. Bass was the first black man Waisman had ever
seen. He touched his face to determine that he was real. For Bass,
given the fact that he was a black soldier in a segregated army, his
personal pain took on another perspective. Bass, now a history teacher,
comments: "Human suffering is universal. Your pain is my pain."
Out of the tragedy of the Holocaust and World War II, Robert Waisman
and Leon Bass offer a hope for a future free from prejudice and hate.

ADL

Music of Auschwitz. 1978. 16 minutes/color/16mm film/video cassette.
16mm film rental $40.00, purchase $325.00, video cassette purchase
$325.00.

In this 60 Minutes segment originally televised by CBS-TV, newsman
Morley Safer accompanies Auschwitz survivor Fania Fenelon on her
return to the infamous concentration camp where, as a young woman,
she was a member of the bizarre Auschwitz women's orchestra. Ms.
Fenelon tells of her journey through the hell of the Holocaust from
her initial imprisonments in Paris as a member of the French
underground to her deportation when it was learned that she was Jewish.
As a member of the orchestra, Ms. Fenelon was a witness to life in
the death camp, playing march cadences by day for prisoners on their
way to the gas chambers and waltz tempos at night for the
entertainment of the Nazi guards. In her uniquely personal account,
Ms. Fenelon captures the experiences of all Holocaust survivors.

ADL CBS CF KSU UA ULI UMI UMIS USF

Night and Fog. 1955. 31 minutes/color/16mm film. Rental $50.00.

A brilliant film on the concentration camp world, in all its piercing
and compelling truth, by one of the foremost French directors, Alain
Resnais. Resnais takes his camera to major concentration camps of
the Nazi era, now hauntingly barren and innocent, and over these scenes
superimposes historic footage evoking the dreadful past. French
narration with English subtitles.

ADL AF BU BYU CWU FI FSU INSU ISU IU LSU MGH MSU NIU SIU
UA UC UCB UI UK ULI UM UMA UMO USF UU UW UWA UWLC

Nightmare: The Immigration of Joachim and Rachel. 1976. 23
minutes/color/16mm film. Rental $40.00, purchase $360.00.

A dramatization of the harrowing experiences of two young orphans
—a brother and a sister—who escape not only from the Warsaw Ghetto

but also from a train carrying passengers bound for certain death. Black and white sequences recall their nightmare while color scenes describe their trip to freedom. Freedom is the United States, where they are welcomed by a caring uncle.

ADL JMS

Poetry of Sonia Weitz. n.d. Audio presentation or 38-page book. $6.00.

This is a selection of poetry about European Jews and the Nazi Holocaust that introduces readers to the family of a surviving Holocaust victim.

DWP

The Rise and Fall of the Third Reich. Four-part series. 1972. 30 minutes per film/b & w/16mm film. Rental $40.00, complete set rental $130.00.

Part I: The Rise of Hitler. Chronicles how Adolf Hitler and his political cohorts in the Nazi Party manipulated events during their country's crises to achieve power.

ADL FI INSU ISU PSU UK ULI UMI UMIS USF UU UWLC

Part II: Nazi Germany: Years of Triumph. Germany between 1933 and 1939, when some sixty-seven million people willingly permitted themselves to become puppets of the Third Reich.

INSU ISU PSU SU UA UI UK ULI UMI UMIS USF UWLC

Part III: Gotterdammerung: Collapse of the Third Reich. In the four years between 1941 and 1945, Hitler's dream of a "thousand-year Reich" turned into the nightmare of World War II. By the spring of 1945, the Allies were victorious and Hitler was dead. Many of his closest followers were imprisoned.

INSU ISU PSU SU UA UK ULI UMI UMIS USF UTA UU UWLC

Part IV: Nuremberg Trial. Traces the trials and attempts to establish that those who conspire to wage war stand guilty of crimes against humanity.

KSU PSU UI ULI UMIS USF UWLC

Scenes from the Holocaust. n.d. 10 minutes/color/16mm film. Rental $20.00, purchase $115.00.

Searing testimony to the hell of the Holocaust has survived in the pen, pencil, and charcoal sketches drawn by Jewish artists who were among the millions sent to the death camps. These sketches form the visual component of this documentary film, set against a musical soundtrack. With minimal narration in the film, the sketches speak for themselves. They evoke emotions that transcend the power of the traditional documentary on the Holocaust. Each sketch is a personal scream of anguish from a victim of the Holocaust--the artist.

ADL

Survivors of the Holocaust. n.d. 25 minutes/color/video cassette. $75.00.

From the Holocaust Resource Center of Buffalo, this documentary features the moving testimony of Holocaust survivors and the children of survivors. Interspersed with their narration—which details their lives before, during, and after World War II—are photographs and footage actually shot in concentration camps. Originally aired on WTVB-TV, written and produced by Rich Newberg, photographed and edited by Dan Summerville.

ADL

Teaching about the Holocaust: Toward a Methodology. n.d. 49 minutes/cassette. $7.50.

Henry Friedlander, author of On the Holocaust and Professor of History at Brooklyn College, takes the position that the Holocaust is a major historical event, similar in its impact to the Fall of Rome or the French Revolution. Dr. Friedlander stresses that "the study of the Holocaust must involve both the event and its impact."

ADL

Then and Now: The Experiences of a Teacher. n.d. 50 minutes/cassette. $7.50.

Elie Wiesel, noted author, teacher, and death-camp survivor, talks about the Holocaust and those who would deny that it happened.

ADL

34 Years after Hitler. 1979. 19 minutes/color/16mm film/video cassette. 16mm film rental, $40.00; purchase film, $375.00; purchase video cassette, $375.00.

This CBS 60 Minutes report documents the resurgence of Nazism in West Germany today, where eighty to ninety groups preach Hitler's anti-Semitism and work toward the day when they can take control of the government. Included are sequences showing their activities, clandestine meetings, hatemongering street rallies, indoctrination camps for youngsters, and military maneuvers using arms and armaments purchased from war surplus. Propaganda material is traced to a neo-Nazi organization operating out of Lincoln, Nebraska, revealed as a conduit for funds from supporters around the world.

ADL CBS CF KSU UA UCB ULI UMI

Through the Weapons of the Spirit: Le Chambon, 1940-1944. n.d. 20 minutes/color/16mm film.

Jewish filmmaker Pierre Sauvage has brought to life a mountain community that helped save the Jews during the Holocaust. This small town in France became a haven of refuge for the oppressed, where over five thousand Jews were given life by five thousand Christians.

FLC

Warsaw Ghetto. 1966. 51 minutes/b & w/16mm film. Rental $30.00.

Film footage, taken from 1940 to 1943, of the mile-square, walled-off Warsaw Ghetto, into which the Nazis herded the city's 600,000 Jews. Assembled over a period of twenty years by Alexander Bernfes, a Ghetto survivor and narrator of the film, the photographs and motion pictures of life and death in the Ghetto were taken by cameramen of the German army, the S.S., and the Gestapo. Produced by BBC-TV.

ADL UA ULI UM UP USU UW UWA

Witness to the Holocaust. 1983. 17-20 minutes for each section/b & w/video formats with 7 sections. Rental $150.00 for entire episode for one week, purchase entire series $600.00.

CG

C. Israel

Abraham's People. 1983. 53 minutes/color/16mm film/video cassette. 16mm film rental $35.00, purchase $425.00, video cassette $325.00.

For more than four hundred years Jews have lived in or close by this one small corner of earth called Israel. Although they were dispersed by the Roman Emperor Titus in 70 C.E., they held tight to their religious and cultural heritage, always looking longingly over their shoulders to the land of their origins. In a series of absorbing, informative, and graphically illustrated interviews with scholars who trace a long history in the Middle East during the Diaspora, we learn of the Sephardim, who for almost two thousand years participated in and contributed to the culture, economy, learning, and well-being of nations from Persia to Morocco to Syria, Turkey, Italy, and Spain. Destiny kept them effectively separated until the end of the nineteenth century, when at last they began to regroup in Palestine. They brought with them some of the culture and many of the traditions of the lands in which they had dwelt, in addition to their religion, which had succored them and kept them one people despite their wanderings. In 1948, Abraham's people finally reunited as Jewish citizens in the State of Israel.

ADL

After the War. n.d. 28 minutes/color/16mm film. Rental $25.00, purchase $400.00.

Between 1948 and 1973, Israel fought four wars against belligerents whose aim was the total destruction of the Jewish state. For each victory many of Israel's men died. This poignant documentary tells the stories of the survivors: parents, wives, children, and friends. They talk about their memories of their loved ones, how each bears the tragedy, and what their sacrifice means for themselves, their country, and the Jewish people.

ADL

__Among Sacred Stones.__ n.d. 7 minutes/color/16mm film. Rental $30.00—
minimum two days.

A short silent film that distinguishes the attitudes and beliefs of the
Jewish people by looking at their grief during visits to the Wailing
Wall and military cemeteries.

AM

__Exodus.__ 1960. 207 minutes/color/16mm film. $75.00.

The struggle of German Jews to reach Palestine. Directed by Otto
Preminger, it stars Paul Newman and Eva Marie Saint.

UART WSU

__Israel--Covenant and Conflict.__ 1969. 30 minutes/b & w/16mm film.

This film, a series of discussions with Dr. Franklin Littell, Father Edward
Flannery, and Mitchell Krauss, is concerned with Christianity's
relationship with Israel. It also touches on significant issues such as
biblical prophesies, Jerusalem's future, and the Arab refugee problem.

ADL SUCB

__Israel: The Right to Be.__ n.d. 52 minutes/color/16mm film. Rental $35.00,
purchase $350.00.

The history of the country since its establishment in 1948 and the
mood of its people at the midpoint of the 1970s are the subjects of
this documentary film. Written and produced by Dore Schary, Broadway
and Hollywood writer-director-producer, it explores issues of the past
and the present. Among them: the legal rights to the land, the human
rights of the Palestinians, and the religious rights of all people. In
focusing on the search for a lasting peace in the Middle East, the film
is of concern to all people.

ADL

__The Israelis.__ 1973. 35 minutes/color/16mm film/video cassette. Rental
$30.00, purchase $575.00, video cassette $575.00.

Amos Elon, distinguished journalist and author of The Israelis: Founder
and Sons, narrates this documentary aired over the CBS-TV network
after the Yom Kippur War. Elon's unique perception of his country
and its people reveals the paradoxes and complexities of life in Israel.
The film focuses on Israeli Arabs and Jews as well as Arabs living
in the occupied areas. They are painfully honest in verbalizing the
emotional toll taken by the Holocaust and twenty-six years of war.

ADL CF UA UCB UCO UI UM USF

Jerusalem: City of David. n.d. 21 minutes/color/16mm film. Rental
$20.00, purchase $250.00.

Produced by WPVI-TV, Philadelphia, this film treatment of the ancient
city of Jerusalem combines both its history and contemporary life.
The film depicts the significance of Jerusalem to Jews, Christians,
and Moslems. Featured is the late Reverend Douglas Young, then
President of the American Institute for Holy Land Studies, who resided
in Jerusalem. Reverend Young describes the role of the Israelis as
administrators of the Holy City.

ADL

My Father's House. n.d. 28 minutes/color/16mm film. $20.00.

In the Old City of Jerusalem, young Americans have come to study
Torah, the sacred books of Judaism, and to re-identify with their
ancient spiritual heritage. This film documents young people who
searched for an ethical, moral, and spiritual guide and found it in
the Torah, which affects all aspects of their lives. Filmed following
the Yom Kippur War, the search for peace is uppermost in their
conversation. They also talk about ethics and morality in Western
society, personal freedom within moral responsibility, and how to
live life to its fullest potential.

ADL

Palestinians and the P.L.O. 1975. 28 minutes/color/16mm film.

The refusal to accept the PLO as the legitimate representative of
the Palestinians is explained by Joseph Tekoah, Israel's former United
Nations Ambassador.

ADL SUCB

A People Chosen: Who Is a Jew? 57 minutes/color/16mm film. $78.50.

Jews born in many different countries and with faiths ranging from
agnostic to orthodox discuss the issue of "Who is a Jew?" The variety
of answers shows a great diversity within Judaism.

KSU MF POSU UI ULI UMI

The People of Nes Ammim. 1979. By Bill Moyers Journal. 60
minutes/color/16mm film.

UTSV

A Promise Shared. n.d. 24 minutes/color/16mm film $17.50.

ADL

<u>This New Frontier</u>. n.d. 27 minutes/color/16mm film. $17.50.

Winner of the 1971 George Foster Peabody Award for distinguished television, this is a film about the people of Israel seen from a fresh point of view. It covers the length and breadth of Israel—from military/ agricultural settlements on the Golan Heights to the beaches of Eliat, from Jerusalem's holy shrines to cosmopolitan Tel Aviv—and captures what the people are all about. Produced by WWL-TV, New Orleans.

ADL

D. Anti–Judaism

<u>An American Girl</u>. 1958. 29½ minutes/b & w/16mm film. Rental $20.00.

This film, based on an actual incident that occurred in the 1950s, tells the story of an American teenager who is mistakenly believed to be Jewish by her friends and neighbors. The particular incident revolves around anti-Semitism, but the story is basically concerned with irrational prejudice.

ADL

<u>Anti-Semitism in America</u>. 1961. 25 minutes/b & w/16mm film. Rental $20.00.

Dr. Melvin Tumin, Professor of Sociology and Anthropology at Princeton University, presents an in-depth study of the attitudes and motivations behind anti-Semitism. Dr. Tumin places special emphasis on the "gentle people of prejudice."

ADL SUCB UP

<u>The Diary of Anne Frank</u>. 1959. 150 minutes/b & w/16mm film. $50.00.

FI

<u>The Hangman</u>. 1964. 12 minutes/color/16mm film. $15.00.

This short film takes Maurice Odgen's poem and uses it to point out a lesson of prejudice; if we ignore repressive measures against minorities, perhaps we will be the next victims.

BU BYU ENM FSU IDSU ISU KSU MGH MHM MSU NIU OSU POSU PSU SU UA UC UCLA UI ULI UMI UNE UNH USF USU UW UWA UWLC UWY WSU

<u>L'Chaim—To Life</u>. 1973. 84 minutes/b & w/16mm film. $50.00 by special arrangement.

Eli Wallach chronicles the plight of the Jews in Czarist Russia, World Wars I and II, the Holocaust, the Warsaw Ghetto, and up to the creation of Israel using photographs and rare motion pictures, archival documents, as well as new footage.

HM ULI

The Mad Adventures of "Rabbi" Jacob. 1974. 96 minutes/color/16mm film. $200.00.

An indirect treatment of anti-Judaism that treats a serious subject with the use of slapstick comedy.

FI

Memorandum. 1966. 58 minutes/b & w/16mm film. $25.00.

To commemorate the twentieth anniversary of their liberation from Nazi concentration camps, a group of survivors returns to Germany. Their pilgrimage is recorded in this Canadian National Film Board documentary, which compares the Germany of the past and the present. The horrors of Auschwitz, Bergen-Belsen, and Treblinka are contrasted with a contemporary court trial where the perpetrators of the Holocaust are set free and absolved from guilt in carrying out Goering's orders in his memorandum on "the final solution." The film is grim evidence that those who did nothing to prevent the Holocaust are as guilty as those who actually committed crimes. And it is a warning that if it can happen in the land of Beethoven and Heine it can happen anywhere.

ADL MGH NFBC POSU PU SH SUCB UCO UM UMI UWA UWY

Oberammergau--The Passion Story and the Jews. 1983. 20 minutes/color/ 16mm film/video cassette. Rental $20.00, purchase $225.00, purchase video cassette, $125.00.

In 1980, an Anti-Defamation League delegation was invited to Oberammergau to attend a preview of the Passion Play, a new production which eliminated, in part, some of the gross anti-Semitic distortions that characterized previous productions. This film documents the delegation's encounters with the mayor of Oberammergau, the monk who supervised the current production's script, and discussions among the delegates on the changes which were made, the revisions which are still needed, and implications for future productions. The documentary, narrated by Professor Leonard Swidler, Professor of Catholic Thought and Interreligious Dialogue of Temple University, is an excellent discussion starter, opening the way for an investigation into the roots of anti-Semitism and its link to the deicide charge.

ADL

E. Immigrant Contributions

Arthur Rubinstein—Love of Life. 1968. 91 minutes/color/b & w/16mm film. $75.00 special rate.

A journey with one of the greatest pianists of all time. This film follows Rubinstein on a concert tour and through his long and extraordinary life.

NYF

Immigrants and Missionaries. 1983. 30 minutes/color/video cassette. $40.00.

An appraisal of the work and milieu of social reformer Jacob Riis. With Dr. Jeffrey Gurock, Associate Professor of Jewish History, Revel Graduate School, Yeshiva University, New York, New York, and Dr. Todd Endelman, Associate Professor of History, University of Michigan, Ann Arbor, Michigan (Indiana University Discussion Series).

ADL IU

Lawyer from Boston—Louis D. Brandeis. 1957. 30 minutes/b & w/16mm film. $19.00.

A film about the discovery of Jewish heritage by Supreme Court Justice and Zionist leader Louis D. Brandeis.

ELF

Rendezvous with Freedom. 1973. 56 minutes/color/16mm film. $65.00, 37 minute version $35.00.

This film is a helpful introduction to the history of the Jews in the United States.

AUB BYU IU KSU PSU

Soviet Dissidents in Exile. 1983. 28 minutes/color/video cassette. $40.00.

In this documentary, five men who dared to challenge the Soviet regime and were exiled for it talk about their days in the U.S.S.R. and what life is like for them now in the U.S.A. In many ways, they epitomize the experiences of all immigrants who have faced the problem of adjusting to a new country, a different culture, and the openness of a democratic society. Yet, these are men with a special point of view, who have lived in the limelight in two countries, as traitors in one and heroes in the other. From their unique perspective they reflect on the past, present, and future—for themselves and for the world.

ADL

Media

170

Addresses

AHC	Alba House Communications Canfield, Ohio 44406
AF	Alden Films 7820 20th Avenue Brooklyn, New York 11214
ADL	Anti-Defamation League of B'nai B'rith Audio-Visual Department 315 Lexington Avenue New York, New York 10016
AM	Arthur Mokin Productions, Inc. 17 West 60th Street New York, New York 10023
AUB	Audio-Brandon Films, Inc. 34 MacQuesten Parkway Mt. Vernon, New York 10550
BU	Boston University Krasker Memorial Film Library 565 Commonwealth Avenue Boston, Massachusetts 02215
BYU	Brigham Young University Audio-Visual Services 101 Harvey Fletcher Building Provo, Utah 84602
CBS	Columbia Broadcasting System 383 Madison Avenue New York, New York 10018
CF	Carousel Films, Inc. 1501 Broadway, Suite 1503 New York, New York 10036
CG	Cinema Guild 1697 Broadway New York, New York 10019
CPU	Cassette Productions Unlimited P.O. Box 66 Pasadena, California 92201
CWU	Central Washington University Media Library Services, IMC Ellensburg, Washington 98926

DWP   Don Weitz Publishing Co.
6083 Village Glen Drive, 4250
Dallas, Texas 75206

ELF   Eternal Light Film Library
United Synagogue of America
155 Fifth Avenue
New York, New York 10010

FI   Films, Inc.
1144 Wilmette Avenue
Wilmette, Illinois 60091

FLC   Friends of Le Chambon
8033 Sunset Boulevard, L784
Los Angeles, California 90046

FSU   Florida State University
Instructional Support Center Film Library
54 Johnson Building
Tallahassee, Florida 32306

HM   Harold Mayer
155 West 72nd Street
New York, New York 10023

IDSU   Idaho State University
Audio-Visual Services
Campus Box 8064
Pocatello, Idaho 83209

INSU   Indiana State University
Audio-Visual Services
Stalker Hall
Terre Haute, Indiana 47807

IU   Indiana University
Audio-Visual Center
Bloomington, Indiana 47405

ISU   Iowa State University
Media Resource Center
121 Pearson Hall
Ames, Iowa 50011

JMS   Jewish Media Service/JWB
14 East 26th Street
New York, New York 10010

KSU   Kent State University
Audio-Visual Services
330 Library Building
Kent, Ohio 44242

LSU	Louisiana State University 16mm Film Library 118 Himes Hall Instructional Resource Center Baton Rouge, Louisiana 70737
MF	Marquis Film Distributors, Inc. 416 West 45th Street New York, New York 10036
MM	Metromedia 250 East 67th Street New York, New York 10021
MMM	Mass Media Ministries 2116 North Charles Street Baltimore, Maryland 21218
MGH	McGraw-Hill Films 110 Fifteenth Street Del Mar, California 92014
MSU	Michigan State University Instructional Media Center East Lansing, Michigan 48824
NCCC	National Council of Churches of Christ in U.S.A. 475 Riverside Drive New York, New York 10115
NFBC	National Film Board of Canada 1250 Avenue of the Americas New York, New York 10020
NIU	Northern Illinois University Film Library Altgeld 114 DeKalb, Illinois 60115
NYF	New Yorker Films 43 West 61st Street New York, New York 10023
OSU	Oklahoma State University A-V Center Stillwater, Oklahoma 74078
POSU	Portland State University Film Library Portland, Oregon 97270

PSU   Pennsylvania State University
                                       Audio-Visual Services
                                       Special Services Building
                                       University Park, Pennsylvania 16802

PU   Purdue University
                                       Film Library
                                       Stewart Center
                                       West Lafayette, Indiana 47907

SU   Syracuse University
                                       Film Rental Center
                                       1455 East Colvin Street
                                       Syracuse, New York 13210

SUCB   State University College at Buffalo
                                       Film Library
                                       Communication Center 102
                                       1300 Elmwood Avenue
                                       Buffalo, New York 14222

SUNB   State University of New York at Buffalo
                                       Media Library, 24 Capen Hall
                                       Buffalo, New York 14260

UA   University of Arizona
                                       Film Library
                                       Audio-Visual Building
                                       Tucson, Arizona 85721

UC   University of Colorado
                                       Academic Services
                                       Box 379
                                       Boulder, Colorado 80309

UCB   University of California
                                       Extension Media Center
                                       2176 Shattuck
                                       Berkeley, California 94704

UCLA   University of California/Los Angeles
                                       Instructional Media Library
                                       Powell Library
                                       Room 46
                                       Los Angeles, California 90024

UCO   University of Connecticut
                                       Center for Instructional Media and Technology
                                       Storrs, Connecticut 06268

UI   University of Iowa
                                       Audio-Visual Center
                                       C-5 Seashore Hall
                                       Iowa City, Iowa 52242

UK   University of Kansas
                            Film Rental Library
                            Continuing Education Building
                            Lawrence, Kansas 66045

ULI   University of Illinois Film Center
                            1325 South Oak Street
                            Champaign, Illinois 61820

UM   University of Michigan
                            Michigan Media
                            400 Fourth Street
                            Ann Arbor, Michigan 48103

UMA   University of Maine
                            Instructional Systems Center
                            12 Shibles Hall
                            Orono, Maine 04469

UMI   University of Minnesota
                            University Film and Video
                            1313 Fifth Street, SE
                            Minneapolis, Minnesota 55414

UMO   University of Montana
                            Instructional Materials Service
                            Missoula, Montana 59812

UN   University of Nevada/Reno
                            Film Library
                            Getchell Library
                            Reno, Nevada 89557

UNE   University of Nebraska/Lincoln
                            Instructional Media Center
                            Nebraska Hall 421
                            Lincoln, Nebraska 68588

UNH   University of New Hampshire
                            Department of Media Services
                            Dimond Library
                            Durham, New Hampshire 03824

UP   University of Pittsburgh
                            Media Services
                            6-20 Hillman Library
                            Pittsburgh, Pennsylvania 15260

USF   University of South Florida
                            Film Library
                            4202 Fowler Avenue
                            Tampa, Florida 33620

USU

Utah State University
Audio-Visual Services
Logan, Utah 84322

UTA

University of Texas at Austin
General Libraries
Film Library
Box W
Austin, Texas 78713

UTSV

Union Theological Seminary in Virginia
3401 Brook Road
Richmond, Virginia 23227

UU

University of Utah
Instructional Services
207 Milton Bennison Hall
Salt Lake City, Utah 84112

UW

University of Wisconsin/Madison
Bureau of Audio-Visual Instruction
1327 University Avenue
P.O. Box 2093
Madison, Wisconsin 53701

UWA

University of Washington/Seattle
Instructional Media Services
237 Kane Hall DG-10
Seattle, Washington 98195

UWLC

University of Wisconsin/La Crosse
Film Rental Library
127 Wing Communications Center
1705 State Street
La Crosse, Wisconsin 54601

UWY

University of Wyoming
Audio-Visual Services
Box 3273 University Station
Room 14 Knight Hall
Laramie, Wyoming 82071

WP

Wombat Productions
Little Lake, Glendale Road
P.O. Box 70
Ossining, New York 10562

WSU

Wayne State University
Media Services
5265 Cass Avenue
Detroit, Michigan 48202

VII.
Syllabi

Syllabi are presented here as a resource for those who teach in the field of Jewish-Christian relations. Except for minor stylistic changes, the syllabi have been left in the form in which they were received from the instructors. Please see the speakers bureau for instructors' addresses, or write in care of the instructor's institution to request information or make further inquiries.

University of South Carolina
RELG 383: The Jewish-Christian Encounter   Carl D. Evans
Fall, 1985   307 Rutledge
Gambrell 247   777-4522 (O)
T-Th 2:00-3:15   776-6295 (H)

CONTENT OF THE COURSE

This course examines the rise of Judaism and Christianity in their classical forms and the encounter between the two religions throughout the centuries. Issues and problems which have emerged in the course of the encounter are placed in context and interpreted in light of their significance for understanding aspects of the Jewish-Christian encounter today.

There are four units of study:

Unit One:	Post-Biblical Judaism and Emergent Christianity
Unit Two:	Rabbinic Judaism in Canonical and Historical Context
Unit Three:	Anti-Judaism in Christianity
Unit Four:	Jews and Christians after the Holocaust

In Unit One we examine the varieties of Judaism in the post biblical period, the emergence of Christianity as (initially) a Jewish phenomenon, the recasting of Judaism in response to the destruction of the Temple in 70 C.E., and the emergence of Christianity as an increasingly Gentile phenomenon in roughly the same period. The parting of the ways between Judaism and Christianity, and the consequences thereof, are explored in anticipation of subsequent units of the course.

Unit Two presents the thesis that aspects of both continuity and change
in the rabbinic system are evident when its canonical texts are studied
in chronological sequence--from the Mishnah to the Tosefta to the
Yerushalmi (Palestinian Talmud) to the compositions of Scriptural exegesis
to the Bavli (Babylonian Talmud). We read selections from the writings
of Jacob Neusner who has pioneered in this type of analysis and consider
whether, as he has suggested, the "constancy and change" in the development
of the rabbinic system can be understood as responses to important events
in the (increasingly Christian) world of formative Judaism.

In Unit Three we take up a variety of issues which are raised by the ways
that Christianity appropriated its Jewish heritage and responded to its
ongoing encounter with Jews and Judaism throughout the centuries. We
study the deicide charge, anti-Judaism in Christian theology, Church Laws
and other manifestations of an anti-Jewish ideology within Christendom,
and Jewish responses to this tragic history.

Unit Four is a study of the variety of ways Christians and Jews have
responded to the Holocaust. The essays we read are written by historians,
theologians, and philosophers--Catholic, Protestant, and Jewish--who ask
searching questions about the meaning of the Holocaust and the role of
religion and its institutions in the post-Holocaust age. The final three
sessions are devoted to post-Vatican II developments, globally and locally,
in the Church's efforts to rethink its relationship to Judaism.

COURSE REQUIREMENTS AND GRADE DETERMINATION

Students are expected to read the assigned materials before each session
of the class and to engage in thoughtful discussion of the readings. Since
the course is designed to be discussion-oriented, class participation is a
significant requirement (see percentages below). There will also be mid-term
and final exams (essay) and a project on "Recent Developments."

The project will be explained more fully in class, but it requires the study
of recent church documents on Christianity's relationship to Judaism and
an interview with clergy of the corresponding denominations in the Columbia
area to ascertain whether, or to what extent, the official church statements
are being implemented locally. A paper which presents the student's critical
reflection on the document(s) and the interview will be due on reading
day, December 13. Those who wish additional credit may present project
reports to the class.

The course grade will be determined as follows:

Mid-term exam	20%
Final exam	30%
Project	30%
Class Participation	20%

Students who choose to present project reports to the class will have 2-5
percentage points added to their final grade, depending on the quality of
the report.

REQUIRED TEXTBOOKS (available for purchase)

    Neusner, Jacob. Judaism in the Beginning of Christianity. 1984.
    Rivkin, Ellis. What Crucified Jesus? 1984.
    Williamson, Clark. Has God Rejected His People? 1982.
    Peck, Abraham J., ed. Jews and Christians after the Holocaust. 1982.
    New English Bible (Oxford Study Edition).

ADDITIONAL REQUIRED READING (on reserve)

    Selections from the following:

    Neusner, Jacob. Invitation to the Talmud (revised edition).
    Neusner, Jacob. Midrash in Context.
    Neusner, Jacob. Messiah in Context.
    Perrin, Norman. The New Testament: An Introduction.
    Ruether, Rosemary. Faith and Fratricide.
    Wilken, Robert. John Chrysostom and the Jews.

SCHEDULE

UNIT ONE:

Post-Biblical   Judaism   and   Emergent
Christianity

Week #1
  Sept. 3   Introduction
  Sept. 5   Judaism and Christianity: Heirs of the Hebrew
                                 Scriptures. Neusner, Judaism in the Beginning
                                 of Christianity, pp. 9-14.

Week #2
  Sept. 10   The Land and the People of Israel under
                                 Roman Rule. Neusner, Judaism in the
                                 Beginning of Christianity, pp. 17-33.

                                 Rivkin, What Crucified Jesus? pp. 16-37.

  Sept. 12   Varieties of Judaism at the Beginning of
                                 the Common Era.
                                 Neusner, Judaism in the Beginning of
                                 Christianity, pp. 35-44.

                                 Rivkin, What Crucified Jesus? pp. 38-55.

Week #3
  Sept. 17   Jesus and the Pharisees.
                                 Neusner, Judaism in the Beginning of
                                 Christianity, pp. 45-88.

                                 Williamson, Has God Rejected His People?
                                 pp. 11-29.

  Sept. 19   Paul and Judaism.
                                 Williamson, Has God Rejected His People?
                                 pp. 47-63. Galatians 1-6, Romans 7, 9-11.

Week #4
Sept. 24
Responses to the Destruction of the Temple.
Neusner, Judaism in the Beginning of Christianity, pp. 89-101.
Perrin, The New Testament, pp. 169-93.

Sept. 26
Conflict and the Parting of the Ways.
Williamson, Has God Rejected His People? pp. 64-85.
John 8-10.

UNIT TWO:
Rabbinic Judaism in Canonical and Historical Context

Week #5
Oct. 1
The Mishnah.
Neusner, Invitation to the Talmud, pp. 28-69.

Oct. 10
The Bavli (Babylonian Talmud).
Neusner, Invitation to the Talmud, pp. 167-270.

Week #7
Oct. 15
What Changes? What Stays the Same? Why?
Neusner, Midrash in Context, pp. 111-37.
Neusner, Messiah in Context, pp. 167-231.

Oct. 17.
Mid-term Exam.

UNIT THREE:
Anti-Judaism in Christianity

Week #8
Oct. 22
The Adversus Judaeos Tradition.
Williamson, Has God Rejected His People? pp. 89-105.

Oct. 24
John Chrysostom, Christian Rhetoric, and the Jews (I).

Wilken, John Chrysostom and the Jews, pp. xv-94.

Week #9
Oct. 29
John Chrysostom (II).
Wilken, John Chrysostom and the Jews, pp. 95-164.

Oct. 31
Crucifixion and the Deicide Charge (I).
Williamson, Has God Rejected His People? pp. 30-46.
Mark 14-15, Matthew 26-27, Luke 22-23, John 18-19.

Week #10
Nov. 5
Crucifixion and the Deicide Charge (II).
Rivkin, What Crucified Jesus? pp. 5-15, 56-124.

Nov. 7
Anti-Jewish Church and State Laws, Crusades, Ghettos, Expulsions, etc.
Williamson, Has God Rejected His People? pp. 106-22.
Ruether, Faith and Fratricide, pp. 183-214.

Week #11
These two films, from the Heritage: Civilization and the Jews television series, provide the transition to the last unit of the course.

Nov. 12   "Roads from the Ghetto" (1789-1917).

Nov. 14   "Out of the Ashes" (1917-1945).

UNIT FOUR: Jews and Christians after the Holocaust

Week #12
Nov. 19   Jews and Religion after the Holocaust: Jewish Perspectives.

Nov. 21   Christology and the Church after the Holocaust. Peck, Jews and Christians after the Holocaust, pp. 25-52.

Week #13
Nov. 26   No Class
Nov. 28   Thanksgiving Recess

Week #14
Dec. 3   Religious Values after the Holocaust. Peck, Jews and Christians after the Holocaust, pp. 53-110.

Dec. 5   Recent Developments: The Catholic Church. Handouts, Class Reports.

Week #15
Dec. 10   Recent Developments: The Protestant Churches. Handouts, Class Reports.

Dec. 12   Recent Developments: South Carolina. Handouts.

Christian Theological Seminary, Indianapolis   1987
T-641: Jews and Christians in Dialogue   Jon Stein and Clark Williamson

The work of this course will be carried out, largely, in seminar-fashion. On occasion the presentation of material in class will be the responsibility of students. Such presentations are indicated on the following pages. The content of the course is the relationship between faithful members of two living traditions, Judaism and Christianity. This relationship will be looked at biblically, historically, and theologically.

The orientation of the course is post-Holocaust. We do our thinking as historical human beings in history, in our particular time and place. We live in the time after the Shoah, that whirlwind of destruction which befell European Jews and which discloses to us demonic tendencies close to the heart of the Christian tradition. The course begins with a session on the Holocaust and then moves to its subject matter.

The theme of the course is dialogue. The course intends to promote a relationship of conversation between members of different strands of two closely related faith-traditions. The assumption is that conversation is a more fruitful and humane relationship than conflict. The other assumption is that it is in the living relations of concrete human beings in prophetic give and take with one another that creative interchange can occur and the true and the good be found.

Term paper: Each student will submit a term paper embodying the results of his/her own critical and constructive reflections on the content of the course. That is, it should show how the student has come to understand the relationship of Judaism and Christianity to each other in the light of the study of Judaism itself, of the first-century scriptures and various scholarly perspectives on them, of the Christian theological tradition and the critique to which that tradition has been subjected of late, of the history of anti-Jewish practice engaged in by Christians and by the Church, and in the light of the critical and constructive reformulations offered by various post-Holocaust theologians. As part of its conclusion, the paper should address three issues: (a) what ought the relationship between Judaism and Christianity, between Jews and Christians, to be?; (b) why should it be so?; and (c) what can you do, practically, to help bring about this kind of relationship?

Due: Wednesday, April 29.

Class procedure: As indicated in the following class schedule, the instructors will be responsible for presenting material for discussion throughout the semester. During class sessions 11 through 15, each student will be asked to report on a book to be chosen from the list at the end of this syllabus. These presentations should seek to raise issues for class discussion. Each presentation should consist of (1) analysis of the structure of the book or article, i.e., of the question or questions it is concerned to answer; (2) an interpretation of the content of the book, i.e., of the answer or answers it gives to its question(s); and (3) a critical, i.e., reasoned response to the book or article.

Grades will be based on term papers, class presentations, and class participation.

Class schedule:

Topic 1: The Holocaust
First session: Audio-visual presentation, discussion.

Topic 2: Introduction to Judaism
Second session: Presentation by Rabbi Stein. Read Steinberg, Basic Judaism.
Third session: Presentation by Rabbi Stein. Read Steinberg, Basic Judaism.

Topic 3: The Rise of Christianity
Fourth session: Anti-Judaism in the New Testament? Read: Williamson, chaps. 1 and 4, Davies, chaps. by Hare and Townsend; presentation by Williamson on Jesus.
Fifth session: An Alternative View of Paul? Read Williamson, chap. 3; Davies, chap. by Gaston; presentation by Williamson on Paul.
Sixth session: Jewish responsibility for the crucifixion? Read Williamson, chap. 2; Williamson presentation on the issue.

Topic 4: The Condition of Jews under Christendom
Seventh session: The Adversus Judaeos tradition in church history. Read
Williamson, chap. 5, Davies, chap. by Efroymson.
Eighth session: Social incorporation of the anti-Jewish "theology."
Read Williamson, chap. 6, Davies, chap. by Davies.
Ninth session: Jewish polemics. Talmudic and midrashic passages; medieval
polemics. Materials distributed in class; presentation by Rabbi Stein.
Tenth session: Jewish responses. Materials distributed in class.

Topic 5: The Holocaust and After
Eleventh session: Read Friedlander, sections one and two.
Twelfth session: Read Friedlander, section three.
Thirteenth session: Read Friedlander, section four.
Fourteenth session: Read Greenberg essay (distributed in class) and section
five of Friedlander.
Fifteenth session: Friedlander, section six, Davies chaps. by Hellwig,
Baum, Pawlikowski, Hall, Anderson, Ruether.
Conclusion
Sixteenth session: Summary discussion.

Yom HaShoah will be observed Friday, April 24 at 8:15 p.m. at Indianapolis
Hebrew Congregation. Members of the class and their families are invited
to a special tour of the congregation beginning at 7:15 that night.

List of books for class presentation:

Eckardt, A. Roy. Elder and Younger Brothers.
Eckardt, A. Roy. Jews and Christians: The Contemporary Meeting.
Eckardt, A. Roy. Your People, My People.
Gager, John G. The Origins of Anti-Semitism.
Klein, Charlotte. Anti-Judaism in Christian Theology.
Littell, Franklin H. The Crucifixion of the Jews.
Rivkin, Ellis. What Crucified Jesus?
Rudin, A. James. Israel for Christians.
Ruether, Rosemary. Faith and Fratricide.
Sanders, E.P. Paul, The Law, and the Jewish People.
Sanders, E.P. Paul and Palestinian Judaism.
Stendahl, Krister. Paul Among Jews and Gentiles.
Thoma, Clemens. A Christian Theology of Judaism.
van Buren, Paul. Discerning the Way.
van Buren, Paul. A Christian Theology of the People Israel.
Vermes, Geza. Jesus and the World of Judaism.

THE JEWISH-CHRISTIAN ENCOUNTER
Religion Studies 151

Legih University   Fall 1985   Alice L. Eckardt

This course seeks to foster critical understanding of relations between
today's Christian and Jewish communities, and to consider the future
of that relationship. Because the present cannot be understood in isolation,

we will examine the historical, religious, and social factors that have both divided and linked the two communities across the centuries. Because we live in the century of the Holocaust, we will try to analyze antisemitism and see how such virulent attitudes and milieux came to exist in "Christian Europe."

The relationship between Jews and Christians has been a complex one on both sides. Issues of self-identity, controversies within the two communities, and changing religious emphases compounded early differences. Nevertheless, commonalities, interaction, and contacts persisted. Probably at no time in the preceding centuries has there been such vitality and innovation in the encounter as at the present, even though the older views still persist in many circles.

* * * * * * * * * *

Class meetings will involve lectures, analyses of study materials, and open-ended discussions. The nature of the course makes it advisable that the student take full part in the class sessions, which will require keeping up with the assigned readings. Moreover, class participation will be taken into account in the final grade, especially in "borderline" grades. The midterm exam (which will be scheduled for about October 16) and the final exam will cover both class materials and all assigned readings.

No term paper is required. However, a student may arrange to write one if 1) the subject is first approved by the professor; and 2) if it is undertaken by Monday, October 21, i.e., approval of subject received and partial list of sources to be used submitted. These papers must be handed in by Wednesday, November 27. Suggestions for topics can be provided by the professor, as well as some guidance regarding materials. If a paper is written, it will count for 30% of the grade, with the remainder divided between the midterm exam (30%) and the final exam (40%).

For students who choose not to write a paper, the midterm exam will count for 40% of the grade and the final exam 60%.

A complete reading of the textbooks (and other assigned readings) is of course expected:

Croner, Helga, ed.   More Stepping Stones to Jewish-Christian Relations.
Flannery, Edward.   The Anguish of the Jews.
Katz, Jacob.   Exclusiveness and Tolerance.
Vermes, Geza.   Jesus and the World of Judaism.
Williamson, Clark.   Has God Rejected His People?
Rousseau, Richard, ed.   Christianity & Judaism: The Deepening Dialogue.

In addition, you will need to have access to the Jewish and Christian Scriptures: The Tanakh (Old Testament) and New Testament.

Hebrew Union College–Jewish Institute of Religion, Cincinnati

Theology 11   Dr. Jacob Petuchowski

ISSUES IN THE CHRISTIAN–JEWISH DIALOGUE

Seminar. Moving beyond the medieval "Battle of the Proof Texts" and
the more recent "Goodwill Movement," this course will examine some
modern Christian theologies of Judaism and Jewish theologies of
Christianity. Attention will be given to current views of Christology,
"Dual covenants," "Succession Theology," proselytization, etc. Class
sessions will be devoted both to lectures by the instructor and to research
and seminar papers presented by the students. Topics will be taken up
in the order listed here. Further books and articles may be added to the
following bibliography.

I. CHRISTIAN THEOLOGICAL BACKGROUNDS

Mackenzie, W. Douglas. "Jesus Christ." Hastings Encyclopedia of Religion
    and Ethics (hereafter H.E.R.E.) 7:505–50.
Goudge, H. L. "Revelation." H.E.R.E. 10: 745–49.
Tennant, F. R. "Original Sin." H.E.R.E. 9: 558–65.
Kilpatrick, T. B. "Salvation (Christian)." H.E.R.E. 11: 110–31.
Brown, W. Adams. "Expiation and Atonement (Christian)." H.E.R.E. 5:
    641–50.
Mackintosh, H. R. "Grace." H.E.R.E. 6: 364–67.
Van Becelaere, E. L. "Grace, Doctrine of (Roman Catholic)." H.E.R.E.
    6: 367–72.
Tillich, Paul. A History of Christian Doctrine. New York: Simon and
    Schuster, 1972.
Whale, J. S. Christian Doctrine. New York: Cambridge University Press,
    1966.

II. CHRISTIAN–JEWISH CONFRONTATIONS IN THE PAST

Samuel, Maurice. The Second Crucifixion. New York: Knopf, 1960.
Talmage, Frank E., ed. Disputation and Dialogue. New York: Ktav, 1975.
Lasker, Daniel J. Jewish Philosophical Polemics against Christianity
    in the Middle Ages. New York: Ktav, 1977.
Jacob, Walter. Christianity through Jewish Eyes. Cincinnati: Hebrew
    Union College Press, 1974.
Fleischmann, Jacob. The Problem of Christianity in Modern Jewish Thought.
    (Hebrew) Jerusalem: Magnes, 1964.
Moore, George Foot. "Christian Writers on Judaism." Harvard Theological
    Review 14 (1921): 199–254.
Baeck, Leo. "Romantic Religion." Essay in Leo Baeck, Judaism and
    Christianity. Philadelphia: Jewish Publication Society, 1958, pp.
    189–292.

III. TWO-WAY TRAFFIC

Stern, Karl. The Pillar of Fire. Garden City, N.Y.: Doubleday, 1959.
Carmel, Abraham. So Strange My Path. New York: Bloch, 1964.

IV. JUDAISM AS SEEN BY MODERN JEWISH CONVERTS TO CHRISTIANITY

Schneider, Peter. The Dialogue of Christians and Jews. New York: Seabury, 1967.
Oesterreicher, John M. The Rediscovery of Judaism. South Orange, N.J.: Seton Hall University Press, 1971.

V. TOWARDS A NEW LOOK IN MUTUAL EVALUATIONS

Stendahl, Krister. "Judaism and Christianity: A Plea for a New Relationship." Cross Currents 17 (1967): 445–58.
Matt, Hershel. "How Shall a Believing Jew View Christianity?" Judaism 24 (1975): 391–405.

VI. THE ONGOING TASK

Thomas, Clemens. A Christian Theology of Judaism. New York: Paulist, 1980.
Borowitz, Eugene B. Contemporary Christologies: A Jewish Response. New York: Paulist, 1980.
Pawlikowski, John T. Christ in the Light of the Christian-Jewish Dialogue. New York: Paulist, 1982.

MAJOR ISSUES IN THE JEWISH-CHRISTIAN DIALOGUE

Rabbi Solomon Bernards   The General Seminary
Prof. John Koenig   New York, New York

Fall, 1986

In this course we shall explore Jewish-Christian relationships from the first century onwards, with an eye toward their historical-theological implications in the present. Particular emphasis will be placed upon contemporary Jewish and Christian interpretations of Jesus within the Jewish world of the first century.

Regular attendance and informed participation in discussions are expected. Each student will be responsible, in addition, for a class presentation of about thirty minutes. Finally, a term paper of 15 pages, the topic of which should be developed in consultation with the instructors, is required.

Sept. 11   Introduction
            A short history of the dialogue.
            The genesis of this course. Goals, methods, resources.

Sept. 18   Vermes, Geza. Jesus and the World of Judaism. Read pp. 1–57.

Sept. 25	Vermes, Jesus and the World of Judaism. Read pp. 58-88; 100-125.
Oct. 2	Sanders, E. P. Jesus and Judaism. Read pp. 1-76.
Oct. 9	Sanders, Jesus and Judaism. Read pp. 123-56; 222-41; 245-69.
Oct. 16	READING WEEK. NO CLASS.
Oct. 23	Sanders, Jesus and Judaism. Read pp. 270-340.
Oct. 30	Flannery, Edward. The Anguish of the Jews. Read pp. 1-6; 117-44; 160-204.
Nov. 6	Flannery, The Anguish of the Jews. Read pp. 205-96.
Nov. 13	For these three sessions topics from the following works may be treated in class reports:

Nov. 20
Dec. 4   Cargas, H. J., ed. When God and Man Failed.
            Lewis, B. Semites and Anti-Semites.
            O'Brien, C. C. The Siege.
            Schweid, E. The Land of Israel.

            Additional topics, such as the following, may also be treated:

            The meaning of covenant for Jews and Christians.
            The Hebrew Scriptures/OT in Christian understanding.
            The impact and literature of the Holocaust.
            Church-Synagogue relations at the grass-roots level.
            Anti-Judaism in Christian liturgy.
            The meaning of mission in Judaism and Christianity.
            Proselytism by Christians (and Jews?).

Dec. 11   Course conclusion
            The continuing agenda(s) for Jewish-Christian relations.

BOSTON UNIVERSITY
Metro College

Rabbi Herman Blumberg
Rev. Michael McGarry

THE HISTORY OF JEWISH-CHRISTIAN RELATIONS

MET HI 307

First Semester, 1984-85

Lecture I	September 6	Expectations, Perceptions, Preliminaries
		a. Written exercises of common terms
		b. Sharing of memories:
		  1) My own upbringing.
		  2) My perceptions of the other.
		  3) Introductions.

Lecture II	September 13	DEVELOPMENT OF JUDAISM. BIBLICAL AND POST BIBLICAL: Themes of Covenant, Torah, Land, Patriarchy, Prophecy, Messiah: Pharisees and Rabbinic Literature, Description of the Jewish World.
Lecture III	September 20	FIRST CENTURY JUDAISM AND CHRISTIANITY: The Ministry of Jesus, Jesus and the Pharisees, The Jewish Christian Church, Christian Understanding of Messiah. Description of Theme Paper.
	September 27	Rosh Hashanah No class
Lecture IV	October 4	FIRST CENTURY JUDAISM AND CHRISTIANITY: The Crucifixion (historical and theological concepts), Paul vs. Peter, The Diaspora, The Emergence of the Polemic.
Lecture V	October 11	THE HISTORY OF THE CHRISTIAN-JEWISH POLEMIC: The Diatribes, The Early Fathers of the Church, The Rights of Jews in the Empire, The Crusades, The Reformation, The Enlightenment, Secularization. FILMSTRIP: "A Troubled Brotherhood."
Lecture VI	October 18	Christian and Jewish Experience in the United States.
Lecture VII	October 25	THEMES/THE HOLOCAUST Film: "The 81st Blow" or "Genocide."
Lecture VIII	November 1	THEMES/THEOLOGY, CHRISTOLOGY AFTER AUSCHWITZ
Lecture IX	November 8	THEMES/ZIONISM AND THE RISE OF THE STATE OF ISRAEL. Historical, Theological, and Social Preparation for the State of Israel; Theology of the Land. Film: "A Wall in Jerusalem."

Lecture X	November 15	THEMES/THE CHURCHES RESPOND: THE SECOND VATICAN COUNCIL, THE WORLD COUNCIL OF CHURCHES, AND OTHER CONTEMPORARY STATEMENTS.
Thanksgiving	November 22	No class.
Lecture XI	November 29	THEMES/MODERN ANTISEMITISM; CHRISTIANS AND JEWS AND THE MODERN ARAB-ISRAELI CONFLICT.
Lecture XII	December 6	THEMES/EVANGELIZATION AND ESCHATOLOGY. CONTEXT AND CONTENT FOR DIALOGUE IN THE 1980s: Why It's Necessary, How to Do It, Themes of Dialogue, Who Does What, How to Live and Transmit the Tradition without Denigrating the Other.
Lecture XIII	December 13	THEMES/MODERN JUDAISM AND CHRISTIANITY ADDRESS CONTEMPORARY ISSUES: Abortion, Modern Warfare, Intermarriage, Death and Mortality.

FIRST SEMESTER CLASSES END MONDAY, DECEMBER 13TH
FINAL EXAMS BEGIN DEC. 13th

Required Readings:

Croner, Helga, and Klenicki, Leon, eds. Issues in the Jewish-Christian Dialogue. New York: Paulist, 1981.

Dimont, Max. Jews, God, and History. New York: New American Library, 1972.

Fisher, Eugene J. Homework for Christians: Preparing for Dialogue. New York: National Conference of Christians and Jews, 1982.

Flannery, Edward H. The Anguish of the Jews. New York: Macmillan, 1964.

Gilbert, A. Homework for Jews: Preparing for Dialogue. New York: National Conference of Christians and Jews, 1973.

Hay, Malcolm. The Roots of Christian Anti-Semitism. New York: Anti-Defamation League of B'nai B'rith, 1981.

Isaac, Jules. The Teaching of Contempt. New York: Holt, Rinehart, and Winston, 1964.

Pawlikowski, John T. What Are They Saying about Christian-Jewish Relations? New York: Paulist, 1980.

Rudin, A. James. Israel for Christians: Understanding Modern Israel. Philadelphia: Fortress, 1983.

Recommended Readings:

Borowitz, Eugene B. Contemporary Christologies: A Jewish Response. New York: Paulist, 1981.

Croner, Helga, and Martin A. Cohen, eds. <u>Christian Mission-Jewish Mission</u>.
New York: Paulist, 1982.

Klenicki, Leon, and Geoffrey Wigoder, eds. <u>A Dictionary of the
Jewish-Christian Dialogue</u>. New York: Paulist, 1984.

Pawlikowski, John T. <u>Sinai and Calvary: A Meeting of Two Peoples</u>. Beverly
Hills, Calif.: Benziger, 1976.

Readings (* Required):

For Lecture II: *The Gospel of Luke
<u>The Common Catechism</u>. New York: Seabury, 1975,
pp. 121-220.

*Dimont, pp. 127-81.

Kung, Hans. <u>On Being a Christian</u>. New York:
Doubleday, 1976, pp. 145-339.

*Hay, chapters 1-2.

*<u>Homework for Christians</u>, pp. 1-13.

*<u>Homework for Jews</u>, pp. 31-40.

*Pawlikowski, pp. 93-108.

For Lecture III: *Dimont, pp. 13-125.

Hellwig, Monika. "Christian Theology and the Covenant
of Israel." <u>Journal of Ecumenical Studies</u> (hereafter
<u>JES</u>) 7 (1970): 37-51.

*<u>Homework for Christians</u>, pp. 38-40.

*<u>Homework for Jews</u>, Preface, pp. 1-4, 41-45.

*Kravitz, Leonard. "The Covenant in Jewish Tradition:
Historical Considerations." Essay in <u>Issues in the
Jewish-Christian Dialogue</u>, pp. 13-37.

For Lecture IV: Ruether, Rosemary. <u>Faith and Fratricide</u>. New York:
Seabury, 1974, pp. 64-116.

*Dimont, pp. 127-81.

Baum, Gregory. <u>Is the New Testament Anti-Semitic?
A Re-Examination of the New Testament</u>. New York:
Paulist, 1965.

*<u>Homework for Christians</u>, pp. 20-24.

*Isaac's articles on deicide and 18 Points.

*Pawlikowski, pp. 1-32.

For Lecture V: *Dimont, pp. 207-342.

Ruether, pp. 117-225.

*Hay, chapters 3-6.

*<u>Homework for Christians</u>, pp. 14-19, 25-28.

For Lecture VI: *Dimont, pp. 354-72.

*Homework for Jews, pp. 19-30.

*Vorspan, Albert. "Concepts of Religious Pluralism and Areas of Conflict in the United States." Essay in Evangelicals and Jews in Conversation. Ed. Marc Tanenbaum et al. Grand Rapids: Baker, 1978, pp. 286-97.

For Lecture VII: Davidowicz, Lucy S. The War against the Jews, 1933-1945. New York: Holt, Rinehart, and Winston, 1975.

*Dimont, pp. 372-90.

For Lecture VIII: McGarry, Michael. Christology after Auschwitz. New York: Paulist, 1977, pp. 1-12.

Fleischner, Eva, ed. After Auschwitz: Beginning of a New Era? New York: Ktav, 1977.

Peck, Abraham J. Jews and Christians after the Holocaust. Philadelphia: Fortress, 1982.

*Pawlikowski, pp. 129-42.

*Polish, Daniel F. "Witnessing God after Auschwitz." Essay in Issues in the Jewish-Christian Dialogue, pp. 134-56.

For Lecture IX: Cohen, Martin A. "The Meaning of Israel after Auschwitz." Essay in Issues in the Jewish-Christian Dialogue, pp. 157-80.

*Dimont, pp. 390-411.

*Hay, chapters 9-10.

*Pawlikowski, pp. 109-28.

*Rudin, chapters 1-3.

For Lecture X: McGarry, pp. 13-54.

*National Council of Churches' Statement on the Middle East.

*World Council of Churches' Statement on Christian-Jewish Relations.

*Wilson, Marvin. "An Evangelical Perspective on Judaism." Essay in Evangelicals and Jews in Conversation, pp. 2-33.

For Lecture XI: *Brockway, Allan. "Theology, Politics, and Israel: The World Council of Churches." (Offprint.)

*Homework for Jews, pp. 49-62.

*Seltzer, Sanford, and Max Stackhouse. "Introduction,"

and Malcolm Diamond, "Christian Silence on Israel: An End to Dialogue?" Essays in Seltzer and Stackhouse, eds. The Death of Dialogue and Beyond. New York: Friendship, 1969, pp. 7-39.

For Lecture XII: Cohen, Martin A., and Helga Croner, eds. Christian Mission-Jewish Mission. New York: Paulist, 1982.

Federici, Tomasso. "Mission and Witness of the Church." Origins 8 (1978): 273-83.

*Pawlikowski, pp. 143-46.

*Homework for Jews, pp. 5-18.

*Berger, David. "Jewish Christian Relations: A Jewish Perspective." JES 20 (1985): 5-32.

*Culbertson, Philip. "Doing Our Homework," JES 20 (1985): 118-23.

*Swidler, Leonard. "The Dialogue Decalogue: Ground Rules for Interreligious Dialogue." JES 20 (1985): 1-4.

For Lecture XIII: *Statements from the Jewish-Catholic Dialogue, Los Angeles, California.

*Grounds, Vernon. "Evangelical Views of Today's Moral Crisis." Essay in Evangelicals and Jews in Conversation, pp. 248-65.

*Rackman, Emanuel. "A Jewish View of the Present Moral Crisis." Essay in Evangelicals and Jews in Conversation, pp. 266-75.

*The Bishops' Pastoral Letter on "War and Peace." (Summary.)

DEPARTMENT OF JUDAIC STUDIES
Brooklyn College
of
The City University of New York

Fall, 1973

CHRISTIAN-JEWISH RELATIONS THROUGH THE AGES

Judaic Studies 75.1
Dr. Esther Feldblum

3 hrs.; 3 credits
Prerequisites: 12.1
or 12.2 or permission of instructor

Bulletin Description:

A historical survey of Jewish-Christian relations from the separation of the early church to contemporary ecumenical trends.

192   Syllabi

Course Outline:

I. Theological Foundations

    1. Beginnings of Christianity and the Jewish Milieu: Common history,
        Palestinian Jewry in the first century; sectarianism and
        messianism; the Pharisees; the historical Jesus; the Gospels.
    2. Judaeo-Christians—The Unresolved Problems: Factional disputes
        in the early church; the Ebionite view of Jesus; tradition and
        law in the community; ambivalences in identity.
    3. The Pauline Development and Versus Israel: The Jew in the
        Graeco-Roman world; the psychology of conversion; Apostle
        to the Gentiles; redefining Israel; the root and the branch.
    4. Conflict of Church and Synagogue: The church fathers of the
        third and fourth centuries; formation of an official attitude
        towards Jews and Judaism; typology in Scriptures; the two
        histories.

Required Reading:

Sandmel, Samuel. A Jewish Understanding of the New Testament. New
    York: University Press, 1960.
Parkes, James. The Conflict of Church and Synagogue. New York: Meridian,
    1961.
Weiss-Rosmarin, Trude. Judaism and Christianity: The Differences. New
    York: Jonathan David, 1965.

Suggested Reading:

Buber, Martin. Two Types of Faith. New York: Harper Torchbook, 1961.
Enslin, Morton S. Christian Beginnings. New York: Harper Torchbook,
    1956.
Goldstein, M. Jesus in the Jewish Tradition. New York: Macmillan, 1950.
Herford, R. Travers. Christianity in Talmud and Midrash. London: Williams
    and Norgate, 1903.
Herford, R. Travers. The Pharisees. Boston: Beacon, 1962.
Isaac, Jules. The Teaching of Contempt. New York: McGraw-Hill, 1965.
Klausner, Joseph. Jesus of Nazareth. New York: Macmillan, 1925.
Klausner, Joseph. From Jesus to Paul. New York: Macmillan, 1945.
Moore, George Foot. Judaism in the First Centuries of the Christian
    Era. Cambridge: Harvard University Press, 1958.
Schoeps, Hans Joachim. Jewish Christianity. Philadelphia: Fortress,
    1969.

II. In Practice

    1. State and Church Law—Jews under Christendom: Roman law
        from Constantine to Justinian (315-531); codes and decrees of
        the Church Councils; the creation of an alien people; theory
        and practices; the exceptions.
    2. The Popes and the Jews: Gregory the Great (590) and the policy
        of Sicut Judaeis non; the Crusades; coercion and conversion;
        the pontificate of Innocent III (1198-1217); papal protection—a
        theological tightrope.

3. __The Devil and the Jew__: The image of the Jew in the Middle Ages; the rationale of contempt and fear; ritual murder, host desecration, and poisoned wells.

4. __Jewish Responses to Christians and Christian Doctrine__: Public disputations and literary polemics; pagans and Christians in Jewish law; the ghetto; crossing the boundaries.

5. The __Crypto-Jews__: The conversions of 1391 and 1497; the Inquisition; religion of the Marranos; the Dutch Jerusalem; apostates or saints?

__Required Reading:__

Parkes, James. __The Conflict of Church and Synagogue__. New York: Maridian, 1961.

Marcus, Jacob R. __The Jew in the Medieval World__. New York: Atheneum: 1969.

Katz, Jacob. __Exclusiveness and Tolerance__. New York: Schocken, 1969.

__Suggested Reading:__

Braude, Morris. __Conscience Trial__. New York: Exposition, 1952.

Flannery, Edward H. __The Anguish of the Jews__. New York: Macmillan, 1965.

Grayzel, Solomon. __The Church and the Jews in the Thirteenth Century__. New York: Hermon, 1966.

Hay, Malcolm. __Europe and the Jews__. Boston: Beacon, 1960.

Parkes, James. __The Jew in the Medieval Community__. London: 1938.

Pinson, Koppel, ed. __Essays on Anti-Semitism__. Third ed. rev. and enl. New York: Conference on Jewish Relations, 1973.

Roth, C. __A History of the Marranos__. New York: Harper Torchbook, 1966.

Schoeps, Hans Joachim. __The Jewish Christian Argument__. Third ed. New York: Holt, Rinehart, and Winston, 1963.

Synan, Edward A. __The Popes and the Jews in the Middle Ages__. New York: Macmillan, 1965.

Trachtenberg, Joshua. __The Devil and the Jews__. New Haven: Yale University Press, 1943.

III. Crises and Change

1. __The Reformation and the Jews__: Biblicism and the Hebrew revival; the charge of Judaizing; "Table Talk" of Martin Luther; Protestant denominationalism and the question of tolerance; Millenarianism.

2. __Enlightenment and the "new" image__: Secularization of Christian Europe; the __philosophes__; metamorphosis of attitudes; Emancipation and the selective application of equality; the Dreyfus Affair; fin de siecle and interbellum developments.

3. __The Impact of the Holocaust on Christian Thinking__: Roots of Nazi anti-Semitism; stances of Christian churches during the Holocaust; the enormity of the Jewish catastrophe; Christian soul-searching; the Ten Points of Seelisberg.

4. __Christianity and Zionism__: Christian millenarians and the restoration of the Jews; anti-Zionism and Vatican policy; Holy Land and Holy Places; rivalry of interests in the Middle East.

5. __Ecumenical trends--their implications__: Definitions of ecumenism; Protestant initiatives; Vatican II; theological reinterpretations and the "two covenant" theory.

Required Reading:

Baron, Salo W. "John Calvin and the Jews." In Harry A. Wolfson, Jubilee
    Volume. Jerusalem: American Academy for Jewish Research, 1965,
    English section, 141-63.
Siirala, Aarne. "Luther and the Jews." Lutheran World 11 (1964): 337-47.
Hertzberg, Arthur. The French Enlightenment and the Jews. Philadelphia:
    Jewish Publication Society, 1968.
Cohn, Norman. Warrant for Genocide. New York: Harper Torchbook,
    1969.
Davies, Alan T. Anti-Semitism and the Christian Mind: The Crisis of
    Conscience after Auschwitz. New York: Herder and Herder, 1969.
Netznyahu, B. The Marranos of Spain, From the Late Fourteenth to the
    Early Sixteenth Century. New York: American Academy for Jewish
    Research, 1966.

Suggested Reading:

Baron, Salo W. "Medieval Heritage and Modern Realities in Protestant-
    Jewish Relations." Diogenes 41 (1968): 32-51.
Berkovits, Eliezer. "Judaism in the Post-Christian Era." Judaism 15 (1966):
    74-84.
Flannery, Edward. "Anti-Zionism and the Christian Psyche." Journal of
    Ecumenical Studies 6 (1969).
Eckardt, A. Roy. Christianity and the Children of Israel. New York: King's
    Crown, 1948.
Eckardt, A. Roy. Elder and Younger Brothers. New York Scribner, 1967.
Gilbert, Arthur. The Vatican Council and the Jews: Cleveland: World,
    1968.
Glock, Charles Y., and Rodney Stark. Christian Beliefs and Anti-Semitism.
    New York: Harper and Row, 1964.

VIII.
Service Groups and
Other Organizations

Organizations have played a key role in initiating and facilitating interreligious dialogue. Below is a list of organizations, arranged alphabetically, that have played some part in keeping the dialogue alive and thriving. The descriptions of the organizations' goals or purposes in most cases has been written by the organizations themselves. Following this list, organizations are listed geographically by state to help facilitate readers' involvement in the dialogue.

A. Alphabetical Arrangement (with description)

American Friends of Nes Ammim
Grange and Chadwick Roads
Teaneck, New Jersey 07666

An international Christian community in the northwest Galilee of Israel. Its goal is to contribute to the creation of a new relationship between Jews and Christians following centuries of alienation and ignorance. Nes Ammim wants to be a concrete sign of solidarity on the basis of a collective, historic responsibility with the Jewish people in the State of Israel.

American Jewish Committee
Institute of Human Relations
165 East 56th Street
New York, New York 10022
(212) 751-4000
(Regional offices listed geographically)

The AJC protects the rights and freedoms of Jews the world over; combats bigotry and promotes human rights for all people; defends pluralism and enhances the creative vitality of the Jewish people; and contributes to the formulation of American public policy from a combined Jewish and American perspective. Founded in 1906, it is the pioneer human relations agency in the U.S.

Anne Frank Institute of Philadelphia
437 Chestnut Street, Suite 221
Philadelphia, Pennsylvania 19106
(215) 625-0411

Interfaith, interracial organization which conducts programs educating
all levels and all sectors of society to the lessons of the Holocaust and
religious freedom. Newsletter--Lest We Forget.

Anti-Defamation League of B'nai B'rith
National Office
823 United Nations Plaza
New York, New York 10017
(212) 490-2525
(Regional offices listed geographically)

Goal of promoting understanding among peoples of different races, creeds,
and ethnic backgrounds. ADL produces and promotes books, pamphlets,
posters, and audio-visual materials that supply accurate information about
racial and ethnic minorities. To further interreligious understanding,
the ADL has established relations with Christian institutions to help them
create programs that reflect sensitivity to and concern for the
Jewish-Christian encounter.

Boulder Council of Churches and Synagogues
2650 Table Mesa Drive
Boulder, Colorado 80303
(303) 499-5611

Umbrella group for thirty-six member congregations that fosters interfaith
activities and exchange. Newsletter--Common Concern.

Bridges for Peace
P.O. Box 33145
Tulsa, Oklahoma 74153
(918) 663-8811

A Jerusalem-based, multi-faceted, evangelical Christian organization
dedicated to the building of sincere relationships between the Christian
and Jewish communities, while encouraging greater concern for the Land
of Israel. Newsletter--Dispatch from Jerusalem.

Center for Holocaust Studies
Documentation and Research
1609 Avenue J
Brooklyn, New York 11230
(718) 338-6494

A research library and archives, open to the public, containing the largest
oral history archives of Holocaust material in the United States with
accompanying oral history subject catalog. The Center has films, slide
shows, videotapes, and filmstrips available to the public, traveling exhibits,

structured class visit program available to schools (grade 9—college), a speakers bureau, reference services, and lecture and performance series open to the public. Newsletter—Center for Holocaust Studies. Bibliography series, Oral History series.

Center for Jewish-Christian Learning
College of St. Thomas
2115 Summit Avenue
St. Paul, Minnesota 55105
(612) 647-5740

Purposes are to teach classes of Jewish life, Judaism, etc.; lecture in various departments of the College; speak at Catholic high schools in the state; hold two community events each year. Lectures published in conference proceedings.

Center for Jewish-Christian Studies
Chicago Theological Seminary
5757 South University Avenue
Chicago, Illinois 60637

Offers resources for scholarly research in Jewish-Christian studies; relationships with scholars throughout the United States, Europe, and Israel; base for continuing education for clergy and laity.

Center for Judaic-Christian Studies
P.O. Box 202707
Austin, Texas 78720

Serves as an educational resource to the Christian community, publishing books and audio and video teaching tapes, and producing seminars, conferences, and television programs. The Center also sponsors and publishes the work of its research extension in Israel, the Jerusalem School for the Study of the Synoptic Gospels.

Christian Clergy for a Better Understanding of Judaism
360 Clinton Avenue, 6S
Brooklyn, New York 11238
(212) 636-4505

An activist Christian fellowship for Christian clergy who reject anti-Judaism in Christian teaching.

Council of Churches and Synagogues
628 Main Street
Stamford, Connecticut 06901
(203) 348-2800

An interfaith organization of member congregations that operate a number of community social-service programs for the poor, hungry, homeless, elderly, and imprisoned of the area; sponsor community forums for education and discussion of current issues of importance; and provides these services out of a shared perspective as people of faith and our commitment to the biblical mandate of Isaiah 58 and Matthew 25.

Ecumenical Institute for Jewish-Christian Studies
26275 Northwestern Highway
Southfield, Michigan 48076
(313) 353-2434

Lectures on intergroup dialogue, antisemitism in Christian thought and
history, Holocaust and Christian response, and Israel and the Middle East.

Friends of Le Chambon
8033 Sunset Boulevard, L784
Los Angeles, California 90046
(213) 650-1774

Purpose is to share with the world what happened in Le Chambon and
why—and thus to explore and communicate necessary lessons of hope
still buried beneath the Holocaust's unavoidable lessons of despair.

Graymoor Ecumenical Institute
475 Riverside Drive, Room 528
New York, New York 10015
(212) 870-2330

or

Graymoor
Garrison, New York 10524
(914) 424-3458

To promote interchurch and interfaith dialogue. From time to time the
Institute also develops resources such as books and pamphlets for those
engaged in active ecumenism and in ecumenical or interfaith studies.
Journal—Ecumenical Trends, Newsletter—At/One/Ment.

The Halina Wind Preston Holocaust Education Committee
Jewish Federation of Delaware
101 Garden of Eden Road
Wilmington, Delaware 19803

In pursuit of the goal of producing educational programming related to
the Holocaust, our organization presents an annual Yom Hashoah program,
provides a resource center of books and audio-visual materials, organizes
seminars for public, private, and parochial school teachers, provides
speakers on the Holocaust to area schools and organizations, administers
the first Garden of the Righteous Gentiles outside Yad Vashem, and much
more.

Holocaust Center
Jewish Federation of the Northshore
76 Lake Street, McCarthy School, Room 108
Peabody, Massachusetts 01960
(617) 535-0003

Created to provide community awareness, information, audio-visual support,
and education about the Nazi Holocaust in order that history not repeat
itself.

Holocaust Memorial Resource and Education Center of Central Florida
851 North Maitland Avenue
Maitland, Florida 32751

The Center helps the schools and universities of central Florida teach the
lessons of the Holocaust by providing video materials and books, curriculum
development, teacher training, seminars and conferences, and exhibits
of Holocaust materials in schools and libraries; by collecting Holocaust
art, memorabilia, and artifacts; by compiling archives of video-taped oral
histories of survivors and liberators; and by presenting an annual Yom
Hashoah Commemoration, television and radio programs, and interfaith
dialogue and projects.

Holocaust Survivors Memorial Foundation
350 Fifth Avenue, Suite 3508
New York, New York 10118

Through education, through the media, through research, through the fine
arts, we are disseminating the true story of the Holocaust to the widest
possible audience. We are remembering, investigating, and reporting the
events of the past to insure that history never repeat itself--in this or any
lifetime.

Holyland Fellowship of Christians and Jews
36 South Wabash Street, Suite 626
Chicago, Illinois 60603
(312) 346-7693

Goals are to serve as an educational bridge to interpret the Jewish
community and faith to Christians, and the Christian community and faith
to Jews; to foster better relations and understanding between Christians
and Jews; and to build a broad network of cooperation and support in America
for the State of Israel. Newsletter--Holyland Fellowship Bulletin.

Interfaith Service Bureau
3720 Folsom Boulevard
Sacramento, California 95816
(916) 456-3815

Organization whose theme is "building bridges of loving services" and in
which the religious community talks and works together. Composed of
Protestant, Roman Catholic, Orthodox, and Jewish congregations or parishes,
denominational judicatories, religious groups or organizations, and individual
members. Newsletter--Interfaith Voice.

International Council of Christians and Jews
Werlestrasse 2, 6148 Heppenheim, P.O. Box 305
Federal Republic of Germany
06252/5041

A voluntary association of representative organizations established to
promote Christian-Jewish cooperation and whose purpose is to coordinate
efforts of its eighteen member organizations in the international and regional

fields, and to undertake joint actions in the sphere of Christian–Jewish understanding, to promote such action, and to seek to remove prejudices and their consequences.

Interweave
31 Woodland Avenue
Summit, New Jersey 07901
(201) 763-8312

An interfaith project in adult education which brings to bear the resources of spiritual tradition on contemporary issues.

National Christian Leadership Conference for Israel
134 East 39th Street
New York, New York 10016
(212) 213-8636

A network of organizations and individuals actively engaged in efforts supporting the State of Israel. NCLCT leadership includes representatives from the Catholic, the "mainstream" Protestant, and the Evangelical communities.

National Conference of Catholic Bishops
Bishops' Committee for Ecumenical and Interreligious Affairs
Secretariat for Catholic–Jewish Relations
1312 Massachusetts Avenue, NW
Washington, D.C. 20005
(202) 659-6857

Established in 1965 in a move towards the implementation of Nostra Aetate, the aim of this office "is to increase our understanding of both Judaism and the Catholic faith, to eliminate sources of tension and misunderstanding, to initiate dialogue or conversations on different levels, to multiply intergroup meetings between Catholics and Jews, and to promote cooperative social action."

National Conference of Christians and Jews
National Office
71 Fifth Avenue, Suite 1100
New York, New York 10003
(212) 206-0006
(Regional offices listed geographically)

Human relations organization engaged in a nationwide program of intergroup education to eliminate prejudice and discrimination. Purpose to build bridges of understanding between all groups, to bring the forces of enlightenment and education to bear upon racial and religious prejudice, and to achieve implementation of the moral law: giving to others the same rights and respect we desire for ourselves. Newsletter—National Conference of Christians and Jews.

National Council of the Churches of Christ in the U.S.A.
Office on Christian-Jewish Relations, Room 870
475 Riverside Drive
New York, New York 10115
(212) 870-2560

The Office on Christian-Jewish Relations seeks to establish and strengthen relations between Christians and Jews in the United States. It promotes and assists in the organization of conversations, dialogue, programs and development of resources among Christians and Jews nationally and in the local and regional spheres. It enables the inclusion and integration of issues emerging from such dialogue in other areas of the life of the Council, and brings to the dialogue issues of relevance emerging elsewhere in the Council. It seeks to help the Council to be aware of issues of concern to Jews and also to help the Jewish community to understand the concerns of the Council. It cooperates with other units of the Council in developing theological perspectives on Christian-Jewish relations for Christian theology. It does its work in consultation with the Jewish community.

National Institute for Catholic-Jewish Education
1307 South Wabash Avenue, Room 224
Chicago, Illinois 60605
(312) 786-0611

The National Institute for Catholic-Jewish Education attempts to foster understanding and respect between Catholics and Jews. It seeks to implement the Vatican II document Nostra Aetate and the subsequent "Vatican Guidelines for Catholic-Jewish Relations" (1975) and the "Statement on Catholic-Jewish Relations" (National Conference of Catholic Bishops, 1977), enhancing the appreciation of Christianity's Judaic heritage.

National Interreligious Task Force on Soviet Jewry
1307 South Wabash Avenue, Room 221
Chicago, Illinois 60605
(312) 922-1983

The Task Force, a major expression of human rights concerns shared by Christians and Jews, works in many ways to achieve freedom for the Soviet Jews and other oppressed peoples. Carries on an intensive program of education, interpretation, and action. Provides guidance and assistance for various interreligious groups throughout the United States and in other parts of the world. Gives workshops on human rights, religious liberty, and the Helsinki Agreement.

Religious Network for Equality for Women
475 Riverside Drive, Room 830A
New York, New York 10115

An interreligious coalition of forty-one Protestant, Jewish, Catholic, and other faith groups who are committed to economic and legal justice for women through legislative change. RNEW, through its member groups, educates and mobilizes the religious community to act on behalf of justice for women and makes visible to policy makers the unified stand of its member groups on particular legislative issues.

Remembrance of the Holocaust Foundation
110 East End Avenue
New York, New York 10028
(212) 744-8727

Our purpose is to raise funds for Holocaust-related activities and further
the cause of Holocaust commemoration.

Rockaway Catholic-Jewish Council
P.O. Box 272
Rockaway Park, New York 11694
(718) 634-1739

Organization exists for dialogue and to cement relations between Jews
and Christians.

Root and Branch Association
142 Sherman Avenue
White Plains, New York 10607

Jews and Gentiles united through faith in the God of Israel and in active
support for the Jewish people and the State of Israel. Newsletter—Root
and Branch Report.

Shalom Ministries
27 Congress Street
Salem, Massachusetts 01970
(617) 744-8131

Dialogues on the Holocaust, the roots of anti-Semitism, and the promises
for the future. Builds bridges in both Jewish and Christian communities.
Newsletter—Shalom Ministries.

South Hills Interfaith Ministries
5171 Park Avenue
Bethel Park, Pennsylvania 15102
(412) 833-6177

Helps people help themselves through training, counseling, and creating
a mutually supportive spirit among persons of all races, creeds, ages,
and religious backgrounds.

Southeastern Florida Holocaust Memorial Center
Florida International University
Bay Vista Campus
NE 151st Street and Biscayne Boulevard
North Miami, Florida 33181
(305) 940-5690

Educating the population about the meaning of the Holocaust, how it scarred
the conscience of the world, and why such an event must never happen
again. This is being done through the educational and administrative skills
of college presidents and school officials, the theological and philosophical

insights of clergymen, the community awareness of civic leaders, and the financial expertise of business men and women.

Student Struggle for Soviet Jewry
210 West 91st Street, 4th Floor
New York, New York 10024
(212) 799-8900
   or
118 Avenue J
Brooklyn, New York 11230
(212) 253-3800

SSSJ stages numerous rallies and demonstrations; runs educational programs in—and shares its expertise with—schools, universities, organizations, and communities; works closely with Congress, and encourages programs to deal sensitively with the absorption of Russian Jews into Israel and North America.

Synagogue Council of America
Committee on Interreligious Affairs
327 Lexington Avenue
New York, New York 10016
(212) 686-8670

Founded in 1926, the Synagogue Council of America is the national representative body of the three branches of American Judaism: Conservative, Orthodox, and Reform. Its constituent organizations, both rabbinical and congregational, represent more than four million American Jews before the nation and the world—representing Jews not as an ethnic group, but as a religious entity. Conducts ongoing consultations with Christian clergy and church organizations on the centrality of Israel to Judaism and Jewish life and interprets current issues to them. Works with other national and international religious bodies to resolve interreligious conflicts.

United States Conference for the World Council of Churches
475 Riverside Drive, Room 62
New York, New York 10115
(212) 870-2560

To promote dialogue between the Church and the Jewish people at all levels. It does so within the context of the three hundred member churches and as such attempts to further information about an understanding of the relation of the Jewish people to the Church within the worldwide Christian ecumenical movement.

United States Holocaust Memorial Council
2000 L Street, NW, Suite 588
Washington, D.C. 20036

The United States Holocaust Memorial Council was established by Congress in 1980 to plan and build the United States Holocaust Memorial Museum in Washington, D.C., and to encourage and sponsor observances of an annual, national, civic commemoration of the Holocaust, known as the Days of

Remembrance. The Council also engages in Holocaust education and research programs. It consists of fifty-five members of all faiths and backgrounds appointed by the President, plus five U.S. senators and five members of the House of Representatives.

B.   Geographic Locator (listed by state)

Alabama

National Conference of Christians and Jews (Regional)
2151 Highland Avenue, South, Suite 204
Birmingham, Alabama 35205
(205) 933-6958

Arizona

American Jewish Committee (Regional)
4710 North 16th Street, Suite 117
Phoenix, Arizona 85016
(602) 279-9696

Anti-Defamation League of B'nai B'rith (Regional)
The First Interstate Tower, 3550 North Central Avenue, Suite 914
Phoenix, Arizona 85012
(602) 274-0991

National Conference of Christians and Jews (Regional)
1509 North Central Avenue, Suite 101
Phoenix, Arizona 85004
(602) 271-0980

Arkansas

National Conference of Christians and Jews (Regional)
103 West Capitol Avenue, Suite 907
Little Rock, Arkansas 72201
(501) 372-5129

California

American Jewish Committee (Regional)
6505 Wilshire Boulevard, Suite 315
Los Angeles, California 90048
(213) 655-7071

American Jewish Committee (Regional)
1100 Main Street, Suite D-1
Irvine, California 92714
(714) 660-8525

American Jewish Committee (Regional)
1551 Camino del Rio South, Suite 108
San Diego, California 92108
(619) 296-6800

American Jewish Committee (Regional)
121 Steuart Street
San Francisco, California 94105
(415) 777-3820

Anti-Defamation League of B'nai B'rith (Regional)
6505 Wilshire Boulevard, Suite 814
Los Angeles, California 90048
(213) 655-8205

Anti-Defamation League of B'nai B'rith (Regional)
7851 Mission Center Court, Suite 320
San Diego, California 92108
(619) 293-3770

Anti-Defamation League of B'nai B'rith (Regional)
2700 North Main Street, Suite 500
Santa Anna, California 92701
(714) 973-4733

Friends of Le Chambon
8033 Sunset Boulevard L784
Los Angeles, California 90046
(213) 650-1774

Interfaith Service Bureau
3720 Folsom Boulevard
Sacramento, California 95816
(916) 456-3815

National Conference of Christians and Jews (Regional)
2125 Santa Fe
Long Beach, California 90510
(213) 435-3404

National Conference of Christians and Jews (Regional)
635 South Harvard Boulevard
Los Angeles, California 90005
(213) 355-0491

National Conference of Christians and Jews (Regional)
3440 Irvine Avenue, Suite 210
Newport Beach, California 92660
(714) 852-9151

National Conference of Christians and Jews (Regional)
635 "C" Street, Suite 404
San Diego, California 92101
(619) 232-6113

National Conference of Christians and Jews (Regional)
465 California Street, Suite 705
San Francisco, California 84104
(415) 391-2850

National Conference of Christians and Jews (Regional)
777 North First Street, Mezzanine
San Jose, California 95112
(408) 286-9663

National Conference of Christians and Jews (Regional)
P.O. Box 1307
Santa Monica, California 90406
(213) 458-2772

Colorado

American Jewish Committee (Regional)
300 South Dahlia, Suite 201
Denver, Colorado 80222
(303) 320-1742

Anti-Defamation League of B'nai B'rith (Regional)
300 South Dahlia Street, Suite 202
Denver, Colorado 80222
(303) 321-7177

Boulder Council of Churches and Synagogues
2650 Table Mesa Drive
Boulder, Colorado 80303
(303) 499-5611

National Conference of Christians and Jews (Regional)
940 Logan Street
Denver, Colorado 80203
(303) 861-1742

Connecticut

Anti-Defamation League of B'nai B'rith (Regional)
419 Whalley Avenue
New Haven, Connecticut 06511
(203) 787-4281

National Conference of Christians and Jews (Regional)
200 Bloomfield Avenue
West Hartford, Connecticut 06511
(203) 243-4031

Delaware

National Conference of Christians and Jews (Regional)
P.O. Box 747, 11th and Market Street
Wilmington, Delaware 19801
(302) 655-0039

District of Columbia

American Jewish Committee (Regional)
2027 Massachusetts Avenue, NW
Washington, D.C. 20036
(202) 265-2000

Anti-Defamation League of B'nai B'rith (Regional)
1640 Rhode Island Avenue, NW
Washington, D.C. 20036
(202) 857-6660

National Conference of Catholic Bishops
Bishops' Committee for Ecumenical and Interreligious Affairs
Secretariat for Catholic-Jewish Relations
1312 Massachusetts Avenue, NW
Washington, D.C. 20005
(202) 659-6857

National Conference of Christians and Jews (Regional)
Anacostia Professional Building
2041 Martin Luther King Avenue, SE, Suite 302
Washington, D.C. 20020
(202) 678-9400

United States Holocaust Memorial Council
425 13th Street, NW, Suite 832
Washington, D.C. 20004

Florida

American Jewish Committee (Regional)
3000 Biscayne Boulevard, Suite 412
Miami, Florida 33137
(305) 576-4240

Anti-Defamation League of B'nai B'rith (Regional)
150 South East 2nd Avenue, Suite 800
Miami, Florida 33131
(305) 373-6306

Anti-Defamation League of B'nai B'rith (Regional)
5002 Lemon Street, Suite 2300
Tampa, Florida 33609
(813) 875-0750

National Conference of Christians and Jews (Regional)
7491 West Oakland Park Boulevard, Suite 208
Ft. Lauderdale, Florida 33319
(305) 749-4454

National Conference of Christians and Jews (Regional)
2250 Oak Street
Jacksonville, Florida 32204
(904) 388-2233

National Conference of Christians and Jews (Regional)
9300 South Dadeland Boulevard, Suite 511
Miami, Florida 33156
(305) 667-6438

National Conference of Christians and Jews (Regional)
501 East Jackson Street, Suite 215
Tampa, Florida 33602
(813) 223-2721

Georgia

American Jewish Committee (Regional)
3355 Lenox Road, Suite 880
Atlanta, Georgia 30326
(404) 233-5501

Anti-Defamation League of B'nai B'rith (Regional)
805 Peachtree Street, NE, Suite 660
Atlanta, Georgia 30308
(404) 262-3470

National Conference of Christians and Jews (Regional)
1365 Peachtree Street, NE, Suite 310
Atlanta, Georgia 30309
(404) 881-1144

Illinois

American Jewish Committee (Regional)
55 East Jackson Boulevard, Suite 1870
Chicago, Illinois 60604
(312) 663-5500

Anti-Defamation League of B'nai B'rith (Regional)
222 West Adams Street
Chicago, Illinois 60606
(312) 782-5080

Center for Jewish-Christian Studies
The Chicago Theological Seminary
5757 South University Avenue
Chicago, Illinois 60637

Holyland Fellowship of Christians and Jews
36 South Wabash Street, Suite 626
Chicago, Illinois 60603
(312) 346-7693

National Conference of Christians and Jews (Regional)
203 North Wabash Avenue, Suite 904
Chicago, Illinois 60601
(312) 236-9272

National Institute for Catholic-Jewish Education
1307 South Wabash Avenue, Room 224
Chicago, Illinois 60605
(312) 786-0611

National Interreligious Task Force on Soviet Jewry
1307 South Wabash Avenue, Room 221
Chicago, Illinois 60605
(312) 922-1983

Iowa

National Conference of Christians and Jews (Regional)
1041 Eighth Street
Des Moines, Iowa 50314
(515) 244-7227

Kansas

American Jewish Committee (Regional)
2200 West 75th Street, Suite 218
Prairie Village, Kansas 66208
(913) 236-8313

National Conference of Christians and Jews (Regional)
212 North Market, Suite 512
Wichita, Kansas 67202
(316) 264-0356

Kentucky

National Conference of Christians and Jews (Regional)
3357 Hunter Road
Lexington, Kentucky 40502
(606) 277-4434

National Conference of Christians and Jews (Regional)
233 West Broadway, Room 606
Louisville, Kentucky 40202
(502) 583-0281

Louisiana

Anti-Defamation League of B'nai B'rith (Regional)
535 Gravier Street, Suite 501
New Orleans, Louisiana 70130
(504) 522-9534

National Conference of Christians and Jews (Regional)
7075 Boyce Drive
Baton Rouge, Louisiana 70809
(504) 924-2602

National Conference of Christians and Jews (Regional)
611 Gravier Street, 912 International House Building
New Orleans, Louisiana 70130
(504) 522-3760

National Conference of Christians and Jews (Regional)
240 Symphony Lane
Shreveport, Louisiana 71105
(318) 861-1129

Maryland

American Jewish Committee (Regional)
829 Munsey Building, Fayette and Calvert Streets
Baltimore, Maryland 21202
(301) 539-4777

National Conference of Christians and Jews (Regional)
1316 Park Avenue
Baltimore, Maryland 21217
(301) 523-1000

Massachusetts

American Jewish Committee (Regional)
72 Franklin Street
Boston, Massachusetts 02110
(617) 426-7415

Anti-Defamation League of B'nai B'rith (Regional)
72 Franklin Street, Suite 504
Boston, Massachusetts 02110
(617) 542-4977

Holocaust Center, Jewish Federation of the Northshore
76 Lake Street, McCarthy School, Room 108
Peabody, Massachusetts 01960

National Conference of Christians and Jews (Regional)
Statler Office Building, 20 Park Plaza, Suite 600
Boston, Massachusetts 02116
(617) 542-7110

National Conference of Christians and Jews (Regional)
90 Main Street
Worcester, Massachusetts 06108
(617) 753-1681

Shalom Ministries
27 Congress Street
Salem, Massachusetts 01970
(617) 744-8131

Michigan

American Jewish Committee (Regional)
163 Madison Avenue
Detroit, Michigan 45226
(313) 965-3353

Anti-Defamation League of B'nai B'rith (Regional)
4000 Town Center, Suite 420
Detroit, Michigan 48075
(313) 355-3730

Ecumenical Institute for Jewish-Christian Studies
26275 Northwestern Highway
Southfield, Michigan 48076
(313) 353-2434

National Conference of Christians and Jews (Regional)
150 West Boston Boulevard
Detroit, Michigan 48202
(313) 869-6306

Minnesota

Anti-Defamation League of B'nai B'rith (Regional)
15 South 9th Street Building
Minneapolis, Minnesota 55402
(612) 338-7816

Center for Jewish-Christian Learning, College of St. Thomas
2115 Summit Avenue
St. Paul, Minnesota 55105
(612) 647-5740

National Conference of Christians and Jews (Regional)
100 North 6th Street, Suite 531B
Minneapolis, Minnesota 55403
(612) 333-5365

Missouri

American Jewish Committee (Regional)
7750 Clayton Road, Suite 103
St. Louis, Missouri 63117
(314) 647-2519

Anti-Defamation League of B'nai B'rith (Regional)
10922 Schuetz Road
St. Louis, Missouri 63146
(314) 432-6868

National Conference of Christians and Jews (Regional)
306 East 12th Street, Suite 814
Kansas City, Missouri 64106
(816) 221-0688

National Conference of Christians and Jews (Regional)
721 Olive Street, 915 Chemical Building
St. Louis, Missouri 63101
(314) 241-5103

Nebraska

Anti-Defamation League of B'nai B'rith (Regional)
333 South 132nd Street
Omaha, Nebraska 68154
(402) 333-1303

National Conference of Christians and Jews (Regional)
127, The Center
Omaha, Nebraska 68105
(402) 346-3357

Nevada

National Conference of Christians and Jews (Regional)
4220 South Maryland Parkway, Suite 210
Las Vegas, Nevada 89109
(702) 732-1359

National Conference of Christians and Jews (Regional)
3710 Grant Drive, Suite E
Reno, Nevada 89509
(702) 827-1111

New Jersey

American Jewish Committee (Regional)
303 Milburn Avenue
Milburn, New Jersey 07041
(201) 379-7844

Anti-Defamation League of B'nai B'rith (Regional)
513 West Mount Pleasant Avenue
Livingston, New Jersey 07039
(201) 994-4546

Institute of Judaeo-Christian Studies
Seton Hall University
South Orange, New Jersey 07079
(201) 761-9569

National Conference of Christians and Jews (Regional)
1124 Atlantic Avenue, 7th Floor, P.O. Box 1881
Atlantic City, New Jersey 08404
(609) 345-3003

National Conference of Christians and Jews (Regional)
40 Ferry Street
Newark, New Jersey 07105
(201) 344-6699

National Conference of Christians and Jews (Regional)
5 Patterson Street
New Brunswick, New Jersey 08901
(201) 246-3110

National Conference of Christians and Jews (Regional)
44 Washington Street, P.O. Box 1189
Toms River, New Jersey 08753
(201) 244-1836

New York

American Jewish Committee (Regional)
48 Mamaroneck Avenue
White Plains, New York 10601
(914) 948-5585

American Jewish Committee, Institute for Human Relations (National)
165 East 56th Street
New York, New York 10022
(212) 751-4000

Anti-Defamation League of B'nai B'rith (National)
823 United Nations Plaza
New York, New York 10022
(212) 490-2525

Anti-Defamation League of B'nai B'rith (Regional)
98 Cutter Mill Road
Great Neck, New York 11021
(516) 829-3820

Center for Holocaust Studies
1609 Avenue J
Brooklyn, New York 11230
(718) 338-6494

Christian Clergy for a Better Understanding of Judaism
360 Clinton Avenue, L6S
Brooklyn, New York 11238
(212) 636-4505

Graymoor Ecumenical Institute
Graymoor
Garrison, New York 10524
(915) 424-3458

National Christian Leadership Conference for Israel
134 East 39th Street
New York, New York 10016
(212) 679-4822

National Conference of Christians and Jews (National)
71 Fifth Avenue
New York, New York 10019
(212) 206-0006

National Conference of Christians and Jews (Regional)
360 Delaware Avenue, Suite #106
Buffalo, New York 14202
(716) 853-9596

National Conference of Christians and Jews (Regional)
71 Fifth Avenue, Suite 1150
New York, New York 10003
(212) 807-8440

National Conference of Christians and Jews (Regional)
5132 Lewiston Road
Niagara Falls, New York 14092
(716) 285-3734

National Conference on Soviet Jewry
10 East 40th Street
New York, New York 10016

National Council of the Churches in Christ in the U.S.A.
Office on Christian-Jewish Relations, Room 870
475 Riverside Drive
New York, New York 10115
(212) 870-2560

Religious Network for Equality for Women
475 Riverside Drive, Room 830A
New York, New York 10115

Remembrance of the Holocaust Foundation
110 East End Avenue
New York, New York 10028

Rockaway Catholic-Jewish Council
P.O. Box 272
Rockaway Park, New York 11694
(718) 634-1739

Root and Branch Association
142 Sherman Avenue
White Plains, New York 10607

Student Struggle for Soviet Jewry
210 West 91st Street, 4th Floor
New York, New York 10024

Synagogue Council of America, Committee on Interreligious Affairs
327 Lexington Avenue
New York, New York 10016
(212) 686-8870

United States Conference for the World Council of Churches
475 Riverside Drive, Room 62
New York, New York 10115
(212) 870-2560

Union of American Hebrew Congregations
Department of Interreligious Affairs
838 Fifth Avenue
New York, New York 10021

North Carolina

National Conference of Christians and Jews (Regional)
700 Parkwood Avenue
Charlotte, North Carolina 28205
(704) 332-4420

National Conference of Christians and Jews (Regional)
305 North Edgeworth Street
Greensboro, North Carolina 27401
(919) 272-0359

Ohio

Anti-Defamation League of B'nai B'rith (Regional)
505 Terminal Tower
Cleveland, Ohio 44113
(216) 579-9600

American Jewish Committee (Regional)
105 West Fourth Street
Cincinnati, Ohio 45202
(513) 621-4020

American Jewish Committee (Regional)
625 Hanna Building
Cleveland, Ohio 44115
(216) 781-6035

Anti-Defamation League of B'nai B'rith (Regional)
1175 College Avenue
Columbus, Ohio 43209
(614) 239-8414

National Conference of Christians and Jews (Regional)
230 East 9th Street, Room 306
Cincinnati, Ohio 45202
(513) 381-4660

National Conference of Christians and Jews (Regional)
3645 Warrensville Center Road, Suite 205
Cleveland, Ohio 44122
(216) 752-3000

Oklahoma

Bridges for Peace
P.O. Box 33145
Tulsa, Oklahoma 74153
(918) 663-8811

National Conference of Christians and Jews (Regional)
6301 North Western, Suite 170
Oklahoma City, Oklahoma 73118
(405) 840-3861

National Conference of Christians and Jews (Regional)
707 South Houston, Suite 301
Tulsa, Oklahoma 74127
(918) 583-1361

Oregon

American Jewish Committee (Regional)
1220 South West Morrison, Suite 930
Portland, Oregon 97205
(503) 295-6761

Pennsylvania

American Jewish Committee (Regional)
1616 Walnut Street, Suite 2106
Philadelphia, Pennsylvania 19103
(215) 732-4000

American Jewish Committee (Regional)
300 South Craig Street, Suite 224
Pittsburgh, Pennsylvania 15213
(412) 683-7927

Anne Frank Institute of Philadelphia
437 Chestnut Street, Suite 221
Philadelphia, Pennsylvania 19106
(215) 546-4789

Anti-Defamation League of B'nai B'rith (Regional)
2225 South 15th Street
Philadelphia, Pennsylvania 19102
(215) 735-4267

Anti-Defamation League of B'nai B'rith (Regional)
Allegheny Building, 429 Forbes Street, 7th Floor
Pittsburgh, Pennsylvania 15219
(412) 471-1050

National Conference of Christians and Jews (Regional)
421 Brookville Drive
Millersville, Pennsylvania 17551
(717) 872-6250

National Conference of Christians and Jews (Regional)
311 South Juniper, Suite 627
Philadelphia, Pennsylvania 19107
(215) 546-3377

National Conference of Christians and Jews (Regional)
1945 Fifth Avenue, 2nd Floor
Pittsburgh, Pennsylvania 15219
(401) 351-5120

South Hills Interfaith Ministries
5171 Park Avenue
Bethel Park, Pennsylvania 15102
(412) 833-6177

Rhode Island

National Conference of Christians and Jews (Regional)
345 Blackstone Boulevard, Hall Building
Providence, Rhode Island 02906
(401) 351-5120

Tennessee

National Conference of Christians and Jews (Regional)
P.O. Box 50572, 6324 Papermill Road
Knoxville, Tennessee 37919
(615) 588-8911

National Conference of Christians and Jews (Regional)
3373 Poplar Avenue, Suite 414
Memphis, Tennessee 38111
(901) 327-0010

National Conference of Christians and Jews (Regional)
100 Oaks Office Tower, 719 Thompson Lane, Suite 332
Nashville, Tennessee 37204
(615) 297-9751

Texas

American Jewish Committee (Regional)
12870 Hillcrest Road, Suite 101
Dallas, Texas 75230
(214) 387-2943

American Jewish Committee (Regional)
2600 South West Freeway
Houston, Texas 77098
(713) 524-1133

Anti-Defamation League of B'nai B'rith (Regional)
12800 Hillcrest Road, Suite 219
Dallas, Texas 75230
(214) 960-0342

Anti-Defamation League of B'nai B'rith (Regional)
4211 Southwest Freeway, Suite 101
Houston, Texas 77027
(713) 627-3490

Center for Judaic-Christian Studies
P.O. Box 202707
Austin, Texas 78720

National Conference of Christians and Jews (Regional)
P.O. Box 26482
Austin, Texas 78755
(512) 322-0025

National Conference of Christians and Jews (Regional)
202 Oleander Street
Corpus Christi, Texas 78404
(512) 883-1329

National Conference of Christians and Jews (Regional)
4319 Oak Lawn Avenue, Section E
Dallas, Texas 75219
(214) 526-6745

National Conference of Christians and Jews (Regional)
409 Executive Center Boulevard, Suite 202
El Paso, Texas 79901
(915) 532-6637

National Conference of Christians and Jews (Regional)
410 West 7th Street Building, Suite 618
Fort Worth, Texas 76102
(817) 332-3271

National Conference of Christians and Jews (Regional)
4848 Guiton, Suite 212
Houston, Texas 77027
(713) 960-9244

National Conference of Christians and Jews (Regional)
118 North Broadway, Suite 623
San Antonio, Texas 78205
(512) 226-9135

Utah

National Conference of Christians and Jews (Regional)
1530 Jamestown Drive
Salt Lake City, Utah 84121
(801) 272-6769

Virginia

Anti-Defamation League of B'nai B'rith (Regional)
1703 Parham Road, Suite 204
Richmond, Virginia 23229
(804) 288-0366

National Conference of Christians and Jews (Regional)
4912 West Broad Street, Room 200, P.O. Box 6505
Richmond, Virginia 23230
(804) 359-2137

Washington

American Jewish Committee (Regional)
1404 Joseph Vance Building
Seattle, Washington 98101
(206) 622-6315

Anti-Defamation League of B'nai B'rith (Regional)
1809 7th Avenue, Suite 1609
Seattle, Washington 98101
(206) 624-5750

National Conference of Christians and Jews (Regional)
P.O. Box 1384, 9725 Southeast 36th, #113
Mercer Island, Washington 98040
(206) 232-3464

Wisconsin

American Jewish Committee (Regional)
759 North Milwaukee Street
Milwaukee, Wisconsin 53202

C. International Organizations

American Jewish Committee
4, rue de la Bienfaisance
75008 Paris
France
1 43-87-38-39/45-22-92-43

American Jewish Committee
9 Ethiopia Street
Jerusalem 95149
Israel
02 228862/233551

American Jewish Committee
Av. Ejercito Nacional 533/302-303
Mexico 5 D.F.
905-531-0733/531-4776

Anti-Defamation League of B'nai B'rith
30 King David Street
Jerusalem
Israel
011-972-2-224-844

Anti-Defamation League of B'nai B'rith
4 bis rue de Lota
75016 Paris
France
011-33-1-45-53-03-02

Anti-Defamation League of B'nai B'rith
Via Romagna 26/7, 00187
Rome
Italy
011-39-6-4741104 or 011-39-06-4742330

Anti-Defamation League of B'nai B'rith
15 Hove Street, Suite 210
Downsview, Ontario
Canada, M3H 4Y8
(416) 633-6227

Bridges for Peace
Box 7304
Jerusalem
Israel
(02) 240-077

Canadian Council of Christians and Jews
49 Front Street
Toronto, Ontario
Canada M5E 1B3

Ecumenical Theological Research Fraternity
P.O. Box 249
Jerusalem 66308
Israel

International Council of Christians and Jews
Martin Buber House, Werlestrusse 2
D-6148 Heppenheim 1767
West Germany
06252/5041

Nes Ammim
Christian Settlement in Israel
Doar Na Ashrat 25225
Israel

Root and Branch Association
P.O. 6273
Jerusalem 91062
Israel
(02) 636510

World Council of Churches
Consultation on the Church and the Jewish People
P.O. Box 66, route de Ferney
CH-1211 Geneva 20
Switzerland
(022) 98 94 00

IX.
Speakers Bureau

This list of speakers has been organized to be of use to beginning dialogue groups, temples, synagogues, churches, colleges, universities, schools, and national, state, and local conferences who are seeking speakers on the dialogue.

It is the responsibility of the organization to establish contact with individual speakers.

This list contains speakers of national reputation and those that would be willing to help with beginning dialogue groups. They represent several different denominations of Christianity as well as different branches of Judaism.

The speakers themselves have supplied their correct title, address, institutional affiliation, relevant publications, and areas of expertise. In some cases they also indicated geographical limitations, expected compensation, and in a few cases, lead time. If any information is missing it is because individual speakers did not supply it. This list is current as of the summer of 1987.

Entries are organized in the manner presented below:

Speaker. Title. Address (Institution and/or Organization and/or Home).
Publications:
Expertise:
Limitations:

Larry E. Axel. Professor of Philosophy, Purdue University, West Lafayette, Indiana 47907, (317) 494-4286 or 615 Kossuth, Lafayette, Indiana 47905, (317) 742-7048.
"Christian Theology and the Murder of the Jews." Encounter 40 (1979): 129-41.
Jewish-Christian dialogue; East-West dialogue.

Robert H. Ayers. Emeritus Professor of Religion, Peabody Hall, University of Georgia, Athens, Georgia 30606, (404) 542-5356 or 450 Milledge Heights, Atlanta, Georgia 30602, (404) 543-2047.
Judaism and Christianity: Origins, Developments, and Recent Trends. Lanham, Md.: University Press of America, 1983. Language, Logic and Reason in the Church Fathers. New York: George Olms, 1979.
Philosophical and historical theology.
Anywhere in the United States, but preferably in the Southeast.

Judith Hershcopf Banki. Associate National Director, Interreligious Affairs, American Jewish Committee, 165 East 56 Street, New York, New York 10022, (212) 751-4000.
"The Image of Jews in Christian Teaching." Journal of Ecumenical Studies 21 (1954): 437-51 (available as reprint from the AJC). "Jews & Catholics: Taking Stock." Commonweal 112 (1985): 463-68. "Religious Education Before and After Vatican II." Chapter in Twenty Years of Jewish-Catholic Relations. New York: Paulist, 1986. "The Church and the Jews: The Struggle at Vatican Council II." In The American Jewish Year Book. New York: American Jewish Committee, 1965.
Catholic-Jewish relations; the impact of Vatican II; how Christians and Jews teach about one another; the Oberammergau Passion Play; seminary education and Christian-Jewish relations; the impact of Israel on Christian-Jewish relations.

Norman A. Beck. Professor of Theology and Chairman of the Department of Theology and Philosophy, Texas Lutheran College, 1000 West Court Street, Seguin, Texas 78155, (512) 379-8713.
Mature Christianity: The Recognition and Repudiation of the Anti-Jewish Polemic of the New Testament. Selinsgrove, Pa.: Susquehanna University Press, 1985. Scripture Notes: For Use with Common, Lutheran, and Roman Catholic Lectionaries. Lima, Ohio: C.S.S., 1956.
Biblical theology; anti-Jewish polemic in the New Testament and how it can be repudiated; anti-Roman cryptograms in the New Testament and their significance for Jewish-Christian dialogue; interreligious dialogue. No limitations.

Solomon S. Bernards. Professor. 70 East 10th Street, Apartment 16V, New York, New York 10003 or Rabbi, Friends of Congregation Mevakshei Derech of Jerusalem, 225 Park Avenue, South, 17th Floor, New York, New York 10003, (212) 674-7400.
"The Jewish-Christian Agenda." Theology Today 41 (1984): 271-74.

Joseph Blenkinsopp. John A. O'Brien Professor of Biblical Studies, Department of Theology, University of Notre Dame, Notre Dame, Indiana 46617.
A History of Prophecy in Israel. Philadelphia: Westminster Press, 1983; "Old Testament Theology and the Jewish-Christian Connection." Journal for the Study of the Old Testament 29 (1984): 3-15.
Second Temple studies; early Judaism and the emergence of Christianity; Judaism in biblical theology; Jewish-Catholic relations.

Lawrence Boadt. Reverend, C.S.P. Associate Professor of Biblical Studies, Washington Theological Union, 9001 New Hampshire Avenue, Silver Spring, Maryland 20910, (301) 439-0551 or Editor-in-charge of Jewish-Christian Publishing, Paulist Press, 997 Macarthur Boulevard, Mahwah, New Jersey 07430, (201) 525-7300.

Reading the Old Testament, New York: Paulist, 1984. Biblical Studies: Meeting Ground of Jews and Christians. New York: Paulist, 1950.
Biblical aspects of the dialogue: Christian and Jewish approaches to reading the Bible; the importance of the Bible for future dialogue; biblical studies and their influence on the dialogue; specific biblical themes, such as afterlife, redemption, salvation, hope, God's kingdom, messiahship, etc.; specific biblical authors: the prophets, the wisdom tradition, etc.; Jewish-Christian publishing and dialogue opportunities.
Any area is negotiable, although the Northeast corridor is my preferred area. Travel expenses plus a reasonable stipend.

Mary C. Boys. Associate Professor, Institute of Religious Education and Pastoral Ministry, Boston College, Chestnut Hill, Massachusetts 02167, (617) 552-8440.
"Questions 'Which Touch on the Heart of Our Faith.'" Religious Education 76 (1981): 636-56. Biblical Interpretation in Religious Education. Birmingham, Ala.: Religious Education Press, 1950.
Working with clergy and teachers.
Willing to travel.

Robert L. Brashear. Reverend. Executive Director, South Hills Interfaith Ministries, 5171 Park Avenue, Bethel Park, Pennsylvania 15102, (412) 833-6177.
"Corner Stone, Stumbling Stone: Christian Problems in Viewing Israel." Union Seminary Quarterly Review 38 (1983): 203-24.
Local interfaith dialogue; Christians and Israel; intermarriage.
No limitations.

Christopher R. Browning. Professor of History, Pacific Lutheran University, Tacoma, Washington 98447, (206) 535-7635.
Fateful Months: Essays on the Emergence of the Final Solution. New York: Holmes and Meier, 1955. The Final Solution and the German Foreign Office. New York: Holmes and Meier, 1978.
History of the Holocaust with particular focus on the evolution and implementation of the Final Solution.

C. Hassell Bullock. Professor, Wheaton College, 1111 North Washington Street, Wheaton, Illinois 60187.
An Introduction to the Old Testament Poetic Books. Chicago: Moody, 1979. An Introduction to the Old Testament Prophetic Books. Chicago: Moody, 1956.
Prophets and wisdom literature; Judaism.
Chicago metropolitan area.

Robert W. Bullock. Pastor, Our Lady of Sorrows Church, 59 Cottage Street, Sharon, Massachusetts 02067, (617) 784-2265.
Catholic-Jewish relations; Israel; the teaching of the Holocaust.

John H. Burt. Retired Bishop of Ohio. Middle Island Point 450, Marquette, Michigan 49855, (906) 226-2413.
The Christian roots of anti-Semitism; Christianity and the fresh approach to the Hebrew Scriptures; issues in the Middle East for Christians; highlights for Christians in the Land called Holy (with slides).
Since I live in the northern peninsula of Michigan, I would need travel expense reimbursement for any trips to engagements; an honorarium is not necessary.

Harry James Cargas. Professor. Associate Editor, Holocaust and Genocide Studies, Webster University, 470 East Lockwood, St. Louis, Missouri 63119, (314) 968-7014.
The Holocaust: An Annotated Bibliography. Chicago: American Library Association, 1986. A Christian Response to the Holocaust. Denver: Stonehenge, 1981. Harry James Cargas in Conversation with Elie Wiesel. New York: Paulist, 1976. When God and Man Failed: Non-Jewish Views of the Holocaust. New York: Macmillan, 1981.

John Tully Carmody. Senior Research Fellow in Religion, University of Tulsa, Tulsa, Oklahoma 74104, (918) 592-6000, #2959.
Ways to the Center. Belmont, Calif.: Wadsworth, 1984. Exploring the New Testament. Englewood Cliffs: Prentice Hall, 1986.
Catholicism; comparative philosophy of religion; spirituality.
Central and Southwest preferred. Heavy writing commitment so comfortable lead-time appreciated.

James Anderson Carpenter. Professor of Systematic Theology. Director, Center for Jewish-Christian Studies and Relations, General Theological Seminary, 175 Ninth Avenue, New York, New York 10011, (212) 243-5150 or (212) 282-0792.
Jews and Christians: Suggestions for Dialogue. Cincinnati: Forward Movement, 1979. On Jews and Christians in Dialogue. Editor, Anglican Theological Review 64 (1982): 445-576.
Judaism and Christian identity; impact of Judaic Studies on Christian theology and self-understanding; reconsiderations in Christology arising from the dialogue; relation of law and grace; theology of the covenant; Christian triumphalism and Jewish realism; Christian response to the Holocaust; "teaching of contempt" and Christian consciousness; dialogue at the grassroots.
The Northeast would be convenient, but I am willing to go anywhere to further the dialogue.

Nancy Gabriela Carroll. Professional lecturer. 377 Walnut Street, Winnetka, Illinois 60093, (312) 441-4577.
Israel and Jewish-Christian relations.
I am willing to speak to any legitimate group within the U.S.A. and Canada. In addition to a lecture fee, my transportation must be paid if the engagement is more than a 1-½ hour drive from my home. I request that local overnight accommodations be provided, as necessary, by the host organization.

Leonard F. Chorobot. Reverend. Professor of Sociology, Department of Social Science, St. Mary's College, Orchard Lake, Michigan 48033, (313) 682-1885.
Polish American-Jewish American Affairs.
Midwest.

Michael J. Cook. Rabbi. Professor, Hebrew Union College—Jewish Institute of Religion, 3101 Clifton Avenue, Cincinnati, Ohio 45220, (513) 221-1875 or home (513) 954-1754.
Mark's Treatment of the Jewish Leaders. Leiden: Brill, 1975. "Anti-Judaism in the New Testament." Union Seminary Quarterly Review 38 (1983): 125-38.

Rabbinic Judaism and Gospel studies; the Jewish Bible and Christian missionaries; modern Passion plays; gospel narratives and Jewish-Christian relations: the Jews and Jesus' trial; was the Last Supper a Passover seder?; the virgin birth and resurrection traditions.

Philip L. Culbertson. Reverend. Professor, School of Theology, University of the South, Sewanee, Tennessee 37375, (615) 598-0780, (615) 598-5931 or Rehov Sukkat Shalom 9, 94305 Jerusalem, Israel, (02-244416, summers only).
"The Pharisaic Jesus and His Gospel Parallels." Christian Century 102 (1985): 74-77. "Rethinking the Christ in Jewish-Christian Dialogue." Ecumenical Trends 13, (1984): 1-5.
Second Temple studies and the Parables of Jesus; the history of Christian-Jewish relations; Protestant attitudes toward Judaism and Israel; what Jews and Christians teach about each other; the theology of Christian-Jewish dialogue; Christianity in the Middle East; Jewish and Christian mysticism; family law in the state of Israel; teaching and preaching Christian-Jewish issues.

Barry D. Cytron. Rabbi, Adath Jeshurun Congregation, 3400 Dupont Avenue South, Minneapolis, Minnesota 55408, (612) 824-2685.
"Nostra Aetate, the Jews and the Future of Dialogue." Conservative Judaism 38 (1985): 21-29. When Life Is in the Balance: Life and Death Decisions in the Light of the Jewish Tradition. New York: United Synagogue of America, 1986. Forthcoming, book on lay Jewish-Christian dialogue for Stimulus series Studies in Judaism and Christianity.
Lay Jewish-Christian dialogue; adult faith development; contemporary American Judaism; biomedical ethical issues and the Jewish tradition.

Paulina K. Dennis. Reverend. Christian Clergy for a Better Understanding of Judaism, 360 Clinton Avenue, 6S, Brooklyn, New York 11238, (718) 636-4505.
The integration of Jewish studies into the Christian seminary curriculum; understanding the Jewish roots of Christianity; Reform Christianity and Orthodox Judaism; a Reform Christian looks at Orthodox Judaism; the Hebraic/Talmudic roots of American constitutional and civil law.
Availability: Weekends in the Northeast area (New York, Connecticut, New Jersey, Boston, and Philadelphia).

Joseph W. Devlin. Monsignor. 22 East Clinton Avenue, Haddon Township, New Jersey 08107 or Assistant Professor of Religion, Department of Religion, La Salle University, 20th and Olney Avenue, Philadelphia, Pennsylvania 19141, (215) 951-1342 or 951-1350.
Cross cultural studies: ethics and biomedical ethics; Jewish-Christian relationships; history of religion in America (including the relationships of Catholics and Jews to the mainstream culture); world religious dialogue; history of world religious traditions.

Robert F. Drinan. Professor of Law, Georgetown University Law Center, 600 New Jersey Avenue, NW, Washington, D.C. 20001, (202) 662-9073. Honor the Promise: America's Commitment to Israel. New York: Doubleday, 1977. God and Caesar on the Potomac: A Pilgrimage of Conscience. Wilmington, Del.: Michael Glazier, 1985.

Alice L. Eckardt. Professor Emerita of Religion Studies, Maginnes Hall #9, Lehigh University, Bethlehem, Pennsylvania 18015, (215) 758-3353 or Beverly Hill Road, Box 619A, Coopersburg, Pennsylvania 18036, (215) 282-1363 (please use home address).
Jerusalem: City of the Ages. Lanham, Md.: University Press of America, 1987. Long Night's Journey into Day: Life and Faith after the Holocaust. With A. Roy Eckardt. Second, rev. ed. New York: Holocaust Library, 1988.
History of Jewish-Christian relations; contemporary efforts at repairing the damage of almost 2,000 years of antisemitism; State of Israel; the Holocaust and post-Holocaust thinking.
No limitations.

Yechiel Eckstein. Rabbi. President, The Holyland Fellowship of Christians and Jews, 36 South Wabash Street, Suite 626, Chicago, Illinois 60603, (312) 346-7693.
What Christians Should Know About Jews and Judaism. Waco, Tex.: Word Books, 1984. "What Christians Need to Know About Jews." Christian Life Magazine 46 (1984): 41-44.
Jewish-Christian relations today: facing the test of Israel; the Christian Right: the Jews' best friend or greatest adversary?; confronting the threat of Jews for Jesus and other missionary groups.

Frank Eiklor. President, Shalom Ministries, 27 Congress Street, Salem, Massachusetts 01970, (617) 744-8131.
Hebraic roots of Christianity; the Holocaust as a predictable event in light of 1,900 years of "Christian" contempt towards Jews; the history of anti-Semitism; the new code word of those who hate Jews called anti-Zionism.
No limitations as to travel; would have to schedule engagements way in advance.

David Ellenson. Associate Professor of Jewish Religious Thought, Hebrew Union College--Jewish Institute of Religion, 3077 University Avenue, Los Angeles, California 90007, (213) 749-3424.
"Christianity Through Jewish Eyes: Historical and Theological Views." Chapter in Jewish Civilization: Essays and Studies. Edited by Ronald Brauner. Philadelphia: Reconstructionist Rabbinical College Press, 1985. "The Role of Reform in Selected German-Jewish Orthodox Responsa: A Sociological Analysis." Hebrew Union College Annual 53 (1982): 357-80.
Christianity through Jewish eyes: historical and theological views.
Happy to speak anywhere.

Anna Marie Erst. Sister, S.H.C.J. Director, National Institute for Catholic-Jewish Education, 1307 South Wabash Avenue, Room 224, Chicago, Catholic-Jewish education.
I would be willing to go anywhere in the United States, though, hopefully, transportation expenses would be provided, especially if the distance is great.

Carl D. Evans. Associate Professor, Department of Religious Studies, University of South Carolina, Columbia, South Carolina 29208, (803) 777-4522 or 7005 Devon Road, Columbia, South Carolina 29209, (803) 776-6295.

Scripture in Context: Essays on the Comparative Method. Ed. with William
W. Hallo and John B. White. Pittsburgh: Pickwick, 1980. "The Church's
False Witness Against Jews." Christian Century 99 (1982): 530-33.
Jewish and Christian appropriations of a common Scriptural heritage;
Christian misunderstandings of Judaism; the "teaching of contempt," Jesus
and the Pharisees.
No limitations.

Robert Andrew Everett. Professor. Pastor, Emanuel United Church of
Christ, 23 Lincoln Place, Irvington, New Jersey 07111, (201) 372-1223.
"A Christian Apology for Israel: A Study in the Thought of James Parkes."
Christian Jewish Relations 72 (1980): 50-64. "The Impact of the Holocaust
on Christian Theology." Christian Jewish Relations 15 (1982): 3-11. "Dealing
Honestly with Judaism and Jewish History: James Parkes as a Model for
the Christian Community." Journal of Ecumenical Studies 23 (1986): 37-57.
Jewish-Christian relations—a history: anti-Semitism and Christian thought;
theology after the Holocaust; Zionism and Christianity; the thought of
James Parkes; future of the dialogue.
Willing to speak in any area.

Randall M. Falk. Rabbi Emeritus, Temple Congregation Ohabai Sholom,
5015 Harding Road, Nashville, Tennessee 37205, (615) 352-7620 or 267
Cana Circle, Nashville, Tennessee 37205, (615) 356-7175.
"Tension and Accord in Jewish-Christian Relations." Newsletter of the
Ecumenical Institute of Wake Forest University. January 1971.
Judaism as Jesus lived it; Jewish-Christian relations: an historical
perspective and contemporary concerns.
Willing to speak in any area.

Eugene J. Fisher. Executive Secretary, Secretariat For Catholic-Jewish
Relations, National Conference of Catholic Bishops, Bishops' Committee
for Ecumenical and Interreligious Affairs, 1312 Massachusetts Avenue,
NW, Washington, D.C. 20005, (202) 659-6857.
Faith Without Prejudice: Rebuilding Christian Attitudes Toward Judaism.
New York: Paulist, 1977. Homework for Christians Preparing for
Christian-Jewish Dialogue. New York: National Conference of Christians
and Jews, 1982.
Scripture; religious education and Jewish-Christian relations; liturgy; Jesus
and Pharisees; history of anti-Semitism; Christian theology of the Shoah;
and related topics.
No travel limitations depending on schedule.

Edward H. Flannery. Father. 80 Farnum Pike, Esmond, Rhode Island 02197.
Anguish of the Jews: Twenty-Three Centuries of Antisemitism. Updated
and revised edition. New York: Paulist, 1985. "Seminaries, Classrooms,
Pulpits, and Streets: Where We Have to Go." Essay in Unanswered Questions:
Theological Views on Jewish-Catholic Relations. Ed. Roger Brooks. Notre
Dame: University of Notre Dame Press, 1987.
Anti-Semitism; Holocaust; Israel; Zionism.
East Coast preferred.

Eva Fleischner. Professor, Montclair State College, 180 Walnut Street,
Montclair, New Jersey 07042.
Judaism in German Christian Theology Since 1945. Metuchen, N.J.:
Scarecrow, 1975. Auschwitz: Beginning of a New Era? Ed. New York:
Ktav, 1977.

The Holocaust and the churches; the "teaching of contempt"; Christian anti-Semitism; Christians who saved the Jews.
No geographical limitations, provided expenses are paid and comes at a time I can fit into my schedule.

Lawrence E. Frizzell. Reverend. Professor, Department of Judaeo-Christian Studies. Seton Hall University, South Orange, New Jersey 07079, (201) 761-9463.
Standing Before God: Studies on Prayer in Scripture and Tradition. New York: Ktav, 1981. "History and Philosophy of Jewish Education: A Bibliographical Essay." Journal of Dharma 9 (1984): 336-47. "Law at the Service of Humankind." SIDIC 19 (1956): 4-7.
Qumran Scrolls and Jewish literature of Second Temple period; Bible; early Christianity; law and ethics; peace and war in Bible and Jewish and Christian traditions; Jewish-Christian relations.
No geographical limitations if schedule is amenable to travel and expenses are covered.

Stephen Fuchs. Rabbi, Temple Congregation Ohabai Sholom, 5015 Harding Road, Nashville, Tennessee 37205, (615) 352-7620.
"Prayer for Peace in Judaism." With Annette Daum. Essay in The Challenge of Shalom for Catholics and Jews. Ed. Annette Daum and Eugene J. Fisher. New York: Union of American Hebrew Congregations, 1985. "Teaching Judaism to Lutheran Seminarians." Christian Jewish Relations, 72 (1980): 43-46.
Interfaith marriage; teaching Judaism to non-Jews.
I would be willing to travel assuming that the date would fit my schedule and my travel expenses would be paid.

Martin T. Geraghty. Reverend. Academic Dean, Cathedral College of the Immaculate Conception, 7200 Douglaston Parkway, Douglaston, New York 11362, (718) 631-4600.
"Catholic-Jewish Dialogue Under Strain: Arafat and the Pope." The Tablet. 75 (1982). "Catholics and Jews Face Each Other in New Way Twenty Years After Vatican II." The Tablet. 78 (1985).

Ann Gillen. Sister. Executive Director, National Interreligious Task Force on Soviet Jewry, 1307 South Wabash Avenue, Room 221, Chicago, Illinois 60605, (312) 922-1983.
"Rationale for Coalition Building." Essay in Women of Faith in Dialogue. Ed. Virginia R. Mollencott. New York: Crossroad, 1987. "Roman Catholics in the Soviet Union." Essay in The Struggle for Religious Survival in the Soviet Union. Ed. A. James Rudin and Ann Gillen. New York: American Jewish Committee, 1986.

Irving Greenberg. Rabbi. President, CLAL, The National Jewish Center for Learning and Leadership, 421 Seventh Avenue, New York, New York 10001, (212) 714-9500 or 4620 Independence Avenue, Riverdale, New York 10471, (212) 548-4211.
"The New Encounter of Judaism and Christianity." Barat Review 3 (1967): 113-25; "The Relationship of Judaism and Christianity: Toward a New Organic Model." Quarterly Review 4 (1984): 4-22.
Holocaust: Jewish theology; Judaism and Christianity.
Limited time availability.

Thaddeus V. Gromada. Professor of History and Coordinator of Multi-Ethnic Studies, Department of History, Jersey City State College, Jersey City, New Jersey 07305, (201) 547-3251 or (201) 547-2168, or Secretary General, The Polish Institute of Arts and Sciences of America, 59 East 66th Street, New York, New York 10021, (212) 988-4388.
Modern East-Central European history, immigrant history; Polish-American Jewish-American relations in America.
New Jersey, New York, Connecticut, Eastern Pennsylvania.

Donald Hagner. Professor of New Testament, Fuller Theological Seminary, Pasadena, California 91182, (818) 584-5247 or 584-5200.
The Jewish Reclamation of Jesus. Grand Rapids: Zondervan, 1984. "The Jewish View of Paul." Pauline Studies: Essays Presented to Professor F. F. Bruce on His Seventieth Birthday. Ed. with M. J. Harris. Grand Rapids: Eerdmans, 1980.
Jewish-Christian relations.
Willing to speak anywhere if travel funds are provided.

Philip Paul Hallie. Griffin Professor of Philosophy and Humanities, Wesleyan University, Middletown, Connecticut 06457, (203) 347-9411 #2265 or 137 Highland Avenue, Middletown, Connecticut 06457, (203) 346-1513.
Lest Innocent Blood Be Shed. New York: Harper and Row, 1979. The Scar of Montaigne: An Essay in Personal Philosophy. Middletown, Conn.: Wesleyan University Press, 1966. Cruelty. Middletown, Conn.: Wesley University Press, 1982.
Ethics; the French resistance during the Shoah; Christians and Jews in the Shoah.
No preferred geographical area, preferred time for lectures, January 15-August 1.

Douglas R. A. Hare. Professor, Pittsburgh Theological Seminary, 616 North Highland Avenue, Pittsburgh, Pennsylvania 15206, (412) 362-5610.
The Theme of Jewish Persecution of Christians in the Gospel According to St. Matthew. New York: Cambridge University Press, 1967. "The Relationship Between Jewish and Gentile Persecution of Christians." Journal of Ecumenical Studies 4 (1967): 446-56.
Jews and Christians in the first century.
Pittsburgh only.

Katharine T. Hargrove. Sister. Lecturer and writer. Convent of the Sacred Heart, Kenwood, Albany, New York 12202.
The Star and the Cross: Essays on Jewish-Christian Relations. Ed. Encino, Calif.: Bruce Publishing, 1966. "The Torah: A Bridge." Christian Jewish Relations 15 (1982): 41-50.
Work with International Speakers Association and International Council of Christians and Jews; a Christian approach to the Talmud.

Walter Harrelson. Professor, The Divinity School, Vanderbilt University, Nashville, Tennessee 37240, (615) 343-3988 or 305 Bowling Avenue, Nashville, Tennessee 37205, (615) 383-8218.
Interpreting the Old Testament. New York: Holt, Rinehart and Winston, 1964. The Ten Commandments and Human Rights. Philadelphia: Fortress, 1980.
Hebrew Bible and its importance for contemporary culture and ethics.
Limited availability.

Maria Harris. Howard Professor of Religious Education, Andover Newton Theological School, 216 St. Paul Street, Brookline, Massachusetts 02146, (617) 964-1100.
Portrait of Youth Ministry. New York: Paulist, 1981. The DRE Reader: A Sourcebook in Education and Ministry. Winoma, Minn.: St. Mary's, 1980.
The education of adults; the use of imagination and the arts in education; the activity of teaching.
No area preferred.

George G. Higgins. Reverend, Monsignor. Curley Hall, The Catholic University of America, Washington, D.C. 20064, (202) 635-5660.

R. W. Huebsch. Associate Professor and Chairman of Religious Studies, Niagara University, Niagara University, New York 14109.
"The Testament of Moses: A Soteriological Consideration. Proceedings: Eastern Great Lakes Biblical Society 2 (1982): 22-33.
The emergence and inter-relationship of Judaism and Christianity in Graeco-Roman Palestine between 200 B.C.E. and 200 C.E., and how this early formative period has affected the interrelationship of Judaism and Christianity.
No limitations except scheduling.

Morris Alton Inch. Executive Director, Institute of Holy Land Studies, Mount Zion, P.O. Box 1276, 91012 Jerusalem, Israel, (02) 718628.
"Jews and Evangelicals." Christianity Today 23 (1979): 24-26. The Literature and Meaning of Scripture. Grand Rapids: Baker, 1981.
Jesus and his times; Israel and the Church; the promised land.
When present in the United States or otherwise as groups tour Israel.

Darrell Jodock. Professor of Religion, Muhlenberg College, Allentown, Pennsylvania 18104, (215) 821-3432 or 821-3100.
"The Modernist and Alternative Views of the Bible." Three Discussions: Biblical Exegesis, George Tyrell, Jesuit Archives. Mobile, Ala.: Spring Hill College Press, 1981. "The Impact of Cultural Change: Princeton Theology and Scriptural Authority Today." Dialog 22 (1983): 21-29.
The impact of the Holocaust in Christian theology; Jewish identity and Jewish-Christian relations; the roots of anti-Judaism in the events of the first century; Jews and Christians in relation to American culture; the history of Christian thought; the authority of the Bible.

Alan F. Johnson. Professor, Wheaton College, Wheaton, Illinois 60187, (312) 260-3766 or 14 Circle Avenue, Wheaton, Illinois 60187, (312) 653-5547.
"The Historical-Critical Method: Egyptian Gold or Pagan Precipe." Presidential Address, Evangelical Theological Society. Journal of the Evangelical Theological Society 26 (1983): 3-15. "The Bible and War in America: A Historical Survey." Journal of the Evangelical Theological Society 28 (1985): 169-81.
Biblical and theological aspects of Israel and the Church; Evangelical-Jewish dialogue; Christian attitude toward the current Palestinian-Israeli conflict.

Edward Jones. Bishop of Indianapolis, Episcopal Diocese of Indianapolis, 1100 West 42nd Street, Indianapolis, Indiana 46208, (317) 926-5454.
Contemporary issues in Jewish-Christian dialogue.

Harriet L. Kaufman. Program Director, National Conference of Christians and Jews, 366 Terrace Avenue, Cincinnati, Ohio 45220, (513) 751-6381. Jews & Judaism Since Jesus: An Introduction. Cincinnati: Kaufman House, 1978.
Teaching Christians about basic beliefs and values in post-biblical Judaism through stories and excerpts from daily liturgy.
Anywhere.

John J. Kelley. Reverend. Rockaway Catholic–Jewish Council for the Diocese of Brooklyn, P.O. Box 272, Rockaway Park, New York, New York 11694, (718) 945-2800 or Beach 111 Street, Rockaway Park, New York, New York 11694.
"The Relation of Christians and Jews." Brochure. Dayton, Ohio: University of Dayton Press, 1972. "Social Justice and the Prophets." Essay in The Future of Jewish-Christian Relations. Ed. Norma H. Thompson and Bruce K. Cole. Schenectady, New York: Character Research, 1982. "Christian Strategy on the Passion Plays." The Ecumenist 24 (1986): 38-44.
Christian strategy on passion plays; Christian perspective on the Holocaust; the ERUV; social justice; Catholic social thought; organization of local groups.
No limitations.

Joseph G. Kelly. Professor, Department of Religious Studies, Nazareth College of Rochester, 4245 East Avenue, Rochester, New York 14610, (716) 586-2525.
"Lucan Christology and the Jewish/Christian Dialogue." Journal of Ecumenical Studies 21 (1984): 688-708. "The Two Covenants." New Catholic World 288 (1985): 203-7.
Old Testament (Hebrew) Scriptures; relation between Old Testament (Hebrew) Scriptures and New Testament (Christian) Scriptures; Roman Catholic teaching on Jewish-Christian dialogue; Roman Catholic theology after the Holocaust.
No limitations; need to plan around teaching schedule at the College.

Barry Kenter. Rabbi, Greenburgh Hebrew Center, 515 Broadway, Dobbs Ferry, New York 10522, (914) 693-4260.
Jewish history, rites and ceremonies; comparative religion.
Metro New York, Northeast. No Friday night, Saturday or Jewish holiday.

Leon Klenicki. Rabbi. Director, Department of Interfaith Affairs, Anti-Defamation League of B'nai B'rith, 823 United Nations Plaza, New York, New York 10017, (212) 490-2525.
Spirituality and Prayer: Jewish and Christian Understandings. Ed. with Gabe Huck. New York: Paulist, 1983. A Dictionary of the Jewish-Christian Dialogue. Ed. with Geoffrey Wigoder. New York: Paulist, 1984.
Rabbinic theology and the religious formation of Jesus: God person and peoplehood—Dimensions of Jewish spirituality; Jewish understandings of Christianity from the Rabbis to our days.

Paul F. Knitter. Professor of Theology, Xavier University, Department of Theology, Cincinnati, Ohio 45207, (513) 745-3491.
No Other Name? A Critical Survey of Christian Attitudes toward World Religions. Maryknoll: Orbis, 1985. "Roman Catholic Theology at a Crossroads." Christianity among World Religions. Concilium 183 (1985): 99-107.

Interreligious dialogue; Christian attitudes toward other religions; Jewish-
Christian dialogue and the question of Christ.
Anywhere in U.S.A.

Josephine Z. Knopp. Director of Holocaust Education, Southeastern Florida
Holocaust Memorial Foundation, Florida International University, Bay
Vista Campus, NE, 151 Street and Biscayne Boulevard, Miami, Florida
33181, (305) 940-5690 or 1201 Northeast 191 Street, Apartment 304-G,
Miami, Florida 33179. The Trial of Judaism in Contemporary Jewish
Writing. Champaign: University of Illinois Press, 1975. In Memoriam:
A History of the Greek Jews of Salonika. New York: Holocaust Library
Publications, 1987.
Jewish studies: thought, history and literature; Holocaust studies;
comparative religions; contemporary Jewish and Christian thought;
Jewish/Christian relations in any area: historical, religious, theological.
I will travel if expenses paid.

John T. Koenig. Reverend. Professor of New Testament, The General
Theological Seminary, 175 Ninth Avenue, New York, New York 10011,
(212) 243-5150.
Jews and Christians in Dialogue: New Testament Foundations. Philadelphia:
Westminster, 1979. New Testament Hospitality: Partnerships with
Strangers as Promise and Mission. Philadelphia: Fortress, 1985.
Major issues in the Jewish-Christian dialogue; interdependence of New
Testament studies and the Church's ministry.
Anywhere.

Andre LaCocque. Professor of Old Testament, Director of the Center
for Jewish-Christian Studies, Chicago Theological Seminary, 5757 University
Avenue, Chicago, Illinois 60637, (312) 752-5757 or 5555 South Everett,
#8C, Chicago, Illinois 60637, (312) 955-0396.
Contributor, A Dictionary of the Jewish-Christian Dialogue. New York:
Paulist, 1984.
The formative era of Rabbinic Judaism; Judaism and Hellenism; apocalyptic
literature; intertestamental literature; Christian theology after Auschwitz.
No geographical limitations.

Donald Charles Lacy. Reverend. Leesburg United Methodist Church,
P.O. Box 175, Leesburg, Indiana 46538 or P.O. Box 70, 512 West Church,
Hebron, Indiana 46341, (219) 996-7668.
Healing Echoes: Values for Christian Unity. Lima, Ohio: C.S.S. of Ohio,
1986. Mary and Jesus. Lima, Ohio: C.S.S. of Ohio, 1979. Decalogue
for Ecumenical Discipleship: A Call to Daily Commitment. Lima, Ohio:
C.S.S. of Ohio, 1956.
Appreciation and understanding for the rich Jewish heritage that underlies
and supports the Christian faith.
Indiana, Illinois, Michigan, Ohio, Kentucky.

Belden C. Lane. Associate Professor of Theological Studies and American
Studies, Saint Louis University, 3634 Lindell Boulevard, Saint Louis, Missouri
63108, (314) 658-2881 or 6742 Chamberlain Avenue, Saint Louis, Missouri
63130, (314) 727-3404.

"Chutzpa K'lapei Shamaya: A Christian Response to the Jewish Tradition of Arguing with God." Journal of Ecumenical Studies 23 (1986): 567-86. "Rabbinical Stories: A Primer on Theological Method." Christian Century 98 (1981): 1306-10.
American religious history; narrative and metaphor in theological language; storytelling in Jewish, Christian, and other faith traditions.

Gerald A. Larue. Emeritus Professor of Religion. Adjunct Professor, Gerontology, Ethel Percy Andrus, Gerontology Center, University of Southern California, University Park, MC 0191, Los Angeles, California 90089, (213) 743-5156.

William Sanford LaSor. Emeritus Professor of Old Testament, Fuller Theological Seminary, (818) 584-5200 or 1790 East Loma Alta Drive, Altadena, California 91001, (818) 797-9068.
The Dead Sea Scrolls and the New Testament. Grand Rapids: Eerdmans, 1972. "The Conversation of the Jews." The Reformed Journal (1976): 12-14. Foreword to A Time to Speak: The Evangelical-Jewish Encounter. Eds. A. James Rudin and Marvin R. Wilson. New York: Eerdmans, 1987.
Semitic languages; Old Testament (history, geography, archaeology, theology).
Anywhere.

Sara S. Lee. Director, Rhea Hirsch School of Education, Hebrew Union College, 3077 University Avenue, Los Angeles, California 90007, (213) 749-3424.
Forthcoming, co-author of entry on Jewish Education for Harper's Directory of Religious Education.
Religious education; models of developing ecumenism among seminary students of different faiths; interfaith dialogue in secondary schools.
Anywhere.

Jon D. Levenson. Associate Professor of Hebrew Bible, The University of Chicago, The Divinity School, 1025 East 88th Street, Chicago, Illinois 60637, (312) 702-8245 or (312) 677-4798.
Sinai and Zion: An Entry into the Jewish Bible. Minneapolis: Winston Seabury, 1985. "Is There a Counterpart in the Hebrew Bible to New Testament Anti-Semitism?" Journal of Ecumenical Studies 22 (1985): 242-60.
Hebrew Bible.
Limited time availability.

Franklin H. Littell. Professor Emeritus, Temple University, Hamlin Institute, P.O. Box 2147, Philadelphia, Pennsylvania 19103, (215) 546-4759 or P.O. Box 172, Merion, Pennsylvania 19066.
The Crucifixion of the Jews. New York: Harper and Row, 1975. The German Church Struggle and the Holocaust. Ed. with Hubert Locke. Detroit: Wayne State University Press, 1974.
United States religious history; studies in the Holocaust; the Church.
All speaking dates are managed by the Hamlin Institute staff and honoraria go to its work.

Clark Lobenstine. Reverend. Executive Director, Interfaith Conference of Metropolitan Washington, 1419 V Street, NW, Washington, D.C. 20009, (202) 234-6300 or 919 Langley Drive, Silver Spring, Maryland 20901, (301) 445-2114.
"Relations between Christians and Muslims: Our Bond in Covenant with God, Our Hope in Dialogue." Doctor of Ministry Thesis-Article.
Interfaith dialogue and relations among Christians, Jews, and Muslims; Christian-Muslim relations; how leaders and members of these three great monotheistic religions can effectively address together issues of social and economic justice in the community.
None, except my schedule and relevance of request to my expertise.

Hubert G. Locke. Professor. Dean, Graduate School of Public Affairs, DP-30, University of Washington, Seattle, Washington 98195, (206) 543-4900.
The German Church Struggle and the Holocaust. Ed. with Franklin Littell. Detroit: Wayne State University Press, 1974. The Church Confronts the Nazis: Barmen Then and Now. Ed. New York: E. Mellen, 1984. Exile in the Fatherland: Martin Niemoller's Letters from Moabit Prison. Grand Rapids: Eerdmans, 1986. The Barmen Confession: Papers from the Seattle Assembly. Ed. New York: E. Mellen, 1987.
The German Church in the Nazi era and the Christian response to the Holocaust.
Nationally.

James R. Lyons. Reverend. Director, Ecumenical Institute for Jewish-Christian Studies, 26275 Northwestern Highway, Southfield, Michigan 48076, (313) 353-2434.
"Do the Jews Need Jesus?" Christian Jewish Relations 17 (1984): 43-47. "The Holocaust: The Christian Moral Culpability." Glad Tidings (1982).
Anti-Semitism in Christian thought and history; Holocaust and Christian response; Israel and the Middle East.
No geographical limitations.

Donald W. McEvoy. Executive Director, San Diego Region, National Conference of Christians and Jews, 636 C Street, San Diego, California 92101, (619) 232-6113 or 703 Stratford Court, Del Mar, California 92014.
Never Again: A Holocaust Memorial Service for Christians. New York: National Conference of Christians and Jews, 1979. Christians Confront the Holocaust: A Collection of Sermons. Ed. New York: National Conference of Christians and Jews, 1980. Miracle in Denmark. A liturgical drama of the rescue of the Danish Jews. New York: National Conference of Christians and Jews, 1981.
No geographical limitations.

Michael McGarry. Reverend. Rector, St. Paul's College, 3015 Fourth Street, NE, Washington, D.C. 20017, (202) 832-6262.
Christology After Auschwitz. New York: Paulist, 1977. "Contemporary Roman Catholic Understandings of Mission." Essay in Christian Mission/Jewish Mission. Ed. Martin A. Cohen and Helga Croner. New York: Paulist, 1984.
Theology after the Holocaust; Jewish-Catholic relations in general; portraying Jews in Christian preaching; the history of Jewish-Christian relations.
Unlimited.

John C. Merkle. Professor, College of Saint Benedict, St. Joseph, Minnesota 56374.
The Genesis of Faith: The Depth Theology of Abraham Joshua Heschel. New York: Macmillan, 1985. Abraham Joshua Heschel: Exploring His Life and Thought. New York: Macmillan, 1985.
Catholic theology; contemporary Jewish theology, Jewish–Christian dialogue.
Anywhere if expenses are met.

Ronald Modras. Associate Professor of Theological Studies, Saint Louis University, 3634 Lindell Boulevard, St. Louis, Missouri 63108, (314) 658-2880 or 3854 Flad, St. Louis, Missouri 63110, (314) 776-0363.
Paths to Unity: American Religion Today and Tomorrow. New York: Sheed and Ward, 1968. "Pope John Paul II, St. Maximilian Kolbe, and Anti-Semitism: Some Current Problems and Perceptions Affecting Catholic–Jewish Relations." Journal of Ecumenical Studies 20 (1983): 630–39.
Catholic–Jewish relations; Polish–Jewish relations; the Holocaust.
No limitations.

Gabriel Moran. Professor, New York University, 737 East Building, Washington Square, New York, New York 10003, (212) 598-2589 or 6 East 8th Street, 2B, New York, New York 10003, (212) 228-6647.
Religious Education Development. Minneapolis: Winston 1983. Interplay: A Theory of Religion and Education. Winoma, Minn.: St. Mary's Press, 1981.
The idea of revelation; religious education theory; critique of Christian language related to Judaism.
No limitations.

Robert Corin Morris. Episcopal Priest. Interweave, 31 Woodland Avenue, Summit, New Jersey 07901, (201) 763-8312 or 422 Clark Street, South Orange, New Jersey 07079, (201) 763-0416.
Judaic roots of Christianity; Jewish spirituality and mysticism; a new Christian approach to the Hebrew Scriptures.
Hundred-mile radius of New York City (or elsewhere according to appropriate arrangements).

C. Bruce Naylor. Reverend. Executive Director, Evansville Area Council of Churches, 119 West Sixth Street, Evansville, Indiana 47708, (812) 425-3524 or (812) 425-2903.
General Jewish–Christian relations; special interest in Soviet Jewry, traveled in U.S.S.R.
Indiana, Illinois, Kentucky.

David Novak. Visiting Associate Professor of Talmud, Jewish Theological Seminary of America, 3080 Broadway, New York, New York 10027, or 2355 Healy Avenue, Far Rockaway, New York 11691, (718) 471-7771 or (718) 327-0242.
The Image of the Non-Jew in Judaism: An Historical and Constructive Study of the Noahide Law. New York: E. Mellen, 1983. Halakhah in a Theological Dimension. Brown Judaic Studies Series, no. 68. Chico, Calif.: Scholars, 1985.
Jewish views of Christianity, especially in Jewish law.
No limitations.

John M. Oesterreicher. Monsignor. The Institute of Judaeo-Christian Studies, Seton Hall University, South Orange, New Jersey 07079, (201) 761-9569 or (201) 761-9141.
The New Encounter Between Christians and Jews. New York: Philosophical Library, 1986. The Unfinished Dialogue: Martin Buber and the Christian Way. New York: Philosophical Library, 1986.
The drafting of Nostra Aetate; Jewish-Christian relations.

John T. Pawlikowski. Reverend, D.S.M. Professor of Social Ethics, Catholic Theological Union, 5401 South Cornell Avenue, Chicago, Illinois 60615, (312) 324-5000 or 1420 East 49th Street, Chicago, Illinois 60615, (312) 624-0423.
What Are They Saying about Christian-Jewish Relations? New York: Paulist, 1980. Christ in Light of the Christian-Jewish Dialogue. New York: Paulist, 1982.
Christology; Jewish-Christian dialogue.
No geographical restrictions.

Jesse H. Plutzer. Co-Chairman, Rockaway Catholic-Jewish Council, P.O. Box 272, Rockaway Park, New York 11694, (718) 634-1739 or 314 Beach 148 Street, Nesponsit, New York 11694, (718) 318-0833.
Theological roots of anti-Semitism: the "teaching of contempt"; the radio priest of the 1930s: Father Charles Coughlin.
Can speak within the metropolitan area of New York City.

Carol Rittner. Director, Elie Wiesel Foundation for Humanity, 666 5th Avenue, 11th Floor, New York, New York 10103, (212) 399-4485.
The Courage to Care. Ed. Carol Rittner and Sondra Myers. New York: New York University Press, 1986. "Education for Catholic-Jewish Relations." The New Catholic World 228 (1985): 230-34. Executive Director of the film The Courage to Care.
Catholic-Jewish relations: the response of the churches during the Holocaust; teaching about the Holocaust; the work of Elie Wiesel.
Sufficient lead time, honorarium, and expenses required.

Midge Roof. Ph.D. Candidate, Department of English, Indiana University. 620 North Washington Street, Danville, Indiana 46122, (317) 745-2741.
Literature of the Holocaust, particularly Christians and the Holocaust; experience as a Fellow at the Center for Contemporary Theology in Jerusalem, which addressed the issue of Christology for the Jewish-Christian reality.
No geographical limitations.

Alvin H. Rosenfeld. Professor of English and Director of Jewish Studies Program, Goodbody Hall 307, Indiana University, Bloomington, Indiana 47405, (812) 335-0453 or 1026 East Wylie Street, Bloomington, Indiana 47401, (812) 339-8101.
A Double Dying: Reflections on Holocaust Literature. Bloomington: Indiana University Press, 1980. Imagining Hitler. Bloomington: Indiana University Press, 1985.
The Holocaust.

John K. Roth. Russell K. Pitzer Professor of Philosophy, Department of Philosophy, Pitzer Hall, Claremont McKenna College, Claremont, California 91711, (714) 621-8000 or 1648 Kenyon Place, Claremont, California 91711, (714) 626-3071.

A Consuming Fire: Encounters with Elie Wiesel and the Holocaust. Atlanta:
John Knox, 1979. Approaches to Auschwitz: The Holocaust and Its Legacy.
With Richard L. Rubenstein. Atlanta: John Knox, 1987.
Perspectives on the twentieth century: the Holocaust.
Would be able to speak on almost any occasion.

Issac C. Rottenberg. Reverend. National Christian Leadership Conference
for Israel, 134 East 39th Street, New York, New York 10016, (212) 213-8636
or 13 Briar Hill Road, Montclair, New Jersey 07042, (201) 783-9106.
The Promise and the Presence: Toward a Theology of the Kingdom of God.
Grand Rapids: Eerdmans, 1980. "Fulfillment Theology and the Future
of Christian-Jewish Relations." Christian Century 97 (1980): 60-69.
Christians who work for the security and well being of Israel; Christian-
Jewish dialogue.
No limitations.

Richard W. Rousseau. S.J. Professor and Chairman, Department of Theology/
Religious Studies, University of Scranton, Scranton, Pennsylvania 18510,
(717) 961-7449.
Editor/Publisher, Ridge Row Press. Christianity and Judaism: The Deepening
Dialogue. Editor. Scranton: Ridge Row, 1983. Interreligious Dialogue:
Facing the Next Frontier. Editor. Scranton: Ridge Row, 1981.

James A. Sanders. Professor of Intertestamental and Biblical Studies,
Claremont Graduate School, Claremont, California 91711, (714) 621-8000
or Ancient Biblical Manuscript Center, P.O. Box 670, 1325 North College
Avenue, Claremont, California 91711, (714) 621-6451.
"Torah and Christ." Interpretation 29 (1975): 372-90. The Dead Sea Psalms
Scroll. Ithaca, N.Y.: Cornell University Press, 1967. Torah and Canon.
Philadelphia: Fortress, 1972.
Working out for Christians and Jews what monotheizing could really mean
in the late twentieth century; intra-biblical hermeneutics in both First
and Second Testaments; the "new" history of Early Judaism; the junction
of the First Testament in the Second; Dead Sea Scrolls and text criticism.

Pierre Sauvage. President, Friends of Le Chambon, 5033 Sunset Boulevard
#784, Los Angeles, California 90046, (213) 650-1774.
Filmmaker: Through the Weapons of the Spirit (1987). (See media section.)
Lectures include: "On Learning Hope from the Holocaust"; "On Being a
Child of the Holocaust"; "The Sources of Caring"; "On Being a Jewish
Filmmaker."
Anywhere if expenses are paid.

Herman E. Schaalman. Adjunct Professor, Garrett Evangelical Theological
Seminary of Northwestern University and Chicago Theological Seminary,
Chicago University. Rabbi, Emanuel Congregation, 5959 Sheridan Road
at Thorndale Avenue, Chicago, Illinois 60660, (312) 274-5173 or 6145 North
Sheridan Road, Chicago, Illinois 60660, (312) 274-4023.
Theological aspects of Judaism; special emphasis on interpretations of
Shoah; revelation as a modern relevant mode; Christian-Jewish dialogue.
No limitations as long as expenses are included in compensation.

Max Andrew Shapiro. Director of Jewish–Christian Learning, College of St. Thomas, Rabbi Emeritus, Temple Israel, 2324 Emerson Avenue South, Minneapolis, Minnesota 55405, (612) 377-8680 or (612) 926-8795.
A Jewish–Christian learning center: its impact on a community.
Will speak whenever can possibly make it.

George J. Sheridan. Reverend. Regional Director, Interfaith Witness Department, Southern Baptist Home Mission Board, 553 Thoreau Terrace, Union, New Jersey 07083, (201) 964-4629.
Jewish relations with evangelical Christians.

Franklin Sherman. Professor of Christian Ethics. Dean, Lutheran School of Theology at Chicago, 1100 East 55th Street, Chicago, Illinois 60615, (312) 753-0721.
The Promise of Heschel. New York: Lippincott, 1971. "Speaking of God after Auschwitz." In Speaking of God Today: Jews and Lutherans in Conversation. Ed. Paul D. Ophals and Marc H. Tanenbaum. Philadelphia: Fortress, 1985. Luther's Works. Editor. American edition, volume 47. Philadelphia: Fortress, 1971.
Luther and the Jews; theological aspects of the Jewish–Christian dialogue.
No limitations.

Michael A. Signer. Rabbi. Professor of Jewish History, Hebrew Union College–Jewish Institute of Religion, 3077 University Avenue, Los Angeles, California 90007, (213) 749-3424.
"Through the Mirror Brightly." Essay in Unanswered Questions: Theological Views of Jewish–Catholic Relations. Notre Dame: University of Notre Dame Press, 1987. "The Land of Israel in Medieval Jewish Exegesis and Polemical History of Literature." In The Land of Israel and the Jewish People. Ed. L. Hoffman. Notre Dame: University of Notre Dame Press, 1986.
Biblical interpretation—Jewish and Christian; history of Jewish–Christian relations; biblical spiritual reflection and reading.
Anywhere that pays planefare.

Jeffrey S. Siker. Assistant Professor of Biblical Theology, Department of Theology, Loyola Marymount University, Loyola Boulevard at West 80th Street, Los Angeles, California 90045, (213) 642-4010 or 7051 B West Manchester Avenue, Los Angeles, California 90045.
Ph.D. dissertation: "The Making of Orphans: The Use of Abraham in Early Christian Controversy with Judaism." Princeton Theological Seminary. "Abraham in Graeco-Roman Paganism." Journal for the Study of Judaism, forthcoming (1988). "The Bible and Public Policy." Christian Century 103 (1986): 171-73.
Early Judaism and Christian origins; contemporary Jewish–Christian dialogue; history of biblical interpretation.

Timothy L. Smith. Professor of American Religious History, Director, Program in American Religious History, Department of History, The Johns Hopkins University, Baltimore, Maryland 21218, (301) 338-7554 or 48 West Cedar Street, Boston, Massachusetts 02114.
"An Historical Perspective on Evangelism and Ecumenism." Mid-Stream 22 (1983): 308-25. Revivalism and Social Reform on the Eve of the Civil

War. Baltimore: Johns Hopkins University Press, 1979.
American religious history.

Jack D. Spiro. Professor, Rabbi. Director of Judaic Studies, Virginia Commonwealth University. Rabbi, Congregation Beth Ahabah, 1111 West Franklin Street, Richmond, Virginia 23220, (804) 358-6757.
A Time to Mourn. New York: Bloch, 1985. Dialogue: In Search of Jewish-Christian Understanding. With John S. Spong. New York: Seabury, 1975.
Education; Judaism; Jewish-Christian theology.
No limitations.

John S. Spong. Bishop. The Diocese of Newark, Cathedral House, 24 Rector Street, Newark, New Jersey 07102, (201) 622-4306.
Dialogue: In Search of Jewish-Christian Understanding. With Jack D. Spiro. New York: Seabury, 1975. The Hebrew Lord. San Francisco: Harper and Row, 1987.

Jonathan A. Stein. Rabbi. Indianapolis Hebrew Congregation, 6501 North Meridian Street, Indianapolis, Indiana 46260, (317) 255-6647 or 1327 Walston Court, Indianapolis, Indiana 46260, (317) 255-6848.
"In Defense of the Congregational Havurah." Journal of Reform Judaism 30 (1983): 43-49. "No Real Solutions to a Very Real Problem." Phi Delta Kappan 64 (1982): 98.
Experience teaching and speaking with church and other Christian groups.
Availability varies greatly.

Leonard Swidler. Professor of Catholic Thought and Interreligious Dialogue, Religion Department, Temple University, Philadelphia, Pennsylvania 19122. Editor, Journal of Ecumenical Studies, (215) 787-7714.
The Passion of the Jew Jesus. New York: Anti-Defamation League of B'nai B'rith, 1984. "The Pharisees in Recent Catholic Writing." Horizons 10 (1983): 267-87.
Jewish-Christian dialogue; Jewish-Christian-Muslim dialogue.

Nechama Tec. Associate Professor, University of Connecticut, Scofieldtown Road, Stamford, Connecticut 06903.
Dry Tears: The Story of a Lost Childhood. New York: Oxford University Press, 1984. When Light Pierced the Darkness: Christian Rescue of Jews in Nazi Occupied Poland. New York: Oxford University Press, 1986.
Anti-Semitism; the Holocaust.

Rose Thering. O.P. Professor of Education and Human Services, College of Education and Human Services, Seton Hall University, South Orange, New Jersey 07079.
"Implementation of the Conciliar Document Nostra Aetate." New York: Anti-Defamation League, 1985.
Catholic-Jewish relations; Holocaust; Israel; Soviet Jewry.
Available on some weekends.

Norma H. Thompson. Professor Emerita, Program in Religious Education, New York University, 737 East Building, Washington Square, New York, New York 10003, (212) 598-2589 or 30 West Avenue, Great Barrington, Massachusetts 01230, (413) 528-0377.

The Future of Jewish-Christian Relations. Ed. with Bruce K. Cole. New York: Character Research, 1982. "Religious Education: Theory and Practice." Religious Education 28 (1984): 26-29. Religious Education and Theology. Editor. Birmingham, Ala.: Religious Education Press, 1982.
The Covenant in Jewish-Christian relations; dialogue: its advantages and limitations; love and law in Judaism and Christianity.
Available most of the time except Christmas to New Year and the Easter season.

John Tolson Townsend. Reverend. Professor of New Testament, Judaism, and Biblical Languages, Episcopal Divinity School, 99 Brattle Street, Cambridge, Massachusetts 02138, (617) 868-3450 or 40 Washington Street, Newton, Massachusetts 02158, (617) 527-6405.
"The Gospel of John and the Jews: The Story of a Religious Divorce." Essay in Anti-Semitism and the Foundations of Christianity. Edited by Alan T. Davies. New York: Paulist, 1979. A Liturgical Interpretation of Our Lord's Passion in Narrative Form. New York: National Conference of Christians and Jews, 1977.
New Testament; Rabbinic Judaism.
Willing to go anywhere as long as expenses are paid.

Paul M. van Buren. Reverend Dr. Honorary Professor, University of Heidelberg. Director, Center for Interreligious Renewal, Shalom Hartman Institute, Jerusalem, Israel or 134 Chestnut Street, Boston, Massachusetts 02108, (617) 723-5852.
A Theology of the Jewish-Christian Reality. Part 1: Discerning the Way. New York: Seabury, 1980; Part 2: A Christian Theology of the People Israel. New York: Seabury, 1983; Part 3: Christ in Context. New York: Harper and Row, 1987.
Theology of the Jewish-Christian relationship.
Twelve-month lead required of all requests.

Manfred H. Vogel. Professor, Northwestern University, 1940 Sheridan Road, Evanston, Illinois 60201, (312) 491-5488 or 2517 Greenwood, Wilmette, Illinois 60091, (312) 251-1781.
"Covenant and the Interreligious Encounter." Essay in Issues in the Jewish-Christian Dialogue. Ed. Helga Croner and Leon Klenicki. New York: Paulist, 1979. "The State as Essential Expression of the Faith of Judaism." Essay in Cities of God: Faith, Politics and Pluralism in Judaism, Christianity and Islam. Ed. Nigel Biggar, Jamie S. Scott, and William Schweiker. New York: Greenwood, 1986.
Jewish-Christian dialogue; modern Jewish theology.
Anyplace in the United States.

H. Eberhard Von Waldow. Professor of Old Testament, Pittsburgh Theological Seminary, 616 North Highland Avenue, Pittsburgh, Pennsylvania 15206, (412) 362-5610 or 2629 Middle Road, Glenshaw, Pennsylvania 15116, (412) 486-0518.
"Social Responsibility and Social Structure in Early Israel." Catholic Biblical Quarterly 32 (1970): 182-204. Forthcoming, form-critical commentary on the Book of Jeremiah for the series The Forms of the Old Testament Literature. Grand Rapids: Eerdmans. "The Concept of War in the Old Testament." Horizons in Biblical Theology 6 (1984): 27-28.

Old Testament prophets and Holocaust studies; Christian theology after the Holocaust.
There are no particular limitations.

Clarence H. Wagner, Jr. Executive Director, Bridges for Peace, P.O. Box 33145, Tulsa, Oklahoma 74153, (918) 663-8811 or Bridges for Peace, P.O. Box 7304, Jerusalem, Israel, (2) 240-077.
Executive Editor of Dispatch from Jerusalem and Dispatch Update Letter.
History of Christian-Jewish relations since the first century C.E.; anti-Semitism in the Church; history and current perspectives of modern Israel; the miracle of modern Israel; God, covenant, and Israel.
I can speak in any area of the United States when I am in the country. Will speak to groups who come to Jerusalem.

Robert Webber. Professor of Theology, Wheaton College, Wheaton, Illinois 60187, (312) 260-5056 or (312) 665-3898.
Moral Majority: Right or Wrong? New York: Cornerstone, 1981. Secular Humanism: Threat or Challenge? Grand Rapids: Zondervan, 1982.
Church and the society; interpreting the religious Right to Jewish people.

Sonia Schreiber Weitz. Co-director, Holocaust Center, Jewish Federation of the Northshore, 7 Felton Street, Peabody, Massachusetts 01960, (617) 535-0003.
Holocaust survivor: Krakow Ghetto, Plaszow, Auschwitz, Bergen-Belsen, Venus-Bergf, Mauthausen.
Teacher-training workshops: "Facing History and Ourselves."
Lecturer: Holocaust awareness programs in public, private, and religious schools, colleges, and civic organizations.

Paul R. Whitham. 3234 Horseshoe Bend, Rockford, Illinois 61109, (815) 874-7860.
Enhancing Christian knowledge of Jews and Judaism in the twentieth century; detailed information on anti-Semitism and the Holocaust.
Weekends, destination open. Some weeknights in Rockford and Chicago.

Marvin R. Wilson. Ockenga Professor of Biblical Studies, Department of Biblical Studies, Gordon College, Wenham, Massachusetts 01984, (617) 927-2300 or (617) 468-3884.
Evangelicals and Jews in an Age of Pluralism. Ed. with A. James Rudin and Marc Tanenbaum. Grand Rapids: Baker, 1984. Evangelicals and Jews in Conversation. Ed. with A. James Rudin and Marc Tanenbaum. Grand Rapids: Baker, 1978.
Jewish-Christian relations; anti-Semitism; evangelical-Jewish dialogue; Hebrew thought; Israel (ancient and modern); Old Testament and archaeology.
Would be willing to consider all invitations.

Michael Wyschogrod. Professor and Chairman, Department of Philosophy, Baruch College, The City University of New York, 17 Lexington Avenue, New York, New York 10010, (212) 505-2157 or 151 West 86th Street, New York, New York 10024, (212) 874-1524.
Jews and "Jewish Christianity". With David Berger. New York: Ktav, 1978. The Body of Faith: Judaism as Corporeal Election. Minneapolis: Seabury-Winston, 1983.

The theology of Jewish-Christian relations; Vatican-Jewish relations; the Mosaic law in Christian thought; a Jewish reading of Paul; a Jewish view of Jewish converts to Christianity.
Would be willing to consider all invitations.

Arthur E. Zannoni. Professor of Religious Studies, Assistant Director, Center for Religious Education, Graduate Programs in Pastoral Studies, College of St. Thomas, P.O. Box 5010, 2115 Summit Avenue, St. Paul, Minnesota 55105, (612) 645-2733.
"Feminine Languaging in the Hebrew Scriptures." Shofar 2, (1984): 5-17.
"The Hebrew Sage: A Model for Lay Campus Ministry." Process 4 (1978): 9-12.
Jewish-Christian dialogue; the use of Hebrew Scripture.
Upper and lower midwestern states.

Ira G. Zepp Jr. Professor of Religious Studies, Department of Philosophy and Religious Studies, Western Maryland College, Westminster, Maryland 21157, (301) 848-7000.
Search for the Beloved Community: The Thinking of Martin Luther King, Jr. With Kenneth G. Smith. Valley Forge, Pa.: Judson, 1974.
"Christian-Marxist Dialogue: Theological Reflections." Journal of Ecumenical Studies 11 (1974): 192-97.
Comparative religion; social justice.
I can speak anywhere with some qualifications, e.g., funds and time. Most of my speaking engagements now are in the Washington-Baltimore area.

Postscript

Up to the last few days of working on this resource book, I was still receiving quite a bit of material for inclusion, and unfortunately had to stop somewhere. This is convincing evidence that the Jewish-Christian dialogue is growing rapidly and promises to be a significant factor in theological and religious study. As the Jewish-Christian dialogue continues to grow, this work will need to be updated. For this reason, if readers have material that they feel should be included in any future edition, they are invited to send it to me in care of Shermis Unlimited, 1016 Riverton Drive, West Lafayette, Indiana 47906.

INDEX OF SUBJECTS

For relations with the Jews see Jewish-.
Syllabi and the geographical directory of service groups have not been
included in the subject or title indexes.

Kingdom: of God, 34, 655, 97,
109, 119, 225, 238; of night,
117
Kinship, 108
Koran, 75

Land: 55, 58, 97, 125, 151, 165;
Holy, 57, 58, 132, 154, 166, 225;
Promised, 58, 232. See also
Israel; Palestine
Language, Languages: 224;
Palestinian, 24; Semitic, 235;
Theological, 235
Last Supper, 85, 102, 227
Latin, 44
Latin America, 92, 127
Law: 3, 4, 19, 22, 24, 34, 35, 36,
37, 75, 97, 100, 115, 124, 128,
149, 226, 230, 242; Civil, 227;
Family, 227; Jewish, 23, 237;
Moral, 200; Mosaic, 224
Layperson, 66, 70, 88
Leadership, 24, 99, 109
Lectionaries: Common, 224;
Jewish, 86; Lutheran, 224; Roman
Catholic, 224
Legal system, Jewish, 39
Legalism, 113
Lent, 108, 129
Liberation, 145, 147, 148, 168
Liberty, Religious, 201
Life cycle events, 107
Literature: 32, 38, 46, 76, 103, 104,
123, 135, 240; Apocalyptic, 31, 41;
Biblical, 139; Catechetical,
81; Christian, 25, 31, 41, 93, 138,
154; Greek, 35; Hebrew, 30;
Holocaust, 50; Imaginative, 104;
Intertestamental, 234; Jewish,
25, 27, 31, 35, 36, 41, 44, 93, 102,
154, 230; Latin, 35; Pagan, 39,
42; Rabbinic, 25, 26, 29, 30, 32,
36, 41, 72, 112; Sacred, 13;
Talmudic, 26; Wisdom, 225
Liturgy: 19, 40, 50, 75, 80, 84-88,
95, 103, 106, 108, 229, 233;
Christian, 86, 87, 112, 156; Holy
Week, 108, 156; Jewish, 86, 87,
156; Lenten, 108
Logic, 224
Lord's Prayer, 87
Love, 2, 4, 64, 84, 115, 124, 130,
242
Lutheranism, 97, 148

Magic, 41, 42
Mankind. See Humanity
Marriage: 82, 83, 84, 105, 107,
109, 127; Mixed, 82, 84, 128.
See also Intermarriage
Mass, 4, 199
Media, xiv, 63, 67, 199
Medieval era. See Middle Ages
Messiah, xiv, 3, 4, 13, 19, 24, 28,
30, 33, 41, 73, 81, 95, 100,
115, 118, 131, 225. See also
Christ; Savior
Messianic: age, 115; hope, 19,
108; idea, 155; types, 25
Metaphysics, 92
Middle Ages, 41, 43-47, 62, 103,
104, 145
Middle East, 59, 164, 165, 198,
225, 227, 236
Midrash, 26, 38, 120
Midrashim, Minor, 44
Minorities, 76, 80, 81, 167, 196
Miracles, 21, 29
Mishnah, 40
Misogynism, 99
Mission: 7, 11, 19, 26, 44, 50,
58, 73, 88-90, 103, 112, 134,
135, 139, 169, 227, 228, 234,
236. See also Witness
Modernity, 150
Monotheism, 29, 96, 153, 236,
239
Moral Majority, 243
Mormons, 5-6
Moslem. See Muslim
Music, 88, 161
Muslim, Muslims, 2, 6, 7, 58,
62, 75, 103, 141, 144, 155,
166, 236. See also Islam
Mysticism: 75, 92; Christian,
227; Jewish, 22, 44, 227, 237;
Merkabah, 37
Myth, 20, 31, 62, 73, 91, 148

Narrative forms, 25, 37, 73,
108, 129, 235
Nationalism: 102, 128; Jewish,
58
Naturalistic position, 9
Nazi: archives, 48;
extermination, 157;
persecution, 48, 54, 55;
policy, 47
Nazis, Nazism, 11, 47, 50, 51,

School of Shammai, 26
Science, 94
Scribes, 18
Scripture, Scriptures: 11, 28, 32,
  33, 72, 75, 77, 80, 85, 99, 100,
  103, 129, 130, 147, 224, 229,
  230, 232; Christian, 18, 22, 36,
  70, 233; Hebrew, 3, 8, 37, 57,
  70, 113, 114, 225, 233, 237, 244
Second Commonwealth, 95
Second Reich, 68
Second Temple Studies, 224, 227,
  230
Second Vatican Council. See
  Vatican Council II
Second World War. See
  World War II
Secular age, 11
Secularization,
Seder. See Passover meal.
Seleucids, 38
Self-government, Jewish,
Seminary: 79; Theological, 95
Semite, xv
Sermon on the Mount, 26–27
Sexism, 99
Sexuality, 94
Shalom, 92, 105. See also Peace
Shavuot, 13
Shoah. See Holocaust
Sikhism, 103
Sin, 4, 21, 94
Sinai, 124
Six-Day War, 58, 93
Social: action, 11, 14, 200;
  commitment, 87; policy, 87, 94;
  service, 14; structure, 102, 242
Society: 34, 40, 63, 97, 101, 127,
  141, 149, 169, 243; American,
  84, 97; Roman, 40
Socio-religious context, 22
Sociology: xiii, 64; Religious, 95
Soteriology, 36
Soviet Union. See U.S.S.R.
Spirituality, 18, 57, 84–88, 103,
  226, 233, 237
State: 44, 46, 97, 151, 242; Jewish,
  ix, 56
Stereotypes, 3–4, 7, 63, 80, 111, 113
Storytelling, 235
Suffering, 78, 161
Supercessionism, 11. See also
  Anti-Jewish polemic
Supernatural beings, 33
Superstition, 42
Syllabi, xiv

Synagogue, 18, 23, 24, 28, 32,
  35, 40, 46, 66, 69, 87, 88
Synoptic Gospels. See Gospels
Systematics, 80

Talmud: 23, 38, 40, 43, 99,
  231; Christians in the, 42
Talmudic period, 40–43, 88, 95
Tanach, 8
Tannaitic period, 27, 46
Taxation, 40
Teacher of Nazareth, 26
Teaching, Christian. See
  Education, Christian
Teaching materials. See
  Instructional materials
"Teaching of Contempt," 7,
  64, 65, 66, 110, 226, 229,
  230, 238
Technology, 94
Temple, 35
Ten Commandments, 231
Terrorist, 2
Textbooks: 80; Christian, 111;
  Jewish, 2, 82; Parochial,
  78; Religious, 2
Theology: xiii, 6, 20, 48, 57, 69,
  70, 74, 75, 102, 103, 120, 124,
  128, 131, 141, 227; American,
  124; Biblical, 55, 134, 224;
  Catholic, 91, 99, 152, 233,
  237; Christian, 2, 49, 61, 62,
  64, 65, 67, 69, 70, 71, 73, 79,
  98, 101, 113, 115, 116, 117,
  127, 130, 150, 154, 201, 223,
  226, 229, 232, 234, 243, 244;
  Christian, of Judaism, 69, 71;
  Covenant, 98, 117, 130, 134;
  Depth, 237; Fulfillment, 37,
  98, 119, 239; German Christian,
  89, 124; Historical, 224;
  Holocaust, 117, 124; Jewish,
  2, 33, 91, 98, 99, 124, 143, 152,
  230, 237, 242; of Jewish
  Christianity, 24, 27, 95;
  Liberation, 126, 148; Medieval,
  99; Modern, 20, 27; Moral, 80;
  New Testament, 28; Old
  Testament, 224; Pauline, 25,
  36; Philosophical, 224;
  Political, 103; Post-Holocaust,
  54, 69, 77, 114, 117, 127, 228,
  229, 236, 243; Protestant, 91,
  124; Rabbinic, 32, 233; Radical,
  54; Reformation, 99;
  Systematic, 71, 115, 116;

INDEX OF
NAMES AND ORGANIZATIONS

Everett, Robert A., 57, 61, 113, 117, 229
Ezorsky, Gertrude, 129

Fackenheim, Emil, 49, 50, 73, 76
Fagan, 4
Falk, Harvey, 25-26
Falk, Randall M., 229
Falwell, Jerry, 125
Farley, James H., 37
al Faruqi, Isma'il Raji, 74
Fasching, Darrell J., 79
Federici, Tomasso, 191
Feeley-Harnik, Gillian, 85
Feingold, Henry L., 125
Feldblum, Esther Yolles, 56, 191
Feldman, Louis A., 26
Fenelon, Fania, 161
Fenig, Ethel C., 136
Fenton, Paul, 75
Fierman, Morton C., 136
Filas, Francis L., 153
Fine, Morris, 14, 106
Finkel, Asher, 26, 85, 102, 156
Finn, James, 102
Fiorenza, Elisabeth Schussler, 26, 43, 49
Fischel, Henry A., 43
Fishbane, Michael, 28
Fisher, Eugene J., 13, 14, 61, 69, 79, 87, 92, 94, 103, 106, 109, 110, 113, 117, 118, 126, 127, 129, 131, 132, 155, 156, 188-189, 229, 230
Fishman, Hertzel, 56
Fitzmyer, Joseph A., 26, 80
Flannery, Edward H., 12, 48, 63, 165, 183, 186, 188-191, 193, 194, 229
Fleck, G. P., 118, 133
Fleischmann, Jacob, 184
Fleischner, Eva, 48, 50, 77, 89, 108, 129, 190, 229
Fleming, E. D., 127
Flender, Harold, 50
Floreen, Harold, 71
Flusser, David, 26, 100, 118
Forster, Arnold, 62, 63
Forsyth, Agnes H., 22
Foss, Helen, 108
Foster, Claude R., Jr., 124
Fournier, Marie H., 118
Frank, Anne, 50, 158, 167
Freedman, Robert O., 156

Frenaye, Frances, 21
Freyne, Sean, 26
Friedlander, Albert H., 50, 77
Friedlander, Gerald, 26, 38
Friedlander, Henry, 50, 163
Friedman, Jerome, 44
Friedman, Maurice S., 77
Friedman, Philip, 50
Friedman, Saul S., 63
Friends of Le Chambon, 198
Fritz, Maureena, 130, 131
Frizzell, Lawrence, 85, 156, 230
Fruchtenbaum, Arnold G., 27
Fuchs, Stephen, 156, 230
Fujita, Neil S., 27
Fuller, Reginald, 126

Gager, John, 63, 155, 192
Garnick, Daniel, 82
Gartenhaus, Jacob, 27
Gass, William, 129
Gaston, Lloyd, 118, 130
Gavin, F., 86
Geanakoplos, Deno J., 128
Geller, Ruth, 128
Genizi, Haim, 50
Genne, Elizabeth, 105
Genne, William H., 83, 105
Georgi, Dieter, 26
Geraghty, Martin T., 230
Gerhart, Mary, 49
Gerstner, John H., 28
Gilbert, Arthur, 60, 72, 74, 188-191, 194
Gilbert, Martin, 51
Gilkey, Langdon, 94
Gillen, Ann, 156, 230
Gillman, Neil, 130
Gittelsohn, Roland B., 82
Glasser, Arthur F., 130
Glassman, Bernard, 63
Glatzer, Nahum N., 36, 77
Glock, Charles Y., 63, 67, 80-81, 194
Goering, Hermann, 168
Goldberg, Michael, 27
Goldbloom, Victor C., 127
Goldhawk, Norman, 18
Goldin, Judah, 26
Golding, Martin P., 129
Goldman, Eric, 154
Goldstein, Morris, 27, 192
Goodenough, E. R., 22
Goodman, Paul, 23, 38
Goppelt, Leonhard, 28

INDEX OF TITLES

INDEX OF MEDIA